W9-ABI-007

Discovering the
God Child
Within

cs

Discovering the God Child Within

A Spiritual Psychology of the Infancy of Jesus

ℭℨ

Eugen Drewermann

Translated by Peter Heinegg

CROSSROAD • NEW YORK

1994

The Crossroad Publishing Company
370 Lexington Avenue, New York, NY 10017

Originally published under the title *Dein Name ist wie der
Geschmack des Lebens: Tiefen-psychologische Deutung der
Kindheitsgeschichte nach dem Lukasevangelium*
© Verlag Herder Freiburg im Breisgau 1986

English translation copyright © 1994 by
The Crossroad Publishing Company

All rights reserved. No part of this book may be reproduced, stored in
a retrieval system, or transmitted, in any form or by any means,
electronic, mechanical, photocopying, recording,
or otherwise, without the written permission of
The Crossroad Publishing Company.

Printed in the United States of America

Library of Congress Cataloging-in-Publication Data

Drewermann, Eugen.
　[Dein Name ist wie der Geschmack des Lebens. English]
　Discovering the God child within : a spiritual psychology of the
infancy of Jesus / Eugen Drewermann ; translated by Peter Heinegg.
　　p.　cm.
　Includes bibliographical references.
　ISBN 0-8245-1388-6 (pbk.)
　1. Jesus Christ–Biography–Early life.　2. Bible. N.T. Luke–
Criticism, interpretation, etc.　3. Jesus Christ–Mythological
interpretations.　I. Title.
BT320.D7413　1994
232.92–dc20　　　　　　　　　　　　　　　　　93-27204
　　　　　　　　　　　　　　　　　　　　　　　　CIP

... *For what is now called the Christian religion existed even among the ancients and was not lacking from the beginning of the human race until "Christ came in the flesh." From that time the true religion, which had already existed, began to be called Christian.*

—Augustine, *The Retractations*, I, 12, 31

Contents

☙

The Text

☙

N O TEXT IN THE BIBLE is as familiar or as controversial as the New Testament Christmas stories. Dogmatized by church tradition and later demythologized by the exegetes, these narratives must strike readers today as strange and contradictory – that is, until we find some way to help us overcome the peculiarly alienating contradiction of thought and feeling, of consciousness and the unconscious. The present study looks to the legacy of ancient Egyptian myths about the birth of a divine man through the choice of a royal virgin. It attempts to dream again, and to relive contemplatively, the primeval images of the mystery of the Incarnation as people imagined and believed them thousands of years before Christianity. Beyond the Egyptian myths the Gospel of Luke draws upon images from the birth of Asclepius, the Greek god of light and the supreme physician, in order to describe the mystery of redemption and make it possible to experience it. In the process texts emerge between dreams and daylight that can't really be understood except in the floating language of poetry and symbols. To posit the birth of the Son of God as real, we have to do away with the boundaries between the truth of the mind and the truth of the heart, between the truth of the Christians and the truth of the pagans, between the truth of the rich and the truth of the poor. Only when the chasm disappears that even today separates history and dogma, will we find our way back to a faith that has the power to change the history of humanity for the better. In the following section I shall concentrate entirely on the narrative parts of the Lucan infancy narrative (Lk. 1:26–38, 39–45, 56; 2:1–20, 21–40, 41–52). In contrast to the tradition of the birth of John the Baptist these texts are not unified. But precisely for this reason, with their many facets and layers, they need and deserve to be carefully viewed against the background of the great mythical traditions of the nations.

The text is my own translation, with the parts from pre-Lucan tradition in italics:[1]

1. The Message of the Angel (1:26–38)

26Meanwhile in the sixth month the angel Gabri-El was sent by God to a city of Galilee called Nazareth, 27to a virgin engaged to a man called Joseph, *from the house of David, and the virgin's name was Miriam.* 28*All of a sudden he came to her and said: Greetings, blessed one, the Lord is with you.* 29But she was frightened by this word and reflected on what this salutation meant. 30Then the angel told her:

Do not be afraid, Miriam, you have found grace with God.
   31*For this is how it is: You will conceive in your womb and bear a son, whose* name[2] you shall call "Jesus" [see Jg. 13:3; Is. 7:14].
   32*He will be great and be called "son of the Most High," and the Lord God will give him the throne of his father* [see Is. 9:6; 2 Sam. 7:12–16],
   33so that[3] he may be king over the house of Jacob forever, for there will be no end to his kingship [see Mic. 4:7; Dan. 7:14].
   34But *Miriam* said to the angel: How can that be – I am not married to any man.
   35*Then the angel answered her:*
Holy Spirit will come upon you,
the power of the Most High will overshadow you.

For this reason too what will come about (in this way) will be called holy, Son of God. 36For this is how it is: Elizabeth, your relative, she too has conceived a son in her old age; and this is already the sixth month for her, the so-called "barren one." 37For "No word from God will be powerless"[4] [Gen. 18:14; Jer. 32:17].

[38]For her part[5] *Miriam* said: So then[6] I am the handmaid of the Lord; let it be unto me according to your word. Then the angel went away from her.

2. The Meeting between Mary and Elizabeth (1:39–45, 56)

[39]For her part *Miriam* set out then[7] and hurriedly went *to the hill country in the province of Judea.*[8] [40]She entered the house of Zechariah and greeted Elizabeth. [41]Then it happened that when Elizabeth heard *Miriam's* greeting, *the baby leaped in her womb,* and Elizabeth was filled with Holy Spirit, [42]so that she cried out in a loud voice:

> *You are praised among women*
> *and praised is the fruit of your womb.*

[43]*But how (has) this (fallen) to me,* that the mother of my Lord comes to me. [44]For[9] you know that when the voice of your greeting rang in my *ear, the baby leaped for joy in my womb.* [45]*Indeed, blessed is she who has come to believe that what the Lord said will find fulfillment.* [56]Miriam stayed with her for about three months; then she went back home.

3. The Holy Night (2:1–20)

[1]Now it happened in those days: An order went forth from the Emperor Augustus to register the whole world for taxation. [2]This tax registration, the first, took place when Quirinius was governor of Syria. [3]*Then* all *went there* to be registered for taxes, each to his city. Joseph too set out from the Galilee, from the city of Nazareth up *to Judea, to the city of David, called Bethlehem, because he was of the house and family of David,* to be registered for taxation along with *Miriam,* his fiancée, who was pregnant. [6]*Then it happened during their stay there: The days of her lying-in were fulfilled,* [7]and she bore her son, the first-born; she wrapped him and laid him in a manger, because there was no room for them in the lodgings.

[8]*Now there were in the same region shepherds, who were spending the night out in the open and keeping watch over*

their flock. [9]*Then an angel of the Lord stepped up to them, so that God's splendor shone around them, and they were afraid — a great fear!* [10]*But the angel said to them:* Fear not. Because in reality[10] I proclaim to you a great joy, which will be (granted) to all people. [11]For born to you *today* is a savior, that is, the Messiah-Lord, in the city of David. [12]*Therefore let this be a sign to you:* You will find a baby, wrapped up, lying in a manger. [13]Then suddenly there was with the angel an abundance of the heavenly hosts, praising God and saying:

> [14]*Glory above for God*
> *and salvation on earth*
> *for people of grace.*

[15]Thus it happened: When the angels had (again) gone from them into heaven, the shepherds said to one another: Let us go over to Bethlehem and look upon the realization of the word that *the Lord* has made known to us. [16]So they quickly went and found *Mary* and Joseph and the baby, lying in the manger. [17]Having seen with their own eyes they themselves now[11] made known the contents of the message that had been given them about this little child. [18]All those who heard *fell into astonishment over what had been told them* by the shepherds. [19] But Mary kept all these words, divining[12] them in her heart. [20]Then the shepherds went back, glorifying and praising God for everything they had been allowed to hear and see, just as they had been told.

4. The Spirit-Prophesying in the Temple (2:21–40)

[21]*Now when* in accordance with the Law of Moses the eight days prescribed for circumcision *were fulfilled, his name was called "Jesus,"* as he had (already) been called by the angel before he was conceived in his mother's womb.

[22]*When* in accordance with the Law of Moses the days of her purification *were fulfilled,* they took him up to *Jerusalem,* to present him to the Lord, [23] as it is written *in the Law of the Lord:*

Every male that opens the mother's womb — shall be called holy to the Lord [Ex. 13:2],

[24]and in order to make an offering in accordance with what is said in the Law of the Lord:

a pair of turtle doves or two young doves [Lev. 12:4–8].

[25]*Surprisingly*[13] *there was a man* in Jerusalem *named Simeon and this man was upright and feared God, one who was waiting for the consolation of Israel.* Indeed, spirit was upon him, a holy spirit, [26]it had been prophesied to him by the sanctuary spirit that he would not see death until he had seen *the Lord's Messiah.* [27]Now he came, spirit-led, into the Temple; and as the parents of Jesus brought in the little child, so that it might be done to him in keeping with the custom of the Law, [28]then he took the child into his arms and praised God; he said:

[29]*Now you release your servant, Lord,*
in keeping with your word in peace.
[30]*for my eyes have seen your salvation,*
[31]*which you have prepared before the face of all the nations,*
[32]*light to enlighten the Gentiles,*
and to glorify your people Israel [see Is. 52:10, 42:6, 49:60].

[33]Then *his father and mother* were full of astonishment over what was said about him. [34]But Simeon praised them, and to *Miriam,* his mother he said: Surely this child is set for the downfall and the rising of *many* in Israel, to be a sign that will be contradicted [35] — indeed, a sword will pass through your own soul — so that the thoughts of many hearts will become *manifest.*

[36]There was also a prophetess there, Anna, a daughter of Phanuel from the tribe of Asher. She was *advanced in years:* she had lived (only) seven years with her husband after her maidenhood, [37]and had remained a *widow* until now, when she was eighty-four years old. *She did not leave the Temple,* serving God day and night with fasting and prayer. [38]She too came along at that same hour, to sing a song of praise to God; and she spoke about him to all those who were waiting for the *redemption of Jerusalem.*

[39]*As they had now* fulfilled everything in accordance with the Law of the Lord, they returned (again) to Galilee, to their town of Nazareth. [40]In the meantime the little child grew up and gathered strength, filled with wisdom, for[14] *the grace of God* was upon him.

5. In His Father's Domain (2:41–52)

[41]*Now* his parents were accustomed[15] to go to Jerusalem every year *for the feast of Passover.* [42]*But when* he (Jesus) had become twelve years old and they had gone up (again), in keeping with the custom of the feast [43] — (already) they had fulfilled the days, on their way back — Jesus, the boy, remained in Jerusalem, without his parents' knowing it. [44]Thinking, of course,[16] that he was in the traveling party, they went a *day's journey* ahead and continually[17] looked for him among their relatives *and acquaintances.* [45]But since they did not find him, they returned to Jerusalem, ever in search of him. [46]Then finally: after three days they found him in the Temple, as he sat amid the teachers, listened to them, and asked them questions. [47]But they were all astonished at his understanding and his answers. [48]When they saw him there, they were beside themselves (with vexation)[18] *and* his mother *said:* Child, how could you do this to us? Don't you see,[19] your father and I had to search for you very painfully.[20] [49]Then he said to them *How is it that you had to search for me? Didn't you know* that I have to be in my father's domain? [50]But they did not understand this word that he spoke to them. [51]Nevertheless he went down with them to Nazareth.[21] And also (in the time that followed) he remained subordinate to them. His mother kept all the words in her heart. [52]Jesus meanwhile grew continually in wisdom and age and *grace with God and man* [1 Sam. 2:26].

Of these texts the two scenes in Nazareth and Bethlehem are obviously the most important. They have had the greatest influence on the Church's teaching; and they represent the documentary basis of Christmas. So first of all we shall have to reexperience and reshape the images and statements that we find in these narratives. By comparison the other details of the so-called history of Jesus' childhood make relatively minor demands on interpretation. On the whole we are not concerned with an exegesis of the narratives in the historical-critical sense.

Rather, while presupposing the findings of that approach, we are looking for the finishing touches and accent shifts that come about when with the help of depth psychology we let *the images speak for themselves against the background of the history of religion.*

Interpretation:
Tuning into and Reflecting on
the Reality of Myth

ℭଽ

HOW ARE WE TO understand a divine secret? We would be well ahead of the game if we could absorb the narratives of the Bible and the symbols of the Church the way the artists, musicians, painters, and poets do, unlike the theologians, who are forever looking for logical reasons, and the researchers, forever looking for historical foundations.

The Humanness of the Divine

When Georg Friedrich Händel began to write the *Messiah* on August 21, 1714, he had just had a miraculous recovery from a severe stroke. Haunted by tormenting self-doubts, he was nonetheless profoundly moved by the sacred words of Scripture that had seized hold of him. Now that he was restored to life, they were like a song of eternity about to become audible to him, "Behold, darkness shall cover the earth." And it did, but amid the crashing of trumpets, the thunder of the organ, and the jubilation of the choir, a mighty sound ascended to heaven, "that once again, as on the first day, the Word, the holy Logos, was awakening men and women, all of them, who . . . were still walking about in darkness and despair."[1] "For the angel of the Lord appeared to them." *That* was how to feel the Word, *that* was how to fill it with sonority, so that his music touched the heart of the audience, as if they themselves were out there in the fields of Bethlehem. Händel experienced in his own flesh what it means to be "born again" in the power of grace and to be given a grateful reprieve. The *Messiah* became his most humble, his most human, his most magnanimous work. He decided that thenceforth the proceeds from its performance would be dedicated to the sick, the prisoners, and the orphanages of London. After all, the Redeemer had come into the world to preach healing to the sick and freedom to prisoners, and to proclaim to all orphans on earth that they too, they in particular, were children of God.

In 1891 Paul Gaugin painted what is probably his loveliest religious painting, entitled *la orana, Maria* (Hail, Mary) in Tahiti.[2] In this work he condensed his expectations and his experiences of a harmony that he thought possible only among the children of nature – the true children of God. Only in them did he find unspoiled the natural capacity and need to revere the holy and to approach it in prayer. So he painted a small, almost private procession of two native women with hands folded, wearing nothing but sarongs around their hips, approaching a Tahitian Madonna. Mary carries the Christ child on her shoulder, with his head resting on her dark hair. Both are looking at us, as if to ask what we see. Can we make out the thin halo that both women see surrounding the figures of mother and child?

Gaugin was penetrated by the "universal value common to all religions," and he attributed more importance to this than to "all dogmas of any one"[3] form of faith. He borrowed the composition of the picture itself from a scene on the temple of Borobodur in Java. Gaugin seems to want to interpret the Christian message in this way: The incarnation of God can mean only that all people have been grasped and gathered up by God. Now, he suggests, they can recognize themselves in their original beauty and natural dignity. Whenever a Madonna treads the earth, the world can be painted only as a freshly discovered Paradise, beyond the Fall, beyond the split between sensuality and morality, between nature and culture, between body and mind. And so Gaugin pictured this earth as God's garden, but with no angel's flaming sword to bar the way to humans. On the contrary, beneath blooming trees, against the background of blue mountains and sun-flooded huts the angel stands with golden yellow wings, directing the Tahitian women to the Madonna and the child. In other words, the angel of Paradise is the same as the angel of the annunciation. The only difference is that the "shepherds in the fields" in Gaugin's vision are women, as if women were by nature better equipped than men for perceiving the holy. What Gaugin is painting is based on the experience of a thoroughly "maternal" view of the world not yet, or no longer, characterized by prohibitions, taboos, and anxiety. The banana trees and their fruit are the very first things that the invited, initiated observer, entering this world of primordial origins, literally runs into. We have to look very carefully to note that the bananas are prepared, arranged in a dish, artfully placed on the edge of a table, bidding us linger and enjoy ourselves. That is how human activity relates to nature's, harmoniously, without transition or conflict. Even the name of the Madonna seems to have found its true melody for the first time, when it rings out in Tahitian, "la orana, Maria." This is a music that, as in Händel, turns into a universal painting of grace,[4] and a painting of grace that becomes the chant of unity sung by all people in the paradise of the world beneath the blessing of a gentle sky. These are interpretations of a divine mystery. They don't figure something out, they transfigure it. They don't prove, they point. They don't aim at comprehending, but are all the better at grasping. For that very reason they are as timeless as the reality that they wish to bear witness to: what it means to be a child of God.

This poetry of the people has always been with us, and still is today. The Romantic movement sought this poetry primarily in fairy tales and legends, which its followers expected to find on peasants' farms, not in princely courts. From the standpoint of literary scholarship they were often wrong on this point.[5] Still, in religion we can observe the goal of all romanticism, the living unity of faith and poetry, in the traditions of the people. Here they manifest such warmheartedness and truth that we are constantly astonished to see how much vital energy and human meaning inhabit the great archetypal images of religion.

And, vice versa, we see what interpretive depths can be reached by the "fantasy" of so-called simple people. In ritual, prayer, and all sorts of holiday customs the "folk" plunge into the mysteries of the divine. But to none of the Christian feasts celebrated by the Western Church are people more attached than to events of Christmas time. Here the popular imagination has molded the almost forgotten *nature symbolism* of the biblical texts onto extraordinarily beautiful and meaningful customs.

The early Church, no doubt influenced by the Mithra cult of the Roman legionnaires[6] as well as by certain oriental rites,[7] decided to celebrate the birthday of the Lord on December 25. Christ was supposed to appear as the true light,[8] as the unconquered sun, which, in keeping with the images of the zodiac,[9] is reborn to new life at the winter solstice. In the Christian world this narrow slice of lived "paganism" has unfolded into a wonderful ensemble of concentrated symbols. For the believing soul, with its sensitivity to dream and myth, the fact that it was "night" when the Christ child came into the world (Lk. 2:8) meant more than a mere indication of time. Rather it described a state of soul, to which it could attach boundless hope. If the Redeemer was "born"[10] during the "night," then for that very reason we could be confident that by his very makeup,[11] as a child of night, Jesus would understand all the darkness and dead-endedness of life. The poetic instincts of piety add that it was *cold* on that night, bitterly cold and lonely. Yet the poverty and wretchedness of the stable[12] are the key to the believer's confidence and comfort.

In purely terrestrial terms Dante's image from *The Divine Comedy* gets things just right[13] when he describes the bottom of hell as a frozen swamp, with the sinners fixed in the ice and the tears on their faces glazed over into an icy mask. Only someone who knows from personal experience how humans become spiritually frozen will be able to find words to melt the ice.[14] And only someone who from the first was born into loneliness and need will be able to say that he was sent, in the words of Isaiah, "to preach good news to the poor, to proclaim release to the captives and recovery of sight to the blind (Lk. 4:18; Is. 61:1–2). You can't deal with the coldness of the world the way you deal with an iceberg. With an axe and dynamite you can at best rearrange the masses of ice, but that won't change the climate. But how much warmth, kindness, and understanding do a people need before they dare to let their tears flow freely and to stop freezing and paralyzing them through relentless compulsions? At least the gentle breath of the animals in the stable — borrowed by folk piety from Isaiah's image of the ox and the ass at their master's crib (Is. 1:2) — would have warmed the child Jesus and animated him with creaturely compassion for all the misery of this world.

It makes no difference what "pagan" customs lie behind the symbol of the Christmas tree.[15] In this context what is "Christian" and what is "pagan" if God himself has "taken on"[16] human nature? According to the Talmud, the angels speak only Hebrew, but the Almighty understands all languages,[17] and the only song of the soul from God is the one that excludes nothing human. Thus in the days when the sun threatens to die, we clothe the world tree with light and decorate it with "angel hair." For the light mustn't die; and we humans are called to warm one another in the cold of the night, confident that the morning will come. If these are not *just* images, the world can live on them.

If only it were possible to interpret God's mysteries in the texts of the Bible this way: after the manner of the musicians, painters, and poets. Then their tidings would touch the heart of *every* person on earth, and God could be heard in songs of joy, in visions of beauty, and in the prayerful poetry of meditation and love. We would stand at the beginning of a Christianity as vast as the sky between sunrise and sunset, as all-embracing as the kindness of God himself, without any separation of "good" and "evil" (Mt. 5:4). But what did we theologians accomplish when over the centuries we kept choosing an increasingly rational and "realistic" language for interpreting religious symbols? The more this language progressed, the more people it had to exclude from the circle of believers.[18]

Three Unfinished Conversations

There are conversations that are like well shafts — full of fear and promise, dangerous and adventurous, in any case guaranteed to change everything. Afterwards, like it or not, you're no longer the same person. Three conversations about faith, more precisely about the New Testament narratives of the Incarnation of the Son of God, had this sort of effect on me.

At a time when the city of Beirut could still claim to be a pearl of the Orient, an island of tolerance, and a nearly successful attempt by Christians and Muslims to live in mutual respect, I met a museum guide in the Musée Nationale Archéologique. She was a thirty-five-year-old woman, the daughter of Italian immigrants, who spoke fluent Arabic along with three European languages, and who had learned Aramaic and Ugaritic as part of her study of archeology. We were standing in the basement of the museum in front of the sarcophagus of King Ahiram of Biblos (ca. 1200 B.C.E.) The sarcophagus was supported by four lions who bared their fangs on each of its four sides,[19] as if to maintain the royal claim to power, now faded, even in death, and to guard the dead king's slumber against possible intruders. The guide pointed out the long side of the sarcophagus, which shows the king sitting on a throne decorated with sphinxes. Ahiram holds a wilted lotus flower in his hand, as a procession of praying supplicants approaches him. "Even back then," she explained, point for point, "people believed in the immortality of the soul. Human life is like a flower that withers but keeps returning to new life. In ancient Egypt the lions might represent the morning sky and the evening sky.[20] Perhaps the king has found his rest in heaven. The individual himself is a winged sphinx, half beast, half angel; he needs prayer to be redeemed." Interpretations of this sort are rarely to be had during museum tours. In fact, they're forbidden, because they lack sufficient scholarly "insurance," and they come too close to the intimate sphere of the personal. The usual policy is to mention the source of the limestone, problems in dating the piece, questions about its place in art history, or aspects of the ideology of kingship and power politics in the thirteenth century B.C.E. Clearly archeology meant more to this woman than knowledge about the past; she was seeking wisdom in the traditions of ancient cultures. "Do you believe in immortality?" I asked her later.

"I'd like to," she softly replied.

"What's stopping you?" I was amazed.

"This thing here." With a gesture of helplessness she pointed to the coffins and the images in the exhibit, now bathed in twilight.

"And what about the explanations you gave before? You spoke with such a peculiar emphasis."

"Are you a Christian?"

"Sometimes. I'm trying."

"I don't know any more. My parents are believers. They never knew any different. And that's how I grew up. When I began to get interested in history, I didn't have any special purpose in mind; it was more out of a sort of nostalgia. Everything in Lebanon has a story to tell about the past. You can't see the waves roll up on the beach without thinking about the Phoenician ships borne by the Mediterranean to the coast of North Africa. Here the present is just a transparent veil; hidden behind it is the radiance of the millennia. I wanted to find the point that it all comes from."

"You didn't find it?"

"No, I lost it. Everything that Christianity teaches is thousands of years older than itself. Have you seen the mother goddesses — Inanna,[21] Cybele,[22] Isis[23]? They all have a child die on them, or a mate, or the god they love. And the world holds its breath; they go down into the underworld and awaken the dead one. These are myths, images, dreams. Can we believe in dreams?"

I tried to say what I had learned: that Christianity wasn't a myth at all; that Christianity differed from all teachings about the gods in that it was historically attested. She shrugged. "I've learned my history. It's the same everywhere. Dreams destroyed and wandering through the underworld. Do you know Pindar? 'Our life is a shadow's dream.' "[24] I never saw the woman again. Perhaps she's long dead: For years now the Lebanese dream has given way to a nightmare.[25] What I wouldn't give to be able to speak to her again. But what is a book except an attempt to continue conversations that couldn't end and in principle never could?

I had an altogether different sort of encounter with an auto dealer from Mersin (Turkey), who years ago drove me from Gaziantep toward Karatepe, to the "Black Mountain" of the Hittites. He was a pious Muslim, and he stopped at noon and turned toward Mecca to pray the opening sura from the ancient Arabic text of the Qur'an. "In the name of Allah, the gracious and compassionate. Praise and glory to Allah, the Lord of (all) dwellers on earth, the gracious and compassionate, who rules on the day of judgment. You alone do we serve, and to you alone do we plead for help. Lead us on the right way."[26]

Years before he had studied the history of religion in London; and J. G. Frazer's *The Golden Bough*[27] was still his favorite book. For him the idea of the *jihad*, the holy war, meant conquering the world for the truth of heaven through kindness and reason.

"But why is the sword of the Prophet revered in the Topkapi Museum in Istanbul?"

"Jesus too said that he hadn't come to bring peace, but a sword" (Mt. 10:34).

"But that's meant symbolically."

"Was it?" His eyes shone with pleasure.

We were standing by the row of free-standing statues at the north portal of Karatepe: coarse, almost clumsy reliefs in the Aramaic style of the eighth century B.C.E., four hundred years after the downfall of the Hittite empire. One of the statues was a naively impressive image of a nursing mother with her child.[28]

"That's not an idol. And yet the Hittites had a mother goddess. Even their predecessors, the Hatti from Anatolia, who weren't Indo-European, prayed to the sun goddess Arinna — called Vurushemu in Hattic — to her spouse, the weather god, and her sons."[29]

"You mean, Christianity isn't quite as new as it claims to be."

He nodded.

"The Old Testament was really new. It declared that there was only one God. All Muhammad had to do was pick up on that idea. God doesn't beget children with a woman, says the Qur'an, and he doesn't make himself the son of a woman.[30] Islam is the first religion that no longer needs myths. From the standpoint of cultural history Christianity is still a part of Asia Minor."

"You understand that as a Christian I can't believe this."

"Do you have to deny the truth to be a Christian?"

He said these words without a smile, quite calmly, as if they were self-evident. He knew exactly what they cost me. And he knew that I would never forget them.

The third of these unforgettable conversations occurred as if by accident in the Indian Museum of Calcutta. I had flown back from Madras with an Indian tourist. We were talking about the great rock reliefs at Mahabalipuram, about the temple of Shiva at Tanjore; and I said I was overwhelmed by the wealth and abundance of Hindu teachings and images. "When you enter a Hindu temple," I told him, "it's as if you were returning to Paradise. You take your shoes off and purify yourself in the large washing area in front of the temple. But then you're considered worthy to see the countless forms of the deity, which, itself without form, makes its appearance in the innermost sanctuary of the temple as the source of indestructible, perpetually self-renewing life."

"You know, don't you, that these images and rites are extremely ancient. Even the oldest cultures in the Indus valley, for example in Mohenjodaro,[31] have this sort of washing area in the priestly district of the city – going back to more than four and a half thousand years ago."

"Yes, I was there. I also saw how in the morning in Benares the people went down to the Ganges to carry out the holy ablutions amid the prayers of the Brahmans. Sometimes it seems to me as if even in Christianity, especially in Catholicism, we're still drinking from these ancient sources of religion, but as if they were flowing only in tiny trickles. When we enter a church, we sign ourselves with the water of rebirth and purification. But our so-called holy water stoups and baptismal fonts look like dried-up pools from the torrents that pour from the head of Shiva."[32]

"Look at this," said my interlocutor, pointing to a picture from the second century B.C.E. that had been found in Bharhut.[33] "Here you see the stages in the Buddha's life: Here's the scene where his mother Mamaya, wife of the Sakya prince Suddhodana, virginally conceives the Buddha after years of infertility in the palace of Kapilavastu. A white elephant approaches her – a symbol of the clouds raining down on and fertilizing Mother Earth. And here" – he pointed to a picture from the Gandhara period in the second century B.C.E. – "look at the famous picture of Mahamaya standing in the sacred grove of Lumbini, bringing the future redeemer into the world,[34] delivering him from her side – in other words, virginally, even during birth.[35] The paradox lies in the fact that the Buddha didn't want people to venerate him or elevate him to a god in this kind of picture. 'You yourselves be your own lamps,' he is said to have told his disciples on his death bed in Kusinara, 'Strive unceasingly.' But obviously there's something in people that forces them to believe and adore the divinity in images that are always the same."

If this Indian is right, I thought at the time, perhaps Christianity is human and true precisely because it makes a primeval music of the spheres and the soul resonate anew. But what is actually new about Christianity, and how does it differ from, say, Buddhism?

Mythical Sources of the Old Testament and Its Earlier Background

Any Christian who reads the story of the Buddha's birth won't hesitate for a moment to recognize in it a *myth,* which, as we have seen, connects certain images of nature with a historical person. But what do we gain by coming to this conclusion? For most thinking people only that these narratives represent untrue, fantastical, and unreal deformations of "actual" history.[36] At most we might credit such traditions with the desire to provide the founder of a religion with special distinctions so as to highlight the loftiness and greatness of his person and teaching. But if this keeps recurring in the most varied religious traditions, the claims to absolute status by the individual forms of faith relativize one another; and we can only maintain an enlightened skepticism toward *all* religious traditions. This was precisely the root of the secret despair felt by the Lebanese woman. She felt that, once applied to Christ, historical criticism had, first of all, destroyed faith in Jesus as the Son of God, and then threatened to unhinge belief in God himself. This is a process that Albert Schweitzer[37] had already agonized through at the beginning of the century and that countless people before him had been compelled to go through since the days of David Friedrich Strauss.[38] Even Christians, with the best will in the world, cannot (for reasons of dogmatic theology, say) claim to read mythical texts like the infancy narratives of Jesus as historical in any straightforward sense. We cannot fly in the face of all we have learned from form history and the history of religion, however often even respected authors may try to.[39] We won't give a religion a solid foundation by seeking the truth of mythical texts in a place where it can't exist: in external nature, as opposed to the *interpretation* of external reality. Anyone who insists on this sort of logical confusion as an article of faith will involuntarily play into the hands of atheism and irreligion,[40] instead of getting closer to the real point of mythical traditions.

Since the days of the Church Fathers the argument has been made that what is merely pious invention (or diabolical delusion) in the traditions of the "heathens" is historical reality in Christianity. But given the findings of the history of religion this has long ceased to hold any water.[41] The question can't be: How can myth be proved to be historical reality? but, How do we understand the truth or the peculiar reality of a myth such as the story of the birth of a divine Redeemer? In the face of myth do we really have just one option: to destroy, as Muslims do, all images in the name of an absolute, invisible God? Is there nothing beyond the Enlightenment dichotomy between myth and history? Can we talk credibly about God only by granting a monopoly to the language of historical facts or by losing ourselves in ahistorical dreams?

Those days should be long gone when, in keeping with the rationalistic faith in progress, the conceptual world of myth (and all of religion) had to be seen as a preliminary stage of scientific thinking.[42] But Christian theology has always had an extraordinarily hard time recognizing the meaning of mythical language. Even today it seems almost impossible to admit the presence of myth in passages of biblical tradition that have been dealt with by Christian dogmatic theology. This attitude leads to the mustering of all sorts of arguments for a kind of intellectual taboo on myth: One defines all the tenets of the Christian faith as "revelation" — while labeling all "pagan" ideas as mere "longing" or wishful thinking, fulfilled or realized only in Christianity.

To take the example of the infancy narratives, it's obviously impossible to equate the difference between "Christianity" and "paganism" with the difference between history (reality) and myth (dream). We have to agree with J. P. Mackey when he says that myth,

> as an expression of faith, is so necessary that clear concepts and the terminology they require, although quite serviceable for analyzing and presenting religious faith, can never completely and adequately replace the myths. Furthermore, lest anyone think that "mythical" is the same as fantastical or untrue, it has to be noted that myth is equally capable of grasping every vision of life and the world that, even if not religious, has the same depth and power of comprehension that religious world-views have. ...The legend of a scientific age that has outgrown all myths is itself a comprehensive myth.
>
> Hence there is no excuse whatsoever...for opposing myth to history, or, as Strauss does, limiting myth to the

night, as he saw it, preceding the dawn of the "historical" age. If myth is an indispensable form of expression for religious faith, . . . then myth also belongs to the raw material that the historian has to work with.[43]

Seen this way, the traditional basic theological formula whereby Christianity tried to understand itself as the sum of myth (promise) and history (fulfillment) is simply not valid. The "history" of "fulfillment" itself can be communicated only as "myth" and has come down to us only in the shape of mythical discourse.

We at most dodge the problem, not solve it, by adopting the hostility to myth typical of Christian theology and attempting to interpret such a highly poetic and highly mythical text as the scene of the annunciation in Luke 1:26–38 exclusively against the background of *Old Testament* prophecy. Even the Old Testament conceptions that when read backwards "point ahead" to the New Testament are located within the periphery of mythical images. Thus the question remains: What do these images mean *in themselves?*

Even *the angel Gabri-El,* who brings Mary the message of the divine birth of the "Savior," bears a name that spells out his mission: "My husband (gabri) is God (El)."

> This says everything that the angel has to say. It corresponds . . . to an old Hebrew tradition that claims the messenger (angel) and the message are identical. For this reason, according to the Talmud's way of thinking, each angel can deliver only *one* message, can complete only *one* mission. The messenger is the message, even and especially in this case, because Mary becomes pregnant by the Holy Spirit through the annunciation itself.[44]

Should we wish to look for models of this scene in the Old Testament, we will have to think of other equally mythical narratives, such as the story of the three angels announcing the birth of Isaac to the barren Sarah (Gen. 18:9–16), or of the angel in the Book of Judges (13:3). The latter angel comes to Manoah to notify him of the future birth of "Samson" (the "little sun"), who will deliver Israel from the hands of the Philistines. We are also reminded of Genesis 6:1–4, that obscure scene before the unleashing of the Flood, when the "sons of God" take to wife such of the beautiful daughters of men that they choose, and with them beget the "giants" of the primordial time.[45]

Likewise the image of the *Holy Spirit* that comes over Mary and will *"overshadow"* her (Lk. 1:35) derives from older myth.[46] "Overshadowing" is a term from the morning of creation (Gen. 1:2), when the Spirit of God "broods" over the waters of primeval chaos like a bird on its nest (the world egg).[47]

> That . . . God is accustomed to have intercourse in the shape of a bird with a daughter of man is well known from the myth of Leda and the swan. To the mind of the ancient world there was nothing scandalous about this. When the text speaks of overshadowing, this suggests the image of outspread wings beneath whose shadow the chosen virgin takes refuge. It also ties in with the Hebrew expression, *bezel kenaphecha* (in the shadow of your wings), a phrase that recurs in Psalms 17, 36, 57, and 63 and in the liturgy of the synagogue.[48]

In these images we find vivid suggestions of protection and security, but, still more, allusions to a *new creation*, a new beginning, as grace-full and wonderful as the beginning of the world.[49] We can ignore for the moment the question (which plays such an important role in the interpretation of the parallel passage in Matthew 1:23) of whether the promise in Isaiah 7:14 should really be understood as a "virgin birth."[50] It is in any case perfectly clear that the Gospel of Luke can't imagine the coming of the Redeemer of Israel otherwise than in the manner of the primeval mythologem of the birth of the divine child or the *divine king* from the blessed virgin.

We moderns, living two centuries after the French Revolution, after the execution of the last absolutist king from the House of Bourbon,[51] may have a hard time understanding how this notion of the virgin birth of a divine king could be self-evident. But all we need do initially is become aware of the contours of this whole mythic picture that makes its way into the infancy narrative of Jesus. The *virgin birth* is in fact inseparably bound up with the idea of the *divine nature of the king,* or the divine nature of a truly royal person. Proof for this can be supplied from the Old Testament. But there we are dealing rather with bold exceptions that at bottom are in complete contradiction with biblical monotheism — erratic remnants of an older mythology thoroughly "blunted" so that they could be set free to work as poetry.[52] In Psalm 2:7, for instance, God speaks to the king at the coronation feast: "You are my son; today I have begotten you."[53] Here we have a sort of second birth, as the king, from the day he takes office, himself becomes God's representative on earth, the incarnate presence of the divine. In this sense the angel first proclaims that Mary's son "will be called the son of the Most High," and the "Lord God will give to him the throne of his father David" (Lk. 1:32). The angel describes as already fulfilled a promise of which the prophet Nathan had held out the prospect (2 Sam. 7:12-16), but that had never become visible reality in all the painful history of the House of Jacob: "I will establish the throne of his kingdom forever. I will be his father, and he shall be my son" (see Is. 9:6). Thus, for those who shared the mythic legacy, speaking of Jesus as the *"son of David"* at the same time meant, in a certain sense, speaking of him as *God's Son.*[54]

Still, despite all such echoes from the Old Testament and late Jewish literature, the stress that the early Church laid on the concept of *Jesus as the Son of God,* beginning with the infancy narratives in the Gospels, simply explodes the Old Testament belief in the Messiah. Faith in the Redeemer's (metaphysical) divine sonship is not rooted primarily in the Old Testament. Instead it borrows from such a broad spectrum of ancient mythology that it can no longer be integrated into the framework of Jewish orthodoxy. With the dogma of God's incarnation from the Virgin Mary Christianity actually becomes what it has since then claimed to be: not a Jewish sect, but a light of revelation to the Gentiles (Lk. 2:32), a religion for *all* people.

To be sure, the filter of the Old Testament still exerts a powerful influence. In fact from the historical perspective there seems to be no direct connection between the ancient oriental and the later Hellenistic mythology of the divine kingship and early Christian faith. Instead, Christianity appears for all the world like a new creation, an authentically fresh revelation. In it the monotheism of Israel, without any loss of biblical coherence and stringency, links and allies itself, by means of certain messianic hopes, with some extremely heterogeneous-looking notions from primeval mythology. With respect to the Old Testament this gives rise to the impression that by teaching Christ's divine sonship Christianity is making a unique and unparalleled claim for itself. Even today, in discussions with notable Fundamentalist theologians one continually hears the argument that Christianity differs specifically from all other religions in its profession of faith in Christ as the Son of God. Paradoxically the truth is quite the reverse: Through its doctrine of the Redeemer's divine sonship Christianity in fact connected to extraordinarily widespread "pagan" ideas.[55] And so the question poses itself to Christian theology all over again: What is meant by this faith in divine sonship in the sense of a mythical symbol?

We can't dodge the responsibility of finding an answer by demythologizing the Lucan text about the virgin birth of God's Son into a mere allegory of God's grace for his people Israel and thus simply evading all of dogmatic theology.[56] That is what (like many other exegetes) Eduard Schweizer, for example, does when he says: "While the virgin birth originally serves to define the uniqueness of the Son of God, as far back as the first narrator of our story, what it really does is describe the grace and kindness of God's Word, which awakens life out of the void."[57] If that was the meaning of discourse about the virgin birth, then we'd have to believe that in its relatively late texts the New Testament adopts mythical notions without actually believing in them. This would mean that only in Christianity's later dogmatic teaching were these texts "remythicized." Such a theory sunders forever exegesis and dogmatic theology, the Bible and the Church, on a central point of Christian doctrine. It also presupposes a "sublimation" of the mythical images that runs directly counter to their concrete history. Isaiah would have had unlimited faith in the all-powerfulness of God's word (see Is. 55:10–11), but not in the virgin birth.[58]

Hence it's impossible to reduce the early Christian confession of faith in Christ as the Son of God to a mere fulfillment of late Jewish messianic theology. Speaking of the annunciation in Luke 1:26–38 Schalom Ben Chorin rightly maintains that "we are dealing here with a myth, whose generative power must not be underestimated. The idea of the Godman, who is a son of the Most High, is evidently one of the archetypal ideals of the soul that are just as real as historical events, only in a different sense."[59] But what is this *different* reality, "woven out of faith, love, and hope, of myth, longing, and archetypal notions, of wis-

dom and childlike simplicity, of dream and prayer?"[60] *That* is
what we now must focus on. Because a religious myth has nothing to do with "facts" but with the meaning of facts. And these
very meanings, which we can get to and experience sensuously
in eternal images, create for seeking and hoping human beings a
self-contained reality, far truer than the world of external facts.

A Christianity as Old as Creation Itself

We can phrase the question another way: What kind of reality
is it that can be expressed *only* in images, which while they
do appear in history cannot be grounded in it? And what kind
of images can alone serve to communicate a divine truth about
human life and human history?

It has already been clearly shown that the proposition from
the Creed "born of the Virgin Mary" belongs on a different level
of reality from the proposition, "This was the first enrollment,
when Quirinius was governor of Syria" (Lk. 2:2). The difference
between the two levels is the same as the one between Creator
and creature, between God and human beings. "In the beginning
God created the heavens and the earth" (Gen. 1:1) is a sentence
that aims to characterize the metaphysical foundations of the
world and the meaning of human existence (and, derived from
that, of all things). The sentence, "About 16–20 billion years ago
the matter of the universe came into existence amid tempera-
tures of more than 10^{32} degrees and 10^{19} billion electron volts of
energy,"[61] is trying to trace back the causal relations in the emergence of the world to an ultimate point of origin in time and
space beyond which we cannot go. Both statements refer to the
existence of the world, but they are thinking of altogether different realms of reality: *Why* something is raises the question of
a logically different order from the question of what something
exists *for.* The first question looks to science (or to the discipline
of history, in the broadest sense) for answers. The second can
only look to religion, and it does so primarily in the language of
symbolic images, in the narrative form of myths.

From ancient times myths have constituted an attempt to give
symbolic expression to the hidden reality, the one concealed
from the senses, of the world of sense experience. Unlike the

philosophy of, say, the Greeks or the Indians, they do not abstract from the world of sense; they transform the sensory world into symbols of the invisible. For myth the world is not something that can be grasped intellectually, as if we could reach some outside vantage point from which to gaze, with the mind's eye, upon the pure, unbroken light of the divine in a uniform white glow. Instead, in the world-view of myth the whole inner space of the universe is perceived like the interior of a cathedral, whose walls open themselves to the sun through their high windows.

The very wealth of images in myth serves to make the walls of the world "thin" and translucent. But the light itself, which pours through the windows in this way, does not become visible as such. It can only flare up in the reflection of all the shapes that appear more or less sharply defined by flowing through the many-colored glass. To round out the comparison, it must be added that in the course of time, depending upon the position of the sun, individual groups of images can appear overly bright while others look clouded over. Then too the meaning of a great many images is hard to make out, even upon the closest inspection. Similarly, the illuminative power of certain mythic images, depending upon the time period, can be perceived as greater or lesser, and can enter into varying contexts of symbolic meanings. But there always remain the places where a bit of heaven becomes visible on earth. The essence of religion consists in this powerful pattern of releasing events and objects in the real world from the narrowness of the earthly realm and transforming them into symbols of infinity.[62]

Upon closer inspection, it turns out that such "windows" cannot be installed at any old spot in the "walls," without damaging the architecture of the "room" and jumbling the laws of statics and aesthetics. And the "pictures" in the windows must be accepted as part of the "spatial layout," in accordance with the temporally conditioned inpouring of light. In other words, mythical symbols are essentially made up of previously available (archetypal) scenes and groups of themes, which cannot be arbitrarily shifted here and there without disturbing the rhythm of life. Such thematic focal points of life are naturally shaped by the most intense moments of experience such as birth, maturation, love, death, rescue, guilt, reconciliation, and so forth.[63] Above all, it is *biological* events, such as generation, conception, motherhood, kinship, and progeny, that myth uses as symbolic models for interpreting and explaining the world. What may appear in the language of philosophers, for example, as a *succession of cause and effect* likes to present itself *in the language of myth* as a *succession of generations.* What is characterized in the language of philosophy as a network of prerequisites, conditions, and occasions can be described in myth as various degrees of relatedness to a common family.

For the interpretation of mythical narratives this simple finding leads to a very important consequence, which continues to be ignored with positively criminal arrogance in historical-critical readings of the Bible. The rule here is that in particular *the mythical genealogies and infancy narratives* must not be read as fantastic biographies but as *symbolic descriptions of the character's nature.*[64] In stories of this sort what the text tells us about the "childhood" of a person does not contain specific reminiscences of his or her youth. Rather it provides a portrait of his or her spiritual position and roots.[65] To that extent the biological (or natural) level of the mythic representation itself must be viewed as a symbol. We must not mistake that level for the essence of the myth, any more than we may read the mythical descriptions of the fate of the sun and moon as mere descriptions of nature.

To be sure, a myth knows, at least implicitly, the whole gamut of its symbolic references. For the believer it possesses a peculiar obviousness that has no need of further reflection and interpretation in order to be intelligible and fascinating. Still, for us moderns there is no longer any direct access to the ways mythical narratives think and speak: Whenever we suppose to take them "literally" we misunderstand them. And whenever we try to read them "symbolically," we risk deflating the seriousness of their claims on us and flattening their unconditional validity into something arbitrary and aesthetic.[66] Nevertheless, a correct translation of the language of myth — natural, oriented to biological models and psychological motivations — is basically no harder than, for instance, understanding that a "noble" or "kingly" person is not defined, as in bygone centuries, by his or her *biological* descent. We readily appreciate that "kingliness" and "nobility" merely represent ciphers of human attitudes and behavior. We always have to interpret the mythical "biology" (or "sociology") as an essential expression of particular possibilities, always remembering that the myths never speak about anything alien or distant. Ultimately they always deal with *our own existence, insofar as it opens itself to the Divine.* In the process we have to shed light on *both* sides, the anthropological and the theological.

If we understand the symbolic language of myth as a window on infinity, then we can also say, stressing the immanent, self-expressive element in myth and recalling Händel's *Messiah,* that myth is something like a song of the soul in the light of morning. That was the point made years ago by Walter Friedrich Otto. Drawing upon the legacy of Friedrich Nietzsche,[67] he pointed to the *analogy between myth and music,* citing in particular the musicality of the creature, the primeval music in the life of every animal:

> The song of the animals is in many cases unmistakably self-sufficient. It serves no purpose and does not aim to produce any effect. Such songs have been pointedly labeled self-representations. They spring from the creature's primordial need to give expression to its nature. But self-representation demands a present reality for whose sake it is performed. This present reality is the environment. No creature stands there for itself alone. They are all in the world, and that means each one in his or her world. The singing creature thus represents itself in and for its world. While representing itself, it becomes aware of the world, happily proclaims it and joyfully lays claim to it. Thus the lark soars up the column of air that is its world, up to dizzying heights, and sings, with no ulterior motive, its song of itself and the world. The language of one's own being is at the same time the language of the world's reality. In the song a living knowledge resounds. No doubt the human musician has a much broader and richer environment. But the phenomenon is basically the same. The musician too must express himself in tones, purposelessly and regardless of whether or not others listen. But self-representation and revelation to the world are here too one and the same. By representing himself, the reality of the existence that wraps the musician round is voiced in his tones.[68]

When a person becomes a song to himself, when he launches himself, in Orphic experience,[69] into the song of the world, or when the music of the world flows through him like a wave, sweeping him up and away into boundless space, then myth comes into existence. Myth is always a union of music, form, and sacred gesture. Hence understanding a myth means transcending the contradictions that rational thought erects between subject and object,[70] between consciousness and the world, between immanence and transcendence. Once again, unlike philosophical thinking, myth is not interested in a distanced judgment of "objects." Myth arises from, and consists in, an extreme heightening of lived experiences of the most intense feeling and imagination, of deep inner emotion. In this experience the essence of a person is laid bare, as his or her remotest origins stand revealed.

But does that mean that mythical images are purely subjective, and nothing more?

This objection is always brought up whenever anyone characterizes the central texts of Christian tradition as "mythical." The answer is that mythical images certainly are subjective, but that in no ways renders them arbitrary or unreal. Modern consciousness has always had a fatefully wrongheaded tendency to maintain that only the activity of the understanding is "objective" and "true," because — at least when properly applied — it is governed by the laws of reason. People with this attitude have evidently not given enough thought to the fact that even the categories of the understanding and the ideas of reason are likewise, strictly speaking, *subjective*. We humans are always the ones doing the thinking; and *our* senses are the ones that give us access to the reality of the world.[71] Above all it's a sign of an extremely narrow consciousness and a mark of intellectual pride to suppose that all that is not thought, the un-conscious, is subject, because of its "irrationality," to whimsical freedom. The religious greatness of myth is grounded precisely in the fact that its images are unconditionally binding: They mean the exact opposite of whimsical wishful thinking.[72]

To understand the psychologically *binding quality* of dreams and myths, perhaps we first have to see how much fear and resistance can be stirred up before we learn, for example, in the course of psychoanalysis, to listen to the images of our dreams and recognize ourselves in them. But this experience of the non-arbitrariness of myth applies still more to the Great Dreams and archetypal images recounted by the myths of the world religions. The greatest insight of psychoanalysis was probably the realization that the images from the unconscious do *not* represent subjective fantasies; they express objectively present truths, which literally decide our happiness or unhappiness, weal or woe, life or death.

K. Hübner rightly observes:

> The psychoanalytical interpretation of myth lent it a new and hitherto unknown importance. Admittedly, psychoanalysis also limited myth to the realm of the purely subjective. But by understanding that myth is a vital form of psychic release, and by believing that it had the power to derive this fact by scientific methods from the laws of psychic life, psychoanalysis conferred on myth the significance of something purely and simply *necessary.* The lost objectively binding nature of myth is thus replaced by its subjective compulsiveness. When myth was considered ... an *unavoidable* childhood disease of language or an *unavoidable* transitional phase of primitive man, it was assigned only a historically limited role. From the standpoint of psychoanalysis, however, myth stretches down into the deepest roots of psychic life and shapes its essence ... for all time.[73]

In this way depth psychology solves a problem that the historical-critical method of biblical interpretation can never manage: It not only shows that the (archetypal) conceptions of the myths *were* necessary in the history of culture. It demonstrates that they are humanly necessary; and at the same time it reveals the meaning of the images in a way that first and foremost does justice to their relevance and binding power for contemporary experience. And so, given the insights of psychoanalysis, it is *essential* for theology to correct and redefine itself in its dogmatic overemphasis on the understanding and in the self-assurance of its historical positivism. In any event, conversely, it is imperative for psychoanalysis to let itself be completed and taken to new depths by theology. Otherwise it will descend into another form of positivism.

Vis-à-vis both human intellectual activity and the ensemble of archetypal ideas in the lower depths of the human psyche, we can assert that we are dealing here with purely human conceptions. *For the individual* these "views" might possess an inner justification and persuasive power, but they would nonetheless remain (in the transcendental sense) subjective and relative. Had the path of evolution accidentally taken an only slightly different course, then (contrary to the opinion of Galileo in the play by Bertolt Brecht),[74] human psychic structures and intellectual capacities would have developed altogether different from the ones we have today. And the world itself would appear to us to have a different foundation and layout.

If this much is granted, a question also arises concerning the validity and truth value of archetypal symbols. This is the same question raised long ago by René Descartes when he wondered how much objectivity he could attribute to human cognitive powers.[75] Ultimately he felt obliged to presuppose that a kindly God – and not a demon – had made humankind. *Consequently* faith was not groundless, and we could know some truth with the help of our sense perceptions and the structures of our thought.[76] We shall have to think in this way about the archetypal images in the depths of the human psyche: They are unquestionably the result of evolution on this our planet earth. They are thoroughly human notions, which have of themselves nothing to do with the existence of God, in its intrinsic makeup. Nevertheless we must and may trust these images, precisely because of their humanity. We may be confident that some truth about God becomes visible in them. We must and may believe that it is theologically justified to say that *God* has given us these particular images "for the road," so that we can find our way in this world and not lose sight of the path back to our eternal homeland.

Of course, it's no secret that this argument involves a theological vicious circle: We believe that God is good, because God has placed images in our souls that show that God is good. And vice versa, the notions of a fatherly (or motherly) God – ideas that could never have arisen without the evolutionary background of warm-blooded mammals – enable us to have a certain trust in the "rightness" of our psychic "equipment." With our longings, hopes, and believing certainties we are no mere "wrong numbers" of nature. To that extent we may and must look upon even (and especially) the archetypal images of the myths, from the theological standpoint, as *objective* – in the sense of given in advance, binding, and not arbitrary.

"Can we believe the myths?"

The answer now must be yes, across the board.

For example, when the traditions of many nations repeatedly speak of *virgin births and sons of God,* who come down from heaven into the world to bring peace and salvation to humanity, then we'll have to say that this vision communicates some truth about human beings and about God. We'll have to acknowledge that this kind of truth can be communicated *only* in such paradoxical images, and so everything depends upon our ability to understand the concrete sense of the corresponding images in themselves.

At the same time *the relation of Christianity to the pagan religions and to history* as a whole must be worked out differently from the way it usually is. We shall no longer be able to say, for example, that the religious symbol of the virgin birth of the divine Redeemer is *based* on Christ. Rather we must acknowledge that the very symbols of faith, including the Christian creed, are as old as the creation of the human race, indeed in a certain sense as old as the creation of the world. On *that* point it looks very much as though the eighteenth-century English deists were right.[77] The fact that something divine is to be communicated in human life doesn't mean that completely new windows have to be cut for this purpose in the narthex of the church. It's enough that the sun's rays stream with new radiance through one given window. And it would be just too naive to think that the "windows" went no further back than the time when they become visible to our eyes. Hence in our search for what *new* foundations have been laid by the historical revelation of God through Christ, we may not go looking on the level of the religious symbols themselves. These images can be found in every person and are expressed, to a greater or lesser extent, in every religion, unless it's utterly imageless. But we can and must ask ourselves what perspective is bound up with the ray of light that the Christian religion sheds on the human soul, for example, through the image of the virgin birth of the divine child Redeemer. It is on the level of "illumination," not the level of form and shape, that the historically conditioned differences between the various religions emerge.

We are looking at an encounter between, on the one hand, the human, the archetypal, and the primordial-eternal, and, on the other hand, the individual, the historical, and the fundamentally new. Only this sort of encounter can give rise to the tension-filled opposition that Christianity expresses with the statement that the eternal Word of God entered time, that in Bethlehem in the land of Judah, in the time of Quirinius, God's Son was born into the world of a virgin. If we wish to experience what such a statement means, we must not look for it in external history. Instead we have to take pains to tap into the images from the history of religion in their valid sense. Othmar Keel is partly right when he says:

> Without realizing it [*sic*], the New Testament has interpreted the millennial discourse of the nations about the true king as an expression of longing for Christ.
>
> The New Testament has transferred the ancient oriental notions of kingship to Jesus through the mediation of the royal psalms, with all their titles and claims. The New Testament believes that Jesus alone has done justice to the mighty dimensions of kingship. He alone is *the* son. He alone has overcome all that is chaotic. Only for the coming of his kingdom can one pray so unconditionally as the royal psalms do.[78]

But then what can the old images, with which the Bible describes the Redeemer, mean in themselves? In order to understand who Christ is, and what the Gospel infancy narratives are trying to say about him, we must, in the following pages, immerse ourselves as concretely as possible in the (archetypal) images from ancient mythology about the virgin birth of royal personages and about the mystery of the divine sonship of the Redeemer. With this in mind the first thing to do is to relate, to reconstruct, and to meditate on the ancient myth that finds expression in various ways, but above all in the scene of the annunciation to Mary (Lk. 1:26–38) and to the shepherds out in the fields near Bethlehem (Lk. 2:1–20).

1

"She Awoke from the Fragrance of God," or the Egyptian Myth of the Birth of the Pharaoh and the Scene of the Annunciation (Lk. 1:26–38)

CB

THE PARADOX PERSISTS, there is no way to dismiss it: In order to understand the substance of the Christian creed we have to go to *Egypt.* As we have seen, the belief that Jesus Christ is God's Son — true man and true God[1] — represents a conviction that could never be derived from any text of Judaism. What Jewish sources may call the messianic king, the son of David, the servant of God, etc.[2] designates a "divine sonship" that is only a pale reminder of the features with which the divine kings in the ancient Near East were clothed. But the actual point of origin of this mythical mode of thought is ancient Egypt. To be sure, the Hellenistic milieu in which Christianity was destined to expand so greatly was likewise familiar with the notion that all great personalities — philosophers like Plato or Pythagoras,[3] statesmen like Alexander the Great[4] and Augustus,[5] miracle workers like Empedocles[6] and Asclepius,[7] founders of states like Romulus,[8] and so forth — could actually be designated *sons of God.*

But even Alexander the Great first had to travel to Egypt to be received as a god,[9] and even Plutarch, in describing the Etruscan priest king Numa, reports the view of the Egyptians as, "not so crude... that the spirit of God could form a union and beget the seeds of life in her, but that on the contrary any bodily connection with a man was completely impossible."[10] The Hellenistic way of speaking of "sons of God" is itself clearly a vulgarized late form, derived from ancient Egyptian ideas. In the Hellenistic world the concept never makes any claim to the absolute status, the cosmic greatness, or the concentration of all reality in a single person that Christianity (once again!) associates with "the Son of God."

To understand the original wealth of meaning in the belief in divine sonship and at the same time to grasp the significance of the central images from Jesus' infancy narrative, we have to turn to Egypt. There we must follow the traces left behind by the people of ancient Egypt from the days when, for the first time in the historiography of a high culture, it believed in the divine sonship of a human being. If ever in the history of religion there was a preparation for Christian doctrines, it would be found growing, alongside the imageless monotheism of Israel, in the image-enraptured millennial culture on the Nile. It was there, among the Copts, not in Palestine, that early Christianity won an unresisting, indeed a passionate acceptance. In all the lands of the ancient world, the Church of Egypt was the only one (a few fringe groups excepted) to survive more than a thousand years of Islamic domination. We owe the crucial dogmas about the nature of the Son of God and the position of the Mother of God to the influence of Alexandria and the great Egyptian Fathers of the Church, such as Athanasius[11] and Cyril,[12] along with Egyptian monasticism.[13]

In his treatment of the history of philosophy[14] and the intellectual evolution of religious history,[15] Hegel argued that Christianity had to come into being from a connection between Rome and Judea: He saw Rome as the principle of expediency, in which the claims of the individual had been bound up with the general welfare only in the abstractness of law. Rome managed to find redemption from the contradictions between the already discovered concept of freedom and the persistent arbitrariness of reality — but only through the Jewish religion, with its idea of the personality and individuality of the Divine. But what if Caesar and Cleopatra had basically been right when they thought the wisdom and beauty of Egypt were needed to fill the power and order of the Roman empire with soul and life?[16] And what if only the synthesis between the prophetic clarity of Israel's belief in God and the religious poetry of ancient Egypt could have brought forth a figure of humanity upon which the principle of Rome,[17] with its unappeasable insistence on power, necessarily came to grief?

The Sacrament of the World

Anyone treading the ground of ancient Egypt meets there a religion that doesn't think "dogmatically," but cultically.[18] Although Egyptian hieroglyphics (mediated by the Phoenicians[19]) taught us the art of writing, the religion of the Egyptians was no book religion. Its mysteries were not written down; they were performed, not narrated but experienced, not taught but celebrated. Since we first find the Christian belief in Jesus' divine sonship attested to in a book, we are a priori in danger of losing sight of the actual cultic or sacramental background of the divine sonship. And if that happens, we are presented with a series of insoluble intellectual problems. In point of fact divine sonship means *the miracle of a transformation,* quite analogous to the miracle of the transformation in the Christian Eucharist. The point has often been made that all the sacraments of the Church are based upon God's taking on human flesh,[20] and that in particular the miracle of the Eucharist continues the miracle of the Incarnation.[21] Such teachings are theologically sound. But anyone who declares the Incarnation to be the "primordial sacrament"[22] really could and should say much more: namely, that "becoming man" can be understood only after the manner and in the experiential space of an essentially sacramental, ritual event. In fact this is the first and most important point that we have to learn from the ancient Egyptians in order to understand ourselves as Christians.

Anyone talking nowadays about ritual and sacraments can't avoid immediately generating a moment of solemn boredom. And the same is true — inevitably — of the doctrinal formulas about the divine sonship of Christ. With their absolute dogmatic rank, these statements have migrated into a territory as incomprehensible as it is unassailable. We are talking about formulas that no longer convey, or aim to interpret, specific experiences. Instead they are now satisfied to do no more than secure verbal conformity with the Christian creed. But at this late date what do we know about the sort of world-view that Christianity, to judge by its words, aims to be? Doesn't Christianity propose a thoroughly sacramental reading of the world in which everything, from the constellations of day and night to the lotus flower and the scarab beetle, could be felt, seen, and sanctified as the locus of a divine epiphany?[23] While believing that such an attitude toward the world was first and foremost based on Christianity, we find that the "sanctification of the world" has hardened into an (undoable) "duty" and "responsibility." The objective holiness of the world is just not part of our experience. And so, working on false assumptions, we run aground and fail to reach the goals we have set for ourselves. The transformation of the world into a cathedral of the divine is not the result of human belief. It is the only thing that empowered faith in the birth of a Son of God to spring forth in the first place.

Presumably the quotation from Plutarch was perfectly on target, and only women are allowed to be physically touched by the spirit of God. Scenes like that of a virgin's conceiving no doubt derive from a matriarchal world, in which the Great Goddess had no need of a man to awaken fertility and life within her.[24] Hence women must have been (and still are!) called to provide binding interpretations of these texts, since they belong to a sort of natural priesthood. A sacramental (or, in the Christian sense, eucharistic) world-view comes down to the attempt to collect and concentrate all the components that make possible, promote, and develop the life of a human being, a world that the Bible describes only in the story of Paradise (Gen 2:4b–25).[25] This is the world of Gaugin, beyond the quarrels and discord of fear, beyond the pains of a soul torn between spirit and sensuality, beyond the naked rivalries for recognition and success that have become the predominant pattern in the patriarchal experience of the world.[26]

But there are certain matriarchal moments when we, like children, as if we had just come into the world, would more than anything like to tenderly caress all things: the grass and the trees, the waves and clouds, the blackbird and the monarch butterfly. We'd like to extend heartfelt thanks to all the things around us for the fact that they exist. So clearly do we sense how little we can take life for granted, how utterly surprising, improbable, and altogether wonderful everything is that we otherwise experience only as "ordinary" and "everyday." But that is exactly how this "maternal" view of the world operates, the view we meet in the images of ancient Egyptian religion as if in an eternal cycle of feast days. Evening after evening, as the world sank into darkness, and the god Atum, now grown old and tired of the day, steered the bark of the sun toward the West, the sky goddess Nut appeared to the eyes of pious Egyptians. She was swathed in the garment of the star-spangled African night, and she arched her body over the earth, as she had since primordial times in order to clasp the beloved god Geb in her arms.[27] The burning heat of the day was replaced by agreeable coolness, and the whole world seemed to rest. Meanwhile at the twelve gates of the underworld the mighty sun overpowered the great Apophis-serpent,[28] the incarnation of non-being in the subterranean depths of all things.[29] The Egyptians considered every single morning a shining victory of light over darkness.[30] Each morning was as much of a miracle as the beginning of creation;[31] and, as the Egyptians saw it, the heart of every sentient creature rose up to heaven when the rays of the sun bestowed the ankh-cross of life upon the images of the gods in the temples.[32] Wasn't the raucous chattering of the baboons in the morning hours on the eastern hills of Old Cairo just this sort of hymn of gratitude?[33] And from time immemorial hadn't these playful children of the moon and night[34] been adepts in the mysteries of the transition from darkness to brightness, in the miracle of the changing phases of the moon, as well as of the transition from thought to figure in the mysterious signs of writing?[35]

The hieroglyphs were, as a matter of fact, precisely what we understand as a *"sacrament"*: In a person's mouth a worldly thing could turn into a sign; and as a symbol, as a spoken word, it could become animated with spirit. That is why the ancient Egyptians covered all their statues with signs, for they saw writing as the body of thoughts, and in turn thoughts became the soul of signs. But everything depended upon never failing to perceive in the things of the world picture-words and word-pictures for the mystery of the divine. Conversely, one had to recognize in God the original model of all created things. Above all, of course, this symbolic openness to the world applied to *the mystery of the sun*. The Egyptians prayed only to the sun, the threefold god:

Hail Ra, great god,
you who run about, indefatigable!
Lord of heaven, eldest in the land of light,
King of Lower Egypt on earth and in the underworld.

Child in the morning,
Lion in the evening,
Chepre with many outward manifestations!
Sun in the day,
Moon ("pillar-like") at night,
There is nothing he does not know about, at every moment.
To you belongs endless time and unchangeable duration,
Life and death are your likeness.
Fair of face, greatly beloved,
Horizontal one, Lord of the eastern mountain!

You are the great power, perfect in birth,
The gracious one, rich in signs and wonders, strong in
    deeds.
Both your eyes shine on our faces,
It is your skin that creates us (?)
Your rays have opened up what is hidden,
Your burning breath has brought down the darkness. . . .
Your color (shines) to earth,
Engraved in our bodies,
Your dew banishes suffering.
Don't set, don't cease with your manifestations!
You are the great "Ba" [the soul] that lives for
Unchangeable duration.

But come in peace, that I may adore your beauty,
That I may tell your Majesty of my wish!

May you . . . irradiate my body, illumine my burial,
May my flesh grow strong through the influence (?) of your
    flesh,
May you open up the caverns of the underworld,
So that I may go in and out great-hearted
And settle down in the place that I want.[36]

In the glow of the threefold sun the Egyptians experienced the eternal beauty of existence, the blessing of the world, the solidarity of all spheres and dimensions of life. For what would beauty be, symbolically speaking, but the work of the sun: the beatification of matter through the animation of light. When the spirit shines out in the transfiguration of the body, when the soul becomes visible in the radiance of the flesh, when purity of heart shines in the gleam of happiness, then beauty begins to enter the world. Beauty is found wherever body and soul fuse together, where a form finds its way back to the truth of its origin, and its inner essence becomes visible to the senses. "Beauty" in this sense is inseparable from the experiential space of the sacrament, because beauty has this power: to make our heart become one with itself and to overcome the opposition between morality and sensuality, between nature and culture, between duty and inclination. These are the contradictions that continually tear our life apart. Only beauty gives us the capacity to experience the world as a whole, so that there is no longer any part in it that would have to be split off and excluded from the Incarnation as something dangerous and subhuman. The divine beauty of the sun and the life-creating poetry of light in all forms of existence were the forces that enabled the Egyptians to overcome even the fear of death.

The Archetype of the "Angel"
and of the "Divine Child"

Only the space of such a "sacramental" world-view can foster the sort of trust that makes it possible for an *angel* to appear to us. The question is not "whence" the angel Gabriel came to Mary, in the context of the history of literature. The question is, how in the first place can an angel say words to us that make mira-

cles grow in the fields of our life. Everything that lends wings
to a person's soul, everything that floods him or her with the
light of heaven, creates a sphere in which angels speak to us. But
this world within the soul is the very one that the myths essentially speak of. And it's clear that we can't believe in such coded
language so long as myth still has to be treated as something "pagan," "antiquated," and "exploded" (perhaps by Christ). In fact
the appearance of the angel is a possibility inherent in every
person. And the angel of God is always sent to us during such
phases of life in the silence of "Nazareth," at times when we can
no longer escape and avoid ourselves.[37]

Nevertheless, such an experience amid the silence counts as
one of the most agitating experiences we can possibly have. In
the famous first *Duino Elegy* Rainer Maria Rilke quite rightly says
that, "Beauty's nothing / but beginning of Terror we're still just
able to bear, / and why we adore it so is because it serenely /
disdains to destroy us. Every single angel is terrible."[38] That is
actually how we feel in the face of the *beauty* of our "angel."
From the standpoint of depth psychology the vision of the *angel
image* allows us to look at a copy of our own nature,[39] an embodiment of the form in which we encounter ourselves on the
way to maturation and fulfillment.[40]

The first sight of what we are actually called to be will always enter the dawn of our life with destructive force. That is
because we seldom dare to really believe in the greatness and
dignity of our own being. It always strikes us as something incomprehensible, mind-boggling, when the veil is torn from our
eyes. We find ourselves facing, at once infinitely remote from,
and inescapably close to, ourselves, the original model of our
own vocation. Hence the message from an "angel" will have to
be the same as in Nazareth, "Do not be afraid, Miriam" (Lk. 1:30).

Historians like to point out that in late Jewish thinking *the
angel Gabriel was a messenger of the last days.*[41] But what's
the use of such outside explanations? Actually there dawns in
every appearance of an angel *a bit of personal eschatology;* and
once again this idea now familiar to us as part of Christian faith
was first conceived by the Egyptians. At the moment of death,
Christianity teaches, the soul of the dead person appears before
the throne of God and has to submit to the "personal judgment"
of its life.[42] The path to this tremendous idea, which confers on

the individual an eternal and inalienable importance, was prepared in ancient Egypt by the mythic image of the weighing of the heart: Under the supervision of the god Thot[43] the heart of the deceased is weighed on a scale against a feather from the hair of Maat, the goddess of truth. Only if the heart of the dead person is as light and unburdened as a feather will it be spared being swallowed up by the crocodile-like devourer of souls, which already stands threateningly by.[44] "My heart of my mother, / my heart of my mother, / my heart of my earthly existence / Rise not up against me as a witness."[45] That was the prayer of the soul, fear-stricken at the judgment of the dead. This scene, along with the ideas about the hellish pains of the wicked, has been taken over as dogma by Christianity (once again in contrast to the Old Testament), in its entirety, down to the last detail.[46] Instead of the goddess Maat Christianity simply has the archangel Michael, who holds the scales of judgment, as we can see, for example, in the impressive painting by Rogier van der Weyden (fifteenth century).[47]

One difference, however, between the religion of the ancient Egyptians and Christianity consists in the fact that the scales held by Michael (or Justice) rise or fall, while on Maat's scales there has to be an equilibrium to avoid condemnation.[48] This difference, which at first seems trivial, is in fact quite meaningful. Depth psychologists will inevitably interpret the wise symbolism of the Angel of Judgment to mean that a person's actual essence is what a person has to face as the standard used in drawing up the final balance sheet of life. Building on this, theologians can add that the "personal judgment" basically consists in seeing one's entire life as a whole beneath the eyes of God and in comparing it with its originally intended essential image. As for the weighing, the ancient Egyptian symbol proves to be more logical than the Christian-Western version, because what is actually at stake here is an inner balance between essence and existence. By contrast, the Christian weighing out of deeds according to good and evil must be viewed as an extremely dubious moralizing of this grand religious vision.[49] The Christian approach seems to be to conquer evil and compensate for it through good works. But for the Egyptians the world, as seen in the figure of Maat, is well-ordered and perfect in itself. Thus for the individual everything depends upon finding and maintaining the harmony, the inner equilibrium of all existing forces and parts of the universe. When the Egyptian faces the goddess of truth, he asks whether his heart is in harmony with the order of the world. But where, we have to wonder, is a person to get the strength to look the truth of his life in the eye, when lies and self-deceit represent the essence of all evils?[50]

One of the wonderful intuitions of Egyptian religion was to portray the divine judge Maat in the figure of a kindly protective angel, as shown, for example, in the grave of Nofretari, the wife of Ramses II, in the "valley of the queens."[51] Maat, the "daughter of the Sun," "the ruler of the shaded land" (i.e., the necropolis), "she who protects a woman, the daughter of a woman" (i.e., "she who protects the wife, the high-ranking one"), "the great royal consort, Nofretari," kneels, squatting on her feet, the black feather in her shoulder-length hair. She is placed in front of the name cartouche of the queen that displays her full name: *Nofretari-merit-n(t)-Mut* — "Nofretari, beloved by Mut (the vulture-headed goddess of Upper Egypt,[52] the wife of Amun, the mother of the divine son Chon at Karnak[53]). The name Nofretari itself is supposed to mean something like "she who belongs to beauty."[54] Maat, the embodiment of the world order, spreads her winged arms in benediction over the name, and hence the person, of the queen. This gesture served as a model for the broad-winged cherubim on the ark of the covenant (Ex. 25:17–20).[55]

Thus the Egyptian goddess Maat represents the primeval form of all the angel images in the Bible and Western religion.[56] And her appearance in the Judgment of the Dead as well as on the walls of the graves of the ancient Egyptians provides a marvelous commentary on the truly "eschatological" meaning of every angelic epiphany: Only beneath the protective wings of the goddess Maat herself will humans finally be able to find their way to the truth of their nature. Only by trusting to a protection that is intended for them, that shields and accepts them, will humans be able to achieve their own measure, their inner equilibrium.[57] In Christian terms, we can also say, borrowing this light from ancient Egypt, that the *"personal judgment"* of an individual consists in being able to view one's own life once again with the eyes of eternal goodness. It means seeing clearly what was meant by one's own existence.

In Luke's annunciation scene the mythical expression for a comparable event *in the midst of life* reads as follows: The angel Gabriel, God's messenger in the last days, enters the life of a person and overcomes the terror of the divine light with the kindly words: "Do not be afraid."

To be sure, if we wish to understand the figure of an "angel," it must be added that, although apparently remote from the sacred scene in Nazareth and yet very closely bound up with it, this figure also includes *the realm of the "demonic."* As in Jacob's wrestling by the stream of Jabbok (Gen. 32:22–32),[58] the "angel" can be something other than "angelic." An angel can embody all the realms and elements of experience that, as in the Grimms' fairy tale of the "spirit in the bottle,"[59] have had to be kept under lock and key for a whole lifetime. Once released, they transform themselves into dangerous "counter-spirits," "deceivers" and "diabolical temptations." Depth psychology interprets the appearance of an "angel" to mean that people who feel a sense of absolute security and the right to live can leave off having to be like "angels" themselves.

Individuals, for example, who suffer from the compulsion never to make mistakes, are constantly forced to satisfy everyone around them by dutiful achievement: That way no one can ever criticize them.[60] But the exaggerated sense of responsibility that results from this in no way simply serves the welfare of others. Its main purpose is to quiet one's own conscience. But sooner or later, despite everything, some discord will arise, an objection, a criticism, a reproach. And then, however reasonable the complaint, one's own perception has to be sufficiently skewed to ignore or justify personal errors, passing them off as somebody else's fault or at least as unavoidable. Thus, under the constant pressure to do everything right there is no way to prevent very serious lapses, though subjectively they go unnoticed. But even worse than this denial is the fading out of all possible motives, wishes, and thoughts that conflict with the compulsion to conform to one's duty. Then the repressed material, which breaks through in seizures, prevails in spite of restraints, creates certain symptomatic character or physical traits, and leads an ever more burdensome and harmful life of its own with ever new anxieties and disturbances. The continual struggle against oneself finally leads to whole regions of the soul becoming literally demonized, while many good and helpful "spirits" are plunged into hell.

By contrast, for all the terror (at oneself) that it causes, the appearance of an "angel" also means that we may, indeed we must, live as human beings. Therefore an essential feature of the appearance of the angel is the word of (an absolute) blessing (Lk. 1:30), a demand for humanness, an unconditional guarantee of recognizing – and, as far as possible, of integrating – all that had previously been avoided and split off from life.

With complete correctness, even from the standpoint of depth psychology, the mythologem of the angelic epiphany indirectly reflects this sort of mode of *self-experience* as a supremely crucial *experience of God.* Because the essential point here is to hear "words" that nobody can say to us, even if we strained all our powers in the effort. We have to listen to a message that none of us can deliver to ourselves, however sensible it may be. We have to live on a permission to exist that in its absoluteness and totality must strike the individual as sheer presumption. Strange as it may sound, achieving the simplest of goals and living an un-inhibited human life requires trust of the sort conveyed by the image of the outspread wings of Maat. Only in such an encounter with the grace of the deity does it seem possible to produce the form of a *human* life. There is nothing a person can take less for granted than being allowed to be a person.

In a depth-psychological meditation that tries its best to do justice to the individual images of a mythical narrative one can understand why in folktales from all over the world the appearance of an "angel" so often introduces *the birth of a divine child.*[61] In the language of myths, fairy tales, and dreams the symbol of the "child" always stands for the basically religious permission to get a fresh start in life. The promise that the "angel" holds out here seems to be fantastic. How's that? Is it possible to be allowed to remember everything that since childhood has never been allowed to live? Can we reimagine life? Is there a chance to learn from old mistakes, to pay old debts, and to use insights developed over the years to build up a new existence? Can we overcome the power of habit, the tug of gravity, and really integrate into our life all the undreamt dreams of love, the unspoken words of tenderness, the barely divined wishes for happiness? Psychologically speaking, the archetypal symbol of the divine child stands for these very realms of the human soul, which spontaneously press their way into consciousness and can neither be "begotten" nor unfolded by mere will power.[62] This is in fact something born in an utterly "virginal" way, something that emerges without the action of a man, where "man" symbolizes the domain of the understanding and the will.[63]

Over any longish period of psychotherapy people whose lives undergo a crucial transformation will almost always report of dreams in which they see themselves confronting the figure of a newborn child. One woman client of mine, for example, had all her life followed the model of her highly suicidal mother and responded to every imaginable conflict with extended death fantasies. In one dream she saw herself going through a barbed-wire enclosure that kept narrowing in front of her until it finally opened as if by itself. Behind the fence stood a woman who handed a foundling to her.

For many weeks my patient felt deeply moved by this dream. "I'm experiencing something like a second birth," she said. "I'm leaving behind my childhood, which was like a concentration camp. I knew that things couldn't go on the way they had been up till now. But in the dream it looks as if I'm allowed to really live again, as if my mother was giving me back to myself. Actually I never had a real mother, but the woman in the dream meant well by me. Somehow I myself was the child."

We spent many sessions after that, luring childhood wishes and longings out of her memory. Naturally, every conceivable fear and guilt feeling came trooping up, previously hampered and blocked by her childish development. The "child" who now grew up was, symbolically speaking, *a sign of contradiction* and a touchstone for "thoughts out of many hearts," as old Simeon put it in the Lucan infancy narrative (Lk. 2:35).

If we want to evaluate properly the real meaning of such experience for the understanding of symbolic religious language, we mustn't look on dream images as purely individual experiences. Rather we have to recognize in them archetypal symbols, which are employed analogously in the religious language of the folk myths. No doubt such dream images have the same importance in the life of the individual as myths do in the life of whole peoples. In particular the degree of binding force is the same in both cases: You *must* follow the image of the newborn child in the dream, or you will squander what may be the last chance to change your life. To that extent the child born "of a virgin" may already be called *divine,* if "divine" means something like inevitable, necessary,[64] in complete agreement with one's own nature.[65]

Above and beyond that, however, in the figure of the child we see initially concentrated the image of one's own "incarnate" nature, making its appearance as a spiritual model in the "angel" of God. Every religious experience that can possibly be had, of gratitude for the gift of existence, of happiness at the fit between being and vocation, of hope for blossoming and becoming whole, of harmony with ourselves and all the world around us — all that is a living presence in this "child." In the face of a world of distress and inner strife, of alienation and compulsive inability to love, of gray frigidity and normalized self-hatred, such a divine child could have no better name than "Jesus," filled as it is with hope and longing. However ordinary a name "Jesus" may have been in the language of his contemporaries,[66] in the mouth of an "angel" it recovers its original literal sense: "savior," "helper," and "redeemer" (Lk. 1:31; 2:21).

For all the introductory remarks about the peculiar nature of mythical discourse and about the ways it understands the world, some readers will no doubt wonder: What are we to make of the Christian *doctrine of the virgin birth of God's Son?* In any event at this point it would be a a a good idea to spell out, in the light of our previous discussion, the actual statement made in the annunciation (Lk. 1:26–38). It has become clear that we neither can nor could gain access to *the experience* of Jesus Christ's divine sonship from certain observations about his birth. Confessing Jesus as the Son of God, in keeping with the mythical language of the "beginnings" of a person,[67] means making a statement, not about the birth, but about the nature of Christ. From the standpoint of depth psychology, the title "Son of God" picks up an *archetypal symbol,* whose inner experiential richness is bound up with the person of Christ so that the content of this archetype is posited in him as real and effective.

Thus the title "child of the virgin" or "Son of God" represents an attempt to interpret the nature of Jesus in such a way as to fuse inseparably with his person all the experiences that have been built into the foundation in the soul of every person, i.e., the realm of new beginnings, regeneration, realization of one's essence, and becoming whole. In other words, we have to assume that the figure of Jesus and what he did were experienced and can be experienced exactly in the way he himself formulates as the key to all his preaching: "Unless you become like children, you will never see how much of a force God could be in your life" (paraphrased after Mt. 18:3). In Jesus' mouth these words cannot have been meant simply as a challenge. Jesus himself, in his person, must have radiated great power (after the manner of a sacrament, in fact). This power must have brought the people who met him, seeking and hoping, a transformation of their entire existence. Thus they were given back to themselves. This sort of child is waiting in every human heart, a child that as such has never been allowed to live and is full of longing to be accepted. All human promise is based on the figure of a still unexhausted life, a never risked and still widely undiscovered life — rather than on all that we have struggled for and wrested from ourselves in order to make ourselves "grown-ups." These "children" at heart[68] were the people to whom Jesus gave the capacity to dare to live.

It's always a feature of the beginning life of such a "child" to trust unconditionally that he or she had the right to be, so to speak, unconditionally loved. This same attitude came alive and took shape in Christ.[69] The mythology of many nations tells of the figure of a *child God,*[70] a divine being, whose child's shape represents something more than a still unfinished prior stage headed for later maturity. Instead the child must be understood here as a valid embodiment of the divine in the transition from non-being to being. Such a "child God" never gets any "bigger" — he remains all his life long the divine child that he is. And in his very childishness a part of the deity reveals itself. In the same sense we can also say of the divine figure of the Christ child that the boy Jesus (despite Lk. 2:40, 52) will never really be "grown-up" in later life. On the contrary, he will always remain the wonderful child who allows and empowers all others to rediscover their true nature.

Characters like Dostoyevsky's Prince Myshkin[71] or Georges Bernanos's country priest,[72] who challenge and question the "grown-up" cruelties of their fellows by their childlike kindness and unbiased understanding, have rightly been described as ideal religious figures.[73] The "teaching" of such "children" is simple, and it holds good for everyone: A child must be loved simply because it is there. A child can do nothing, owns nothing, as yet has nothing to win consideration and respect from others. If we want to love it, we must love it for its whimpering, for its crying, its smiling, for its presence. Otherwise it will come to grief from the lovelessness of humans. This is a truth and an inner attitude that centuries before Christianity the Chinese sage Lao-tzu described with the words:

> Of old those who were the best rulers were subtly mysterious and profoundly penetrating;
> Too deep to comprehend.
> And because they cannot be comprehended,
> I can only describe them arbitrarily:
>
> Cautious, like crossing a frozen stream in the winter,
> Being at a loss, like one fearing danger on all sides,
> Reserved, like one visiting,
> Supple and pliant, like ice about to melt.
> Genuine, like a piece of uncarved wood,
> Open and broad, like a valley,
> Merged and undifferentiated, like muddy water.
>
> Who can make water gradually clear through tranquillity?
> Who can make the still gradually come to life through activity?
> He who embraces this Tao does not want to fill himself to overflowing.
> It is precisely because there is no overflowing that he is beyond wearing out and renewal.[74]

The words of Isaiah (42:2–3) about the "suffering servant," who doesn't make his voice heard in the street or quench a dimly burning wick, could not reflect better the attitude of this sort of divine child. In the New Testament these "eternal children," these trusting *"poor,"*[75] who have become empty for God, who are considered the true representatives and imitators of the "divine child" of Bethlehem – these are the true children of God. But the man we may call "God's Son" is the one who makes it possible for us to become such "children of God" (Jn. 1:12; Gal. 3:26; Heb. 1:5).

Up to this point the spectrum of meanings uncovered by depth psychology in the symbolism of the Son of God or the "divine child" has been limited to the internal world of the mind. Mythical images, however, have two more possible levels of meaning: Their contents are usually projected at once into both external nature and the cultural environment. Thus we have to be familiar with these contents in order to understand what a religious image can have to say, religiously and existentially. In this context *the religion of ancient Egypt*, with the central cosmic and social position of the Pharaoh, once again offers the classic field for investigating the notion of divine sonship. Only by pressing our study further into these connections can we really evaluate, in particular, the scene of the annunciation in the Gospel of Luke (Lk. 1:21–38).

The Myth of the Divine Birth of the Pharaoh

Are there truths that at first shine forth exclusively in a single person and yet are valid for everyone? Are there visions that in their first historical form are visible only in a single individual, although in him we see something of the nature of *all* persons? The belief of the ancient Egyptians in the *divine sonship of their king* seems to be this sort of truth.

We find the first evidence of this idea in a fairy tale from the seventeenth century B.C.E., which tells of the divine origin of the Fifth Dynasty:[76] One day the sun god Ra is unhappy with King Cheops ("he who possesses me": Chnum[77]): "And even if he is willing to grant him another grandson (the builders of the second and third pyramid of Gizeh), nevertheless after these a new race is to come to the throne, a race that will care more for their gods than for their own giant tombs.... Thus Ra will beget with the spouse of one of his priests, Red-dedet, a new race." Ra himself speaks to Isis, Nephthus, and Mesechenet ("place where one settles down" – the birth fairy who determines the fate of a child),[78] to Heket (the frog-headed goddess, the female counterpart of Chnum)[79] as well as to the ram-headed Chnum himself: "Arise, go and deliver Red-dedet of the three children that are in her womb.... They will build your temples, they will attend to your altars and meals, they will make your drinking tables flourish, and they will make your sacrifices great."[80] Then these gods go in the form of musicians to the pregnant Red-dedet, and she bears three children: Userkaf ("strong is his soul"),[81] Sahure ("he who approaches the sun"),[82] and Neferirkare ("he who has been made handsome by the *ka* of the sun")[83] — the first three rulers of the Fifth Dynasty. *Chnum,* who shapes human beings, gives them healthy bodies, *Isis* gives them their names, and *Mesechenet* recognizes them for true kings.[84]

This fairy tale-like story, with identical text and images, was sketched in several temples of the New Kingdom (seventeenth–fifteenth centuries B.C.E.). In the temple of Deir el Bahari it has the following tenor:[85] Amun announces to the Great Nine Deities in heaven his decision to beget a new king for the land of Egypt. Hatsheput (she whom Amun embraces, splendid of face – or as *first of the nobles*)[86] is chosen to be crown princess, the only woman who can lay claim to royal dignity. Amun charges Thot (the god of wisdom) to search for Queen Iahmes (the one born from the moon),[87] the consort of the ruling king. He has chosen her as the future mother of the crown princess. Thot replies that the one chosen is more beautiful than all the women in the country; but her spouse is not of marriageable age, so she herself is still a virgin. Then the messenger god Thot leads the god Amun to the chosen one, the future queen mother. The text reads:

> This glorious god came,
> Amun, Lord of the thrones and lands,
> after taking on the form of her husband (Tutmose I).
> They found her resting in the beauty of her palace.
>
> She awoke from the fragrance of the god
> and laughed before his Majesty.
> He went immediately to her and was inflamed for her.
> He lost his heart to her.
>
> She could look on him
> in the form of a god,
> after he had come near her.
> She exulted to see his beauty.
>
> His love pressed into all her limbs.
> The palace was flooded

with the fragrance of the god.
All his fragrances were (fragrances) of Punt.

The majesty of this god
did everything to her that he wished.
She delighted him with herself
and kissed him.[88]

The royal spouse and mother of the king Iahmes spoke to the majesty of the glorious god Amun, the lord of the thrones of both countries: "My lord, how great is your fame! How glorious is it to look upon your face! You have wrapped my majesty round with your brilliance. Your aroma is in all my limbs." (So she spoke) after the majesty of this god had done all that he wished with me. Then Amun spoke, the lord of the throne of the two lands, to her: "Hatsheput is thus the name of your daughter, whom I have laid in your body, corresponding to the saying of your mouth [i.e., the elements of the mother's first words after conception]. She will exercise the glorious kingship throughout the land. My fame will belong to her. My prestige will belong to her, and my crown will belong to her. She will rule both lands (of Egypt). . . . I will surround her every day with my protection, together with the god of each day."[89]

Thereafter Amun charges the creator god Chnum to shape the promised child out of clay on the potter's wheel and to make for him a body in his likeness.

And Chnum answers him: "I form this your daughter, ready for life, welfare, and health, for food, nourishment, for respect, popularity, and all good things. I sketch her form before that of the gods (kings) in her great dignity of a king of Upper and Lower Egypt."[90]

Accordingly Chnum creates the royal child Hatsheput

and her spirit on the potter's wheel, *and the goddess of the growing life, the frog-headed Heket, presents them with life.* Chnum speaks to her: "I form you with this divine body . . . I have come to you, in order to make you more perfectly than all the gods (kings), I give you all life and happiness, I give you duration and joy, . . . and I make you to appear on the throne of Horus like [the sun god] Ra [himself]. I make you to stand on the summit of all living creatures, when you have appeared as king of Upper and Lower Egypt, as your father Amun-Ra, who loves you, has commanded."[91]

The messenger god Thot (in other words, "the angel") is now sent forth by Amun to announce "the honors and title of the royal mother Iahmes that heaven has settled on her."

He *calls her* the daughter of the earth god, heiress of Osiris, princess of Egypt and mother of the (coming) king of Egypt. Amun, the lord of the throne of the two lands, is content with your great dignity as a princess great in favor, in gaiety, in charm, and lovableness and popularity, *and closes his message to the great royal spouse Iahmes with the wish that she may live, endure, be happy and gay at heart forever.*[92]

Chnum and Heket forthwith accompany the pregnant queen to her birthplace, and Chnum speaks to her the words of blessing: "I surround your daughter with my protection. You are great, but she who opens your womb [i.e., Hatsheput] is greater than all kings before this."[93] The queen then goes into labor and brings her divine child into the world in the presence of Amun and the goddess of birth Mesechenet.

As the newborn son is shown to the earthly father, so now Hathor, as the highest goddess, fetches Amun, *so that he can view...his dear daughter, now that she has been born. Then his heart rejoices,* and he confirms that this is the daughter that he begot. *He kisses her and embraces her and tends to her and loves her above all things.* "*Welcome, welcome,*" he says to her, "*you my own dear daughter*[94] . . . my splendid image who has come forth from me."[95]

Amun entrusts to his daughter the throne of his father, the sun god Ra. On orders from Amun the child is tended by divine nursemaids and suckled by divine cows. Everyone blesses her, prays for her welfare, and hopes that her royal dignity will endure forever. The child has her umbilical cord cut; then she is appointed and acknowledged as crown princess by her earthly father. Her reign will last for millions of years, for all eternity.

This is not the place to show by what route ideas of this sort may have *historically* stimulated the formation of Jewish-Christian legends (perhaps through Egyptian Jewish communities and the Hellenistic Egyptian mystery religions). What we want from this passage is its meaning, not the cultural-historical transference of belief in the Son of God. At first glance only this much is clear: Stories like this one are much closer to the annunciation in Luke 1:26–38 than to any text in the Old Testament. To put the theological relationship in the proper light, we must note in particular that it is the god Amun (in the retinue of the sun god Ra) who is revered as the true father of the king.

In her brief but excellent study on "Pharaoh und Jesus als Söhne Gottes," Emma Brunner-Traut rightly attaches special meaning to this circumstance.

> For who is Amun? — Amun is the wind god, the breath of God's life who is in all things and is nevertheless invisible. By stirring the waters of the primeval stuff, he started the work of creation. He is just as permanent and omnipresent as he is hidden. He is the cause of the psycho-spiritual element in all living creatures; and finally he is the spirit in the sense of the Pneuma [i.e., the Christian Holy Ghost — E.D.]. "You hear his sound without seeing him" (see Jn. 3:8) is the classic description of his nature as a *deus invisibilis.* "No thing is empty; but he, Amun, is in it" expresses his omnipresence. He joins with Ptah and Ra to form the trinity — not threeness — about which a hymn says: "All gods are three: Amun, Ra, and Ptah. God as Amun is hidden; God is Ra before all eyes (as the creator), and Ptah is God's body." This wind god, or in its Hellenistic formulation the *pneuma theou,* in other words the heavenly spirit, is the one who begot in the virgin the new king, God's Son and God himself.[96]

Hence what the Egyptian theologian Athanasius tried to say about the *equality of essence* in the Father and the son also holds true for the Pharaoh: The Son of God (the Pharaoh, the Messianic King) "is of one essence with the Father."[97] Significantly Athanasius also made his point using the image of the son. "Son of my body" is the Egyptian mythological expression for this metaphysical equality of essence, on the strength of which the gods Ra, Amun, and others address the Pharaoh. In the faith of the Egyptians the earthly descent and the heavenly origin of the divine king are not in opposition to one another. Rather they reciprocally condition one another, in exactly the same way that Christian theologians will forcefully stress that Christ is "true man" and "true God."[98]

And yet the approach taken by early Christian theology, with its Greek influences and its orientation to philosophical concepts, was headed for trouble. When it confronted the primeval notion of the Redeemer's divine sonship, as taught by the Egyptians, it found itself in a logical deadlock. Once translated into the language of Aristotelian logic and metaphysics, elements that fit seamlessly together in the ritual, sacramental thought of the Egyptians inevitably became as contradictory as the dogma of the "transubstantiation" of bread and wine in the Eucharist.[99] By contrast, the belief in the divine sonship of the king originally implied no logical contradiction.

This can be readily observed in the complicated *five-member titles of the Egyptian kings' names.* For example, if the Pharaoh was addressed with the name of the falcon-headed god Horus (the one who is found above), even in more ancient times that was not, as some have thought,

> to make the king equal to his god, because the living king [in contrast to the dead king] was never looked upon as god in the full sense of the word. Rather this title conferred on him the capacity to play his role of mediator, which was not possible for a normal mortal.... This is explained by the Egyptian belief in the magical ability of titles to confer power.[100]

Above all the title "son of the Sun God," which prevailed in the course of the Middle Kingdom, was first used as a surname, before it was placed together with the personal name in the royal cartouche.[101] Thus the (civilian) personal name and the (divine) title persist together without contradiction, just like the double name Jesus Christ.

"So long as the later Pharaoh is a crown prince, he is considered the son of his earthly father. Only when he ascends the throne, which reveals his election by heaven, is he called 'Son of God.' Only then is his birth reported as miraculous."[102] In exactly the same way we shall have to say of Christian doctrine that the divine birth of Jesus can be understood only in the light of his resurrection and ascension, his "enthronement" at the right hand of the Father.

> But that also means that as a child Pharaoh is considered the son of his mother, the royal consort. Only from the moment of his enthronement is he considered born of the "virgin," the divine consort. Hence any kind of moral or ethical reasons for his mother's virginity, as fabricated by extravagant Greek fantasy, are utterly out of place here. The virgin is simply an expression of the fact that the Pharaoh can be conceived by nobody else but God. No one but God was involved in the Pharaoh's begetting. Thus the Pharaoh can even have older siblings, sisters or (deceased) brothers, without this calling into question the virginity of the divine consort. And the genealogy of the Pharaoh according to his earthly ancestors stands side by side with his divine origins.[103]

At this juncture I don't want to get into a rough description of the pre-eminent role of the king in ancient Egypt. But to understand the title "Son of God" it is of central importance that the Pharaoh was essentially viewed as the Supreme Priest[104] and the maintainer of the world order. The very title "Gold Horus name" appears to characterize the king as the embodiment of the fiery glow of the sky, as the "scion of the sun-filled sky,"[105] and the cord knotted together that frames the fourth and fifth king's name could be "a sign of the [king's] rule over the sun-circled sky." Or in the form of the sun's course it could symbolize the cyclical return of all life.[106] In fact it was the responsibility of the king to serve, so to speak, as the "brother" of Maat. In this way it was his cultic function to preserve and guarantee the equilibrium of the world in the cycle of becoming and passing away, of birth and death, seedtime and harvest, Nile flood and dry season.[107] As the "lord of ritual" he was the guarantor of the world order, and as with the divine birth, the accession to the throne of a new king was conceived of as a new creation of the world, "which after the death of his predecessor was plunged deep into chaos for lack of anyone to guarantee proper order."[108]

To bring the world back into balance, the crucial point was to reconcile *the fundamental contrariness of all things.* For the Egyptians everything was built up of pairs of opposites *completing each other.*[109] Hence the contradictions of life had to be brought into a fruitful synthesis. For a long time Egyptologists have mistaken this religious or metaphysical dualism for something political and historical: Scholars have thought that it contained a late echo of a period in which there had been two prehistorical kingdoms, Upper and Lower Egypt. But in fact it's almost always misleading to base mythical images on historical events. Rather we have to realize that, conversely, there are mythical images at the bottom of at least the interpretation of history, if not the shaping of history itself.[110] When the Pharaoh of ancient Egypt was styled "lord of both lands," that is because the dualistic wisdom of the Egyptians naturally also demanded a political division of the country.[111] Thus when we understand the Pharaoh, the Son of God, as the "uniter of both lands," this has to be above all in the *psychic,* symbolic sense, as a figure integrating all opposites or as the personification of the human being through whom and in whom all the contradictions of life and experience are transcended in a higher unity.

This point of view literally shows the *sun nature* of the Pharaoh in another "light." It's not just that in the form of the Pharaoh heaven is close to earth. The human heart appears in him as "weighed out" on the scale of Maat, as in harmony with the order of the world. This is not due to some lucky twist of fate, but rather to the virgin birth, through the creation of a new form of man in the act of *becoming conscious.* In mythical terms this meant: through a self-begetting of the sun in human form. According to Egyptian belief, the sun is born every morning to new life in the form of a child from the womb of the sky goddesss Nut.[112] In just the same way the person of the son of the god on the throne of Thebes embodies the form of a person who has gone through the twelve hours of the night, who has been tested by struggling with the powers of darkness, who has been born anew through the sun-bright clarity of the spirit. This person can no longer be understood from "below," but only from "above," to use Jesus' words in his conversation with Nicodemus (Jn. 3:3).

To sum up what the Egyptians thought of the divine nature of the Pharaoh, there is no more beautiful text than the hymn to the king as the priest of the sun. This hymn, which is written on various temples and tombs in Upper Egypt, closes with the words:

> Ra has appointed King N
> on the earth of the living
> for ever and ever;
> on the day of justice for man, when the gods get satisfaction,
> when the truth must out, and sins are destroyed;
> he gives the gods the food of sacrifice,
> dead offerings to the transfigured ones.

> The name of the King N
> is in heaven like (the name of) Ra (like the sun)
> he lives in expansiveness of heart
> like Ra Harachte (*like the sungod*)

> The people exult when they see him
> the folk prepare ovations for him
> in his (cultic role) of the child.[113]

"The king meets the god [that is, Ra, the sun god] in his own form and thus through the exercise of the cult shares the destiny of the god, his rejuvenation and rebirth."[114]

Whose Child Is Anyone?
or the Eternal Witness of Love

Against this background we shall be able to believe in Christ's "divine sonship" only in a way that enables us to become "children of light" ourselves.

Whose child is anyone?

The Egyptians were the first ones to give expression, in the person of the Pharaoh, to the surmise that we don't sufficiently understand someone so long as we characterize that person simply as the child of his or her parents. Persons are not essentially the sum of biological, psychological, and sociological forces. To understand a person it is not enough to be familiar with the hereditary structures, the educational influences as well as the social conditions of his or her life. If the Egyptian image of the birth of a human being from the light of heaven is correct, then it means in principle that a person must be seen as something more than just "earth-born." So long as a person is simply a being "born of the will of the flesh and the will of man" (Jn. 1:13), he will never be able to think of himself as anything more than a transitory part of nature: dully drowsing, and at the mercy of pressures from within and without, a plaything of instinctual impulses and whatever environmental influences happen to be strongest at the time.

In this view a person will be a true inhabitant of the "darkness," the exact opposite of a sun person — the eternal product, never productive, always the creature, never creative, a shape that's merely shown, without any shaping power. In the Egyptian vision of a royal person, by contrast, our existence looks like something that has come down to earth from heaven, flushed with the gleaming sunlight, born to "great-heartedness like Ra," spread out in an ocean of happiness between sunrise and sunset, with the whole world lying at his or her feet. Our brief earthly existence, seen with the eyes of the sun, seems a gift from heaven lent to time. If one were to explain the mythologem of the shaping of the human creature on the potter's wheel of the god Chnum, it would have to be translated into something like this: "Strive to see in the person who faces you a completed work of art, whose original model lies preserved in heaven, elevated above disintegration and death, removed from all woe and untouched by decay."

What we experience on earth will never bring to light more than a limited version of our true being, and much of it will be repressed rather than unfolded. So it is all the more important to learn to look at ourselves and others against the background of the form that the god Chnum formed as our body and our soul. Over the head of every person rests this kind of reflection of the sky. Over everyone's life are spread the gracious wings of the goddess Maat and the protective wings of the goddess Mut. And everyone is called, in a second birth, to ascend the throne of his life and to receive directly from the hands of Amun, the god of the wind and spirit, the claim to personal sovereignty, full authority to make decisions, and freedom. "The wind blows where it wills, and you hear the sound of it, but you do not know whence it comes or whither it goes" (Jn. 3:8).

This thoroughly Egyptian saying is like a late echo of the primeval Egyptian vision of our true origin and destiny: We are children of the light and the wind, born free, with the spirit blowing through us, with an enlightened consciousness, limitless beings, close to the invisible mystery of heaven, the most sublime "material" that could appear on earth.[115]

Perhaps a brief episode from Joseph Roth's novel *Unending Flight* can clarify, in a negative fashion, what experiences can be bound up with this "second birth," the "festival celebrating accession to the throne" of life, of royal origin from light and spirit. Franz Tunda, a first lieutenant in the Austrian army, returns home from Russia years after the end of the First World War. In Vienna in the 1920s he finds a society that is prosperous once again and that has completely abandoned itself to the rules of its game of alienation, which it now takes for granted. Nevertheless at a party one night the conversation turns to Tunda's life in Baku — a wonderful city. "When a wind stirs in Baku. . . . " The talk rolls desolately along on the usual tracks, until a textile manufacturer once again picks up the theme of the wind in Baku:

> "I understood precisely what you . . . meant. . . . Everyone lives here according to eternal laws and against his will. Of course, when he began, or when he got here, everyone had his own will. Everyone arranged his life, in complete freedom, no one ever interfered. But after a while he didn't even notice it, what he had set up in a free decision turned into law, admittedly not a written law, but a holy law — and thereby ceased to be the result of his decision. Everything that occurred to him afterwards and what he later tried to carry out, he had to push through against the law, or else he had to get around it. He had to wait until the law, so to speak, shut its eyes in exhaustion. But you don't know the law yet. You have no idea what frightfully open eyes it has, eyelids stuck fast to brows that never shut."[116]

If you began to be the father of a family out of free will, do you think you could ever stop? . . . When I came here, I had a lot to do, I had to make money, set up a factory. . . . I had no time for the theater, art, music, arts and crafts, religious objects, the Jewish Religious Community, Catholic cathedrals.... Thus I became, so to speak, a boor or a man of action, people admired my energy. The law took over me, ordered me to be coarse and unscrupulous.... The law! Do you think the wind in Baku doesn't interest me more than oil? But may I ask you about winds? Am I a meteorologist? What will the law say to that? So everybody lies the way I do. Everybody says what the law prescribes him to.... When you enter a room and look at the people, you can immediately tell what each one will say. Everyone has his role to play. That's how it goes in our city. The skin you're stuck in isn't your own. And the way it is in our city is also the way it is in a hundred larger towns all over our country."[117]

To the day he died Joseph Roth was pained by this bourgeois ignorance. He was a marvelous storyteller who kept running up against the walls of unimaginativeness, of morally framed emotional insensitivity, of hypocrisy and narrowness of heart. What would people be capable of if they became aware of their true sun-nature and opened the wings of their soul to the wind of light. It would be everyone's vocation to take his or her place on the throne of golden Horus. Surely such a coronation festival would be identical to a second birth from the spirit and truth, as the Gospel of John says (Jn. 3:8; 1 Jn. 3:9). It would be a moment that showed whose "children" we really are.

To be sure, it takes a great deal of inner freedom to really take this step to personal dignity and internal sovereignty. This is an *active doing* (*Tathandlung*) in Johann Gottlieb Fichte's sense: It creates the human being first and foremost as "I," and makes him or her appear as such.[118] It does so by lifting humans out of the controlled herd of the General Public. And how much fear has to be overcome before anyone will dare to be the "uniter of both lands." That means not denying and repressing the inner contradictions, but integrating them into oneself in such a way as to be borne up by them as by the throne of a king.

And yet, in this decisive step of becoming human (incarnation), what's at stake is not "courage" or "decisiveness," but the radically transforming experience of being allowed to live beneath the wings of Maat and being "a beloved of Horus." In no way is the proclaiming of the divine origin of human beings simply an act of becoming conscious. It is above all an experience of love. Here more than anywhere else the rule holds that the psychoanalytical scheme of interpretation must be both confirmed and corrected.

The pioneers of psychoanalysis, as one-sided as they were justified, argued that the dogma of the virgin birth of the Son of God constituted a thoroughly *Oedipal* notion. Ernest Jones saw the idea of a virgin impregnated by the Holy Spirit as a remnant of infantile sexual fantasies.[119] According to Jones, the child thinks that life is begotten in the body of his mother by intestinal gases. Under the pressure of severe anxiety and repression, Jones claims, such notions continue to affect the thinking of neurotics even later in life, partly as fixated passages of psychic development, partly as regressively relived fantasies. But psychoanalysis saw the real meaning of the whole construct of the virgin birth of a godlike royal son primarily as a way of denying the father's role in the process of generation. This denial magically eliminated him as a competitor with the child for the body of the mother. With the help of such fantasies the son made himself the only beloved, and to that extent the divine or divinized son of his mother. And in the sense of the "family romance,"[120] it naturally served the child's narcissism to put a god as his begetter in the place of his hated father.

If we relate this to the Egyptian texts, this view of the divine birth of the Pharaoh finds solid corroboration in the fact that in the mythic vision the god Amun himself, as we have seen, takes on the form of the spouse of the royal mother to replace him by bringing the new son of the gods into the world.[121] A similar account is given by the famous Greek legend of Alcmene, the mother of Heracles. On the night before her husband Amphitryon returned from defeating the Teleboans and the Taphians, she took into her arms not her mortal husband but heavenly Zeus.[122] This "Amphitryon complex" may surely be read as more than an aim-inhibited fantasy of the son. At the same time we can't miss seeing the mother's dream of being able to call her own not just a divine child but above all a divine spouse. But it's also evident from the psychoanalytical perspective that with such wishes for a son and spouse the mother is simply consoling herself for the real limitations and privations caused by everyday married life with a frustrating husband. And so she would posi-tively need a divine child by her side to recoup her losses for her husband's failures as a lover.

There is no question that this sort of psychoanalytical read-ing of the mythologem of the divine birth contains many valid insights. *All* the things Freud saw really do exist. In particular there can be no disputing the fact that in Christian theology and the history of piety (partly, no doubt, under the influence of Bud-dhism, as we shall discuss later [see p. 151] the doctrine of the virgin birth has supplied a nourishing environment and an ideo-logical justification for sexual repression, delusory fears, endless guilt feelings, and masochistic ideal-formations of every kind.

In Christianity venerating the mother of God as a *virgin* no longer meant, as in ancient Egypt, an absolute reverence for the royal son of the god, while completely ignoring the rest of family history or even the love life of the king's mother. Now it meant being allowed and obliged to look up to, in the fig-ure of Mary, a pure, because sexless, image of woman. If the Virgin Mary is the only sinless mortal, this seems to lead, not log-ically but psychologically, to the inevitable conclusion that the loss of virginity, entrance into sexual maturity, and hence sexual experience itself, represents sin pure and simple.

In fact *the doctrine of original sin* espoused by Christian the-ology could never be completely cleared of elements of sexual anxiety and hostility to the instincts. As the mother of the Re-deemer the Virgin Mary was contrasted with Eve in Paradise, the mother of all those born in sin. And while the story paints a sublime ideal of supernatural virtue, this was pitted against the "naturalness" of the feminine, emphatically presented as a temptation to vice and dissipation.

It was very much along theses lines that in 1917 Max Beck-mann represented "the Fall" as the eternal drama between man and woman: Dispensing with the symbolism of the forbidden fruit, he painted with (at the time still) shocking openness the figure of a woman who, along the same line of sight as the ser-pent, offers the man her breast. In excruciating conflict with himself he falls a helpless prey to the magic of desire. Rather than experiencing their own drives, this human couple suffers from them as an irritation, indeed as a disease. They are cursed by the sin of having to be human beings. Everything Freud has written on this subject appears in Max Beckmann's picture as a unique settling of accounts with the neurotic pathology of Christian theology and its compulsion to unnatural behavior, concealed beneath holy phrases.[123]

This depth-psychological critique of the Christian ideal of the Madonna is justified.[124] The Oedipus complex is very well adapted for describing and understanding all the permutations and deviations of the human psyche within *patriarchal* social structures. But it's not equally capable of evaluating the psychology of matriarchal cultures. In particular it takes a rather destructive position vis-à-vis symbolic religious forms. This undoubtedly makes it possible to display in sharp outline the unreal, inauthentic, kitschy-morbid features of a religion. But the original, non-abusive meaning of symbolic religious language must largely get displaced, if not distorted, here. As a matter of fact, the dogma of the virgin birth of the Son of God originally hadn't the least thing to do with the Christian ideal of chastity. And if only for that quite liberating realization our Egyptian excursion should be of considerable profit. Furthermore it is clear that the representational world of such a belief is thoroughly *matriarchal*. Thus it certainly cannot be understood primarily from the standpoint of the (patriarchally based) Oedipus complex. What remains is nevertheless an extremely important experience, which psychoanalysis rightly points to: that *only love* can see another human being as what the Egyptian symbols call a "royal" or "divine" person.

Only for those who love does all the meaning of life and all the value of the world become so concentrated in the presence of the other that even here on earth they believe nearness to him or her is nearness to heaven. Only to those who love does the presence of the other appear like the bark of the sun on the shore of eternity for the passage into the undimming world of light.[125] Only those who love will feel as if over the Yaru-fields of heaven on the banks of the superterrestrial Nile the sun were rising effortlessly in the music of the spheres to an imperishable morning. *Mnj* – "landing" – is what the Egyptians called the process of *dying*. And as a determinative for the hieroglyphic of a landing pole, they added a man who swings a cudgel, because death is always an act of violence.[126] Alongside that they placed a statue of Osiris, because the person is transformed into

Osiris, just as Christians trust they will meet the risen Christ at the moment of death (Rom. 14:7–9). But if a person becomes *Osiris in death,* then he can be said to become *the child of the sun in the middle of life in love,* so magnanimous and light will his heart be. Only in love do our lips spontaneously utter the sort of names that the Egyptians used to designate the king as the center of their existence: "the living sun," or "the image of God living [on earth]."[127] Tutankhamen, who was so insignificant historically, but so well known because of archeology, had the magic name under his title of son of the sun: "living image of Amun," while his consort bore the name Anches-en Amun (she lives for Amun).[128] For everyone who loves, the other appears as the precious artwork of heaven, as the most noble image of the divine, as a sacrament whose embodied experience promises and anticipates all the bliss of paradise.

Hence lovers never stop calling one another by names that with their kaleidoscopic images and their wish for unending repetition might have been taken from the Litany of Loreto. Thus the Egyptian might call the woman closest to his heart: "The golden one who refreshes the heart ... the New Year's star ... sole mistress – The golden one in the bud ... fair truth – who appeared in the sky – lovely is the sky-northwind [i.e., coolness] – house of the moon – queen forever."[129]

Truly religious songs are always love songs, and true love songs always speak to the power of love lying behind all creation. Our heart obviously has this sole energy, which wants to flow through the valley of neediness in the form of a single human partner into the sea of infinity. And every suppression of love, however pious and moral, however pure and holy, however demure and retiring it may act, is always a form of denying and calumniating God. In the eyes of love the fairy tales are right to describe the path of love as a wandering in search of a king's son who is waiting at the end of the world to be discovered in his true nature. They are right when they tell of the beloved wrapping herself on her wedding night in the garment of the stars, the moon, and the sun,[130] exactly as if she herself were the incarnation of the sky goddess Nut. All the beauty of the sky, all the goodness of the world, all the blessings of the deity are gathered together in the person whom we love the most. Nowhere in ancient Egypt are experiences of this sort presented more splendidly than in the sensitive poetry and individual tenderness of the art of Amarna, a unique religion of the sun that flourished during the reign of Amenophis IV (Amun is content), of Ikhnaton (he who is useful or pleasing to the sun disk).[131]

A wonderful feeling of trust and security finds expression here in the way simple scenes of family life now become the site where the deity is revealed. Thus we see, for example, the king and his consort Nefertiti (the beautiful one has come) on cushioned thrones, decorated with the signs of the union of both lands, sitting across from one another. The queen, looking fragile, with an elongated neck and delicate hands and arms, caresses the head of her daughter Meritaton (the beloved of the sun disk), who is standing before her. At that moment Meritaton is receiving with lifted arm an ear pendant from the hands of her father. On the queen's knee stands her second-oldest daughter Meketaton (Atun is protection), who tenderly strokes the queen's chin with her extended hand. Meanwhile the youngest daughter, Anchesaton, who later became the wife of Ikhnaton, sits on her lap and nestles under the protecting left hand of the queen. The whole family is swathed by the gleaming arms of the sun, which arches over the humans, blessing and protecting them, like the royal hands, and holds the ankh up into the breath-wind.[132]

The sun itself, this picture says, is the fluid medium of life, and in the favor of its kindness humans find their way to one another in love. Just as Amenophis IV shaped the inner rooms of the temples in rectilinear fashion, making them face the sun, he also saw human life in all its facets as flooded with light.[133] He himself was the high priest of this religion of the uniquely divine sun. Once again it is the warmth of love that opens the human heart to heaven and makes a person recognize in the other a priest of the sun. Only in the magic of love do powers stream toward a person, transforming the entire world.

Hence in the figure of a person who loves, something of the essence of the divine is visible. Who would have known this better than the Egyptians, believers in a religion more delighted by images and more powerful in using them than any other on earth? One could search the literary history of the nations and never find a more loving and spirit-filled hymn than the love song to the wind-spirit god Amun from a grave in Thebes:

> I wish to see you, lord of the persea trees,
> when your throat brings the north wind.
> You give replenishment without anyone's eating.
> You give drunkenness without anyone's drinking.
>
> My heart would look to you.
> My heart is gay, Amun, you protector of orphans.
> You are the father of the motherless.
> You are the widow's spouse.
>
> It is lovely to say your name.
> It is like the taste of life.
> It is like the taste of bread for a child,
> like a cloth for the neck.
>
> You are like the fragrance of an orchard
> in the time of heat.
> You are like a flower . . .
>   . . .
> Give joy to the heart of man.
> How the face that sees you rejoices.
> Amun, it feasts every day.[134]

Is there any more beautiful way of expressing the theme that keeps ringing in the prayers of the Psalms and the texts of the Prophets: that God protects the orphans and widows and clothes the naked (Ps. 10:14; 68:6; Hos. 14:3; Jer. 49:11, etc.)? Can one find a lovelier expression for the truth that runs through every religion in its depths: that we are "God's race" and "live and move" in God as in the air we breathe (Acts 17:28–29)? One of the grand promises of the New Testament is that at the end of time in the heavenly Jerusalem there will be *no Temple anymore,* but God himself will be the temple (Rev. 21:22). Even in Christianity we are still living in a religion that has to separate out the holy areas from everyday life, so that God can live in them and be available for visits. By contrast, the sun religion of Ikhnaton tried to describe the divine as a temple of light, which flows in blessing and embraces all regions of life. And a Pharaoh like Ikhnaton would have understood the verse from Revelation that the holy city of Jerusalem has no need of the sun or moon, because God himself is its light (Rev. 21:23).

He solemnly named his newly built city Achet-Aton (modern day Amarna), "horizon (light land) of the sun disk,"[135] as if to say: Humans need a place where they can live entirely in the radiance of God. As children of the light they are really at home only in the homeland of the light. It is the task of a king and a priest to show people just this place on earth, where heaven and earth fuse together. This is a wedding of light in the rising and setting of the sun, a never-ending exchange of prayer and answering of prayers, of praise and blessing, of longing and fulfillment. Anyone who calls down heaven to earth and raises the earth to heaven truly deserves the title, "son of the sun," "child of light," "living image of God," "God's Son." But does the *Pharaoh* deserve this title?

The Mighty Ones of the Kingdom and the King of Kings

The whole concept of the Son of God, who is born of a virgin, overshadowed by spirit and light (by Amun-Ra), born into the world was, as we see, completely worked out in ancient Egypt *as an idea* thousands of years before Christianity. And this idea lived on in cultic actions as a vivid reality. If ancient Egyptian theologians had been asked to translate their faith into the conceptual language of Greek philosophy, they would have presumably rejected this strange request as a barbarism. They would have seen it, quite rightly, as the end of living religion. Only when the ancient religion died did people begin, for example, to write down the Osiris myth. Every cult that has to be propped up with explanations, because it isn't self-explanatory, is on its last legs. But suppose the ancient Egyptian theologians had nevertheless tried, against their better judgment, to link their mysteries consistently together and to frame them in the conceptual language of abstract theorems. Had they done so, they would surely have wound up with the sort of formulations that we see the Alexandrian Christians coming up with.

The Christian Egyptians inherited ancestral symbolic patterns that dated back around fifteen hundred years, i.e., a period considerably longer than that between Moses and the Maccabees, the whole span of the Old Testament. No Christian faith can compel one to accept historical dishonesty. Hence we must gratefully acknowledge the fact that the theology of divine sonship was not originally developed by Christianity but borrowed from Egypt. The central concept of Christian faith is thus indebted to the great three-thousand-year-old religion on the Nile. And along with the related teaching by the religion of Osiris of immortality this constitutes the greatest spiritual gift that ancient Egypt could give to the rising force of Christianity. Indeed, in a certain sense Christianity itself is a new embodiment of the old religion of light, the new historical resurrected body of Amun Ra *at the moment of birth* and of Osiris *at the moment of death.*

It is extremely important to see that *on the level of symbols* the saying of Ecclesiastes proves true: "What has been is what will be, and what has been done is what will be done; and there is nothing new under the sun. Is there a thing of which it is said, 'See, this is new'? It has been already, in the ages before us" (Eccl. 1:9–10). The essential dynamic of the history of religion does not consist in inventing new forms of expression. If any religion means and indicates divine things, that comes about only when light from the eternally unchanging (archetypal) figures strikes against the "windows" of the human soul. By contrast, the whole tension, the real wealth, the actual novelty of the history of religion occurs *on the level of the interpretation* of symbols. And *here* Christianity has in fact managed to make visible something decisively new as *its* revelation in the context of the symbol of divine sonship.

What happens when we call Jesus Christ the "Son of God"?

It's clear that in so doing we are not "objectively" defining, once and for all, as it were, the nature of Jesus. Rather we are trying to use an archetypal pre-existent expression to describe a domain of experience whose symbolic expression is concentrated in the idea of the virgin birth of the Son of God. People who say, "I believe in Jesus Christ, the only-begotten Son of God," are basically professing that in their life they have had all the experiences with Christ that the ancient Egyptians bound up with the person of the Pharaoh. At the least they are voicing the hope that they *will be able* to have the corresponding experiences.

In the figure of the Egyptian god-king there awoke for the first time an explicit consciousness of the absolute dignity and free-

dom of the person, of a second birth from the life-giving power
of Amun-Ra, of spirit and light, of a new beginning of "reconciliation" and "union" of the "two lands." This is a balancing out
of all life's contraries on the scale of the world order, a divine
childhood of eternal life "in time and eternity."[136]

Another point must be made concerning the vision of the
"son of the sun": He has come down from heaven and will "go
up" to heaven (see Eph. 1:20–21), as the "first of those who have
fallen asleep" (literally the first of the westerners), as the Egyptians said of Osiris,[137] and the Christians said of Christ in the
same sense (1 Cor. 15:20). It is one and the same interrelated
profession to believe in the divine nature of Christ and to see in
him the source of immortality. If the Christian creed, according
to 1 Peter 3:19, teaches that after his death Christ descended into
the underworld, before he was carried off in view of his disciples
up to heaven (Lk. 24:50–53; Acts 1:4–14), then we are seeing the
ancient Egyptian images of this scene right before our eyes.

We see the bark of the sun gliding through the night, in order,
when morning comes, to cross the ocean of the sky with new
brilliance. Only those whose hearts, in close contact with Christ,
have expanded like the sky between sunrise and sunset will be
able to call Christ the "Son of God." By saying this they declare
that they have in fact experienced the figure of Jesus as "light
shining in darkness" (Jn. 1:5), as the decisive point transforming
their lives from a dead end to confidence, from despair to trust,
from sorrow to joy. Hence for them Jesus occupies the position
indicated in ancient Egyptian religion by the title "son of the
sun." Only when the figure of Christ meets (has met) them so
that they experience themselves as "newborn" can they believe
in the man from Nazareth as "(re)born from the virgin." And only
when people discover the figure of Christ as an opportunity to
start all over, ending a life that in truth looks more like a slow
death, will they be able to call the person of Christ divine. For
what would God be if not the wellspring of life, the source of
light, the condition of truth (Jn. 8:12; 14:6)?

To that extent the *miracle stories* of the New Testament, say,
can serve as examples of the sort of experience that a person
can and must have to come to know and to confess Jesus as
the Son of God.[138] For those who thanks to Christ recover the
courage to stand on their own two feet (Jn. 5:1–9) and to re-

gain the use of their "withered" hands (Mk. 3:1–6), for those who thanks to Christ dare to believe again in their original purity and to "impose" on other people (Mk. 1:40–45), for those who emerge from paralyzing guilt restored to themselves through the word of forgiveness, or who open themselves to life as if they were leaving the cave-tomb as a well nigh rotting corpse (Jn. 11:1–45) – for all such Christ *is* the Son of God, the place where heaven comes close to earth, the high priest (Heb. 4:14–16), the king of kings (Rev. 17:14; 19:16). In this way specific experiences with the person of Jesus Christ are always interpreted by a mythic concept that already had a solid place in the religion of ancient Egypt. Only by extending this concept does it become understandable and internally necessary to hand down the same stories about Christ's birth and ascension that were once ritually commemorated in the person of the Egyptian god-king. This naturally raises once again the question of what distinguishes Christian faith from the religion of the ancient Egyptians.

One thing is clear: Belief in the divine sonship of a person cannot be the fundamental difference between Christianity and the Pharaonic faith of the Egyptians. *On the level of religious symbolism itself there is complete agreement* between the religion of the Christians and the religion of the ancient Egyptians. Indeed, from the standpoint of the *history of religion* one would even have to say that Christianity is totally dependent upon the religion of the ancient Orient for the central statement of Christian tradition. Or rather, one would have to say that Christianity is totally dependent on Egypt, if it weren't for the fact that psychologically it makes much more sense to think of a real rediscovery of the corresponding primeval archetypal thought patterns, as they – independently of one another – *continually* appear in the religions of the world's peoples. This means, first of all, that Christianity *can't* challenge the truth content of, for example, ancient Egyptian religion. It too has at its disposal experiences capable of advancing an ensemble of ideas about the divine sonship of a royal or priestly person from the depths of the human psyche into consciousness.

And one must even grant that the ritual elaboration of the symbolic images in ancient Egypt was staged with incomparably greater richness and intensity than in the relatively thin conceptual scheme of Christian theology. We need to become familiar with the whole content and rich frame of references of the symbolism of divine sonship, virgin birth, promise by the angel, etc. But to do so, it is *altogether indispensable for the understanding of Christian faith* to meditate our way through the corresponding religious images in ancient Egypt. Only from that perspective can we outline the realms of experience to which the Christian vocabulary would point the way. And yet at this juncture the difference *in the interpretation* of the essentially identical idea of the Son of God between Jesus Christ and the Egyptian Pharaoh is unmistakable and of crucial importance. We can call it the difference of *personal depth.*

In his philosophy of history G. W. F. Hegel long ago rightly observed that it was a principle of life in the ancient Near East that one person alone (the monarch) was considered free, while all others were unfree.[139] To be sure, the cause of this radical centralization of all decision-making authority does not lie, as one might first assume, in the individual ruler's subjective desire for power. It is rather the symbolic role itself that lends him his godlike dignity. Hence we can't say that the Pharaoh *usurped* his absolute power over other people. Quite the contrary, as S. Morenz emphasizes, in the New Kingdom it was the kings themselves "who . . . assigned all power to the deity and at the same time spoke of human impotence."[140] If the king is worshipped as a representation of God, this is in the sense of a cultic image.[141] In the time of the Ramessides, for example, prayers were framed

> that tried to make the idea of the immediately experienced transcendent God bearable, even familiar, as their shepherd. Songs of praise were composed that sound like hymns to the Good Shepherd, with details occasionally reminiscent of Psalm 23: "Amun, shepherd, who early cares for his cattle, who drives the hungry to pasture. The shepherd drives the cattle to pasture – Amun, you drive me, the hungry one, to feed, for Amun is a shepherd, a shepherd who is not idle." Or: "How lovely is your appearing, Ra, my Lord, who acts as a shepherd in his pasture. We drink at his water. See, I breathe the air that he gives. . . . Ra, great shepherd! Come, all you cattle. Look, you spend the day at his fodder before him, after he has cleared away all evil."[142]

Such prayers clearly show that, however often they might stress the essential equality of the king with the sun in the sky, the Egyptians readily distinguished between the divine model (Amun-Ra) and his divine reflection (the Pharaoh, the Son of God).

To that extent the claim of the king of ancient Egypt to be the Son of God must certainly not be interpreted as an expression of tyrannical hybris. Instead, for the Egyptians the king held the position of a *corporative person.*[143] That is, he was the ideal embodiment of the image of humanity, as the Egyptians saw it, in humanity's essential vocation. The figure of the king made visibly and corporeally present the share that all men and women had, in accordance with their whole existence, as members of the same religion and same nation.

Only through this mystical unity between the king and his people or between the people and its king can we understand the enormous readiness to identify with the Pharaoh. This was seen most graphically by the way the Egyptians every year by the tens of thousands took upon themselves the strenuous task of building the pyramids and temples. They did so without, like other nations, employing giant reserve armies of prisoners-of-war and slaves. Only in this way can we understand the longing felt by Egyptian officials to find their last rest in the shadow of the pyramids — near and in union with the divine.

Still, for all the grandeur of the Egyptian conception of the Pharaoh's divine sonship *the archaic form of the corporative person,* in which this symbolism first appears, is necessarily ambivalent. And here lies the actual point of departure for new and more advanced development by Christianity. The true essence of being human, its dignity and greatness, is expressed and represented in *an individual.* But the actual form of a second birth of man from the spirit and light makes its appearance as something inherently objective and obligatory. This second birth lays claim to all energies and penetrates all parts of life in human consciousness, and gets from that its necessity and truth. But at the same time the appearance of external objectivity prevents all those energies from being concentrated on a single individual so that the substance of the symbolic intention can become *everyone's* reality. In other words, so long as the symbolic expressive figure is still posited in its archaic external form as the essential element, it is still standing in the way of the appropriation of its spiritual truth.

Thus, for example, the king of Egypt still needed an enormous mass of gold and precious stones, expensive pomp and show, complete political power and triumphal war booty from raids into Nubia and Asia Minor,[144] in order to furnish tangible proof of his title of Son of God. In this way the symbolic truth of the figure of the God-king, precisely because it is at first taken *unsymbolically,* i.e, externally-realistically, leads to a persistent obscuring of its content: The freedom of the person, projected onto a single man, is true in its ideal mode; yet it remains untrue in its real mode where it must assert itself as the unfreedom of all.

That is why the religion of Egypt in its inner contradictoriness wears the face of a sphinx. And the question remains how we are to become aware of the inexhaustible wealth of its images and ideas. If we focus narrowly on the externality of its expression, then, from the historical standpoint, we see a straight line leading from the Egyptian Pharaohs of the New Kingdom to the Assyrians and Babylonians with their boundless adoration of military power,[145] to the Persian court style of Persepolis,[146] to the bold world-conquering campaigns of Alexander "the Great,"[147] and to the divine monarchy of the Roman Caesars.[148] On the other hand if we look to *the inner meaning of the religious symbol* of the Son of God, then we find a straight path from the images of ancient Egypt to the dogmas of the early Church. It is the great achievement of Christianity to have grasped the central symbolism of ancient Egypt in its intellectual content and to have elevated it *in pure inwardness* to the central expression of its own faith.

Who is the "king of kings" (Rev. 17:14), the "king of glory" (Ps. 24:10), the "king forever" (Ps. 29:10)?

Immediately before his passion, at the Lást Supper, after the words instituting the Eucharist and expressing hope for the perfecting of the world in the coming kingdom of God (Lk. 22:16), Jesus responds to a dispute among the disciples by rendering his definitive judgment on earthly power: "The kings of the Gentiles exercise lordship over them; and those in authority over them are called benefactors. But not so with you; rather let the greatest among you become as the youngest, and the leader as one who serves" (Lk. 22:25–26). According to Jesus' critical rejection of all external striving for power, the "great" are those who ask themselves whom they can help by their way of being and acting. Jesus prizes people who don't base their feeling of self-worth, in keeping with royal Psalm 110, on making their fellow humans their "footstool" (v. 1) or "shattering their heads over the wide land" (v. 5). He values those who promote and strengthen the self-esteem of others as much as possible. A true "king" for Jesus is someone who lives the idea of the divine sonship as a *universally valid* truth and strives to perceive the still veiled royal dignity of each person even in the most disfigured human face. He alone will have the power, after the manner of the true "good shepherd," who never robs or plunders, to call every one of his "sheep" by name and lead them out (Jn. 10:2–3).

Incomparably stronger than all the might of rulers is the power of disinterested love in the hearts of people, for only this can penetrate the whole being of the other. Only the person who never wants to rule wins through kindness the trust and affection of everyone. Only those who themselves are so "transparent" that when near them the soul of the other opens to the light are true "priests of the sun." And only someone whose own dedication calls into life all the forces of beauty, of self-respect and of "expansiveness of heart" deserves the name of a "son of Ra."

Franz Werfel once described this attitude of the "children of God" when he programmatically resolved:

> Never again will I
> Laugh a person's face to scorn.
> Never again will I
> Judge the nature of a man.
>
> Yes, there are cannibal brows.
> Yes, there are pimp's eyes.
> Yes, there are glutton's lips.
>
> But suddenly
> From the dull speech
> Of the easily judged man
> From a helpless shrug of the shoulders
> A tender fragrance of linden wafted to me

Out of our distant happy homeland.
And I regretted my crafty judgment.

Even in the most slovenly face
The God-light of its unfolding waits.
The greedy hearts reach for filth —
But in every
Human being born
Is the promise of the Savior's homecoming.[149]

Only those who have themselves renounced "judging" other people (Lk. 6:37) can give others an opportunity to become "more righteous." Only they are siblings of Maat, brothers and sisters of the "daughter of the sun," guardians of harmony on the scale of the world order. Only those who go two miles with someone who forces them to go one (Mt. 5:41) are walking on the royal road of the sun, whose path is as wide as the whole world between sunrise and sunset. Only they are a "Horus on the horizon," as the Egyptians used to say. And only those who freely give to someone who asks (Mt. 5:32) correspond to the image of the Egyptian sun, whose hands spread universally like a flowing benediction of warmth and light over the head of every single person, so that they may all breathe life and drink joy. The one whom we must love with all our heart, with all our mind, and with all our strength (Mk. 12:30), because he gathers together all our thinking, enthralls all our feeling, and unites all our efforts, is in truth the "living image" of God on earth.

Christians believe that anyone who understands who Jesus is can, indeed must, speak in this way about him. What began with the concept of the royal corporative figure of Pharaoh finds its way to reality, so that an individual can say as the Apostle Paul did: "It is no longer I who live, but Christ who lives in me" (Gal. 2:20). What began in ancient Egypt as a single person's claim of freedom is fulfilled in Christianity by a freedom that shatters every yoke (Gal. 5:1). The fundamental principle posited in the divine "son of the sun" in ancient Egypt finds closure when the "children of light" take part in their "adoption as sons" (Gal. 4:5; Eph. 5:8). We can't understand any of these expressions and images without ancient Egypt. But ancient Egypt arrived at the realization of its own truth in the new religion of Christianity, and in that form it lives on. Under its Christian name it conquered the world. The "Cheperu of Ra," the evolving forms of the sun, wrapped themselves in the garment of Christ. For nothing goes under in the realm of the spirit without heading toward a new morning.

Meanwhile it was precisely the political "night" of ancient Egypt from which the "unconquerable sun" of Christianity came forth. It's hard to get a really clear notion of how much Christianity had to distance itself from the spirit of the Israelite royal psalms, with their expectations of political power and their nationalistic hopes, in order to distinguish the "kingdom of heaven" from all the kingdoms of this world. In Jesus' day powerful Jewish factions fought ever more fanatically for the coming of a new Davidic empire. They refused to see that all such messianic promises reach fruition in their religious sense only when understood *symbolically* (instead of "literally," in other words ideologically).

But by this time ancient Egypt had already been practicing for almost a thousand years to learn wisdom within political powerlessness and to recognize the insignia of bygone power in the enduring truth of their spiritual meaning. As far back as the Middle Kingdom the Osiris religion initiated a sort of democratization of Egyptian piety.[150] The faith in the immortality of life was no longer reserved to Pharaoh, but shared with everyone. At the same time the external (magical) arrangements for immortality became increasingly simpler and more internalized. Now there was no longer any need to build pyramids and fill their chambers with vast amounts of treasure in order to be allowed to cherish the hope of being safe and sound in the next world. But this very internalizing of all religious modes of expression in ancient Egypt was silently preparing Christianity's message of the divinity of the Son of man and the immortality of the poorest slave in Rome. Here too the religion of Christ would pick up and complete the religion of Osiris.

Thus the objective loss of power by the Egyptians had a dialectic effect: Externally it created a political vacuum in which Israel, for the very first time, even if only for a few centuries, got a certain amount of breathing room for its autonomy and national greatness. But precisely because of this the people of the Old Testament were thrust into a messianic hope from whose political externals the nation of fellahin on the Nile increasingly distanced itself. The de facto powerlessness of the Son of God on the throne of Egypt thus became the best nurturing soil to prepare the hope for a king whose kingdom was not of this world (Jn. 18:36). And when this king came, he had to flee Israel in order to grow up in Egypt. This is not just a matter of fulfilling a biblical "prophecy" — *inwardly* it seems to correspond to the truth of what Matthew tells us in 2:13–15 about the "flight to Egypt."

To be sure, this poses a problem for Christianity that is an intrinsic part of the tension between the inner and outer side of the ancient Egyptian symbolism of the "Son of God." The flight from the world by the Egyptian Desert Fathers, by which they gave Christianity its essential shape after the time of the persecutions, could not and cannot in itself be the ultimate form of the "truth of the sun."[151] Ever since the first days of the new religion the question arises of how Christian interiority interprets itself for the task of shaping the world, how faith in the kingdom of heaven forms itself into a path on earth. "What shall we do?" (Lk. 3:10). This question of the people to John the Baptist finds its answer in the next scene in the Gospel of Luke: the meeting between the mother of Jesus and the mother of the Baptist. This is a narrative mode that no longer belongs to myth but to legend and hence must be read in a different way.

2

Mary and Elizabeth, or the Meeting of Two Worlds (Lk. 1:39–45, 56)

CB

I CAME TO THE CONCLUSION that what people call life is death and what they call death is life.... Where is it written that a bedbug lives and the sun is dead?" How much hope must have been destroyed, and how much suffering must one have tasted to agree with this résumé by I. B. Singer.[1] "What shall we do?" Ever since humanity began to exist, people have complained that the world is in a bad way, and there has been no lack of attempts to keep the evil in check. The two possible answers, the ethical solution and the religious solution, have been pitted against each other since time immemorial. Nowhere else in world history – with the one exception of the difference between Confucius and Lao-tzu in ancient China – do we find this opposition so clearly and sharply outlined as in the meeting, and the contrast, between John the Baptist and Jesus Christ. And it is this inner tension whose *essence* must be worked out in order to understand the story of Mary's "visitation."

The account of Mary's visit with her "cousin" Elizabeth has been largely evaluated as an attempt to define the relationship between John's disciples and the community of Jesus.[2] John is considered the "elder," because his appearance occurred earlier than Jesus' public career. For that reason, the consensus has been, the Church was intent on claiming for itself the figure of the Baptist as the "precursor" of Christ.[3] The story of Mary's visitation therefore served the purpose of linking the self-contained tradition of John the Baptist[4] to the tradition of Jesus in the sense that even in his mother's womb John joyfully greeted the child Jesus.

Such historical-critical interpretations are surely on the right track in recognizing that "infancy narratives" of this sort are not biographical information, but theological statements. In fact we are not dealing here with historical data from the life of Mary and Elizabeth, but rather with something crucial in their "children's" relationships with one another.[5] But what is "essential" about the person of John the Baptist in relation to, and by contrast with, the figure of Jesus cannot be discussed as a question of the past. Instead we must try to grasp the meaning of John the Baptist in the *transtemporal* thematic and typical sense, so as to understand the eternal "precursory element" in his appearance with regard to Christ. Only then will we comprehend what is really at stake in the meeting between Mary and Elizabeth.

Who *was* John the Baptist?

Readers who ask this question will find themselves confronted in the usual commentaries with a series of plausible hypotheses: He was a man who by all appearances was close to the Essenes, who likewise were familiar with immersion baths and lived in the wilderness.[6] He was a man who, like the Essenes, believed that the messianic kingdom would be dawning soon and rated fidelity to the law of God higher than the priestly cult in the Temple of Jerusalem.[7] He was a man who, like the Essenes, saw the coming judgment of God on the godless right before his eyes. But unlike the Essenes, John cried out to save at the last minute whatever was still savable.[8] In making our way through such historical reconstructions we find various bits of information but not what John the Baptist meant to his contemporaries and what he himself wanted to be: an event, a challenge, a questioning of all of existence for weal or for woe.

Who *is* John the Baptist?

To answer *this* question you have to feel the need, the revolt, the desperate hope that will come over all those who try to measure the course of this world against the criterion of the divine.

In the Old Testament an author whom we call the "Yahwist" (because he always uses "Yahweh" for the name of God) raises the issue of the incompatibility of God's will and human will, of truth and life, of ideal and reality, to a level of lethal consistency. In the story of the Flood,[9] as we read in the Bible's opening pages, God can no longer bear to look on as humans plunge more and more deeply into disaster. Amid a world that could be like a Paradise it is clear that only human beings lack all measure and can't stand being mere creatures. Only human beings strive from sheer anxiety to carve out breathing space for themselves and to press out of themselves something absolute, something ontologically equal to God. Their own creatureliness becomes a terrible torment to them and an inescapable curse: incapable of loving, tortured by shame, at odds with themselves and the world around them.

Thus human beings alone find themselves exiles, refugees, banished from the Paradise of the world. And even the attempt to restore their lost status with sacrifices and accomplishments leads only to the eternal drama of relentless competition and fatal violence (Gen. 4:1–16). Human beings continually find that what was actually designed to ground their happiness becomes their doom: If humans weren't so dependent on one another as man and wife, there wouldn't be the continual curse of mutual humiliations and misunderstandings in the most private and intimate regions of life together (Gen. 3:15–16). If human beings were not so much each other's brothers and sisters, the feeling of menace and reciprocal hostility wouldn't flare out of control (Gen. 4:1–12). If humans didn't have such an infinite need for love, they wouldn't be continually creating for themselves a domain of inescapable, loveless conflicts (Gen. 4:22–24). In the end God seems to have no other option than to eradicate man from the face of the earth because "every imagination of the thoughts of his heart is only evil continually" (Gen. 6:5). Ultimately the Eternal One is sorry to have ever made humankind; and so God decides to send a great Flood over the earth, as if he had to cleanse his world, like Augeas's stable, from the filth of humanity.

Evidently *John's baptism of repentance* expresses a quite

similar idea.[10] As far back as the Fathers of the Church Christian writers repeatedly and rightly recognized in the Flood a prophetic image, an archetype of baptism.[11] John too seems convinced that human beings, such as they are, have actually earned "destruction." Yet can't this knowledge be a source of salvation? Anyone who resolutely tries to begin a new life can find the flood of annihilation turning into a cleansing bath and waters of regeneration. One simply has to have the right insight and the right will in good time. Even if all of our previous life was a failure it's still possible to start all over again. At any rate John cherishes this hope of all prophets, that the announcement of the threatened catastrophe will lead to second thoughts, penance, and conversion; and in this way he represents with special urgency *the demand for ethical renewal.*

For John humans are bad when they don't do the good that they could do. But they can do good only when they understand what is good for them, and when they have the will to follow their insights. Thus John urgently preaches the threat of judgment by the waters of the Jordan. He proclaims a judgment so certain and inevitable that his hearers grow more ready to anticipate it in the form of a voluntary flood and thereby perhaps avoid it after all. With wild language John humiliates and abuses his audience (Jn. 3:7–9): "Brood of vipers" is the label for these ripe descendants of the serpent in Paradise, as John sees them, for a people full of cunning, lies, and duplicity, whose whole essence consists in the dirty dealings of inner conflict and two-facedness. "Sons of Belial"[12] was the correct designation in Qumran for this sort of people. Nevertheless, provided they have been brutally honest in taking note of their own self-abasement, of the continual self-contradiction in their internalized cruelty, can't we expect people to find the courage at last to confess the truth about themselves?

And if they don't have the courage – can't they be helped by the whip of fear? "Even now the axe is laid to the root of the trees," John thunders. The logic here is like burning brush in advance of a prairie fire or trying electroshock for apparently incurable madness. Above all the Baptist tears down any ideological reassurances: "But we are the children of Abraham!" Nowadays one might say in the same vein, "But we're members of the party with the most progressive platform." "But we're the established representatives of the objectively correct interests." "But we simply embody what everybody is saying and doing anyhow." John wants once and for all to unmask this entrenchment in the guarantees of the collective and to show how baseless it is. "God is able from these stones to raise up children to Abraham." In fact it would be easier to awaken stones to life than to soften the hardness of human hearts.

Still, in his striving for the moral renewal of humanity John has carried things further than all the prophets before him: "Among those born of women none is greater than he," Jesus will later say of him (Lk. 7:28). So many people came to him and had themselves baptized. A new life — John must have described this hope as so palpably close. All his directives are so solid, practical, absolutely doable. The demands of some prophets before him who dreamed of moral improvement for humanity may have bordered on the utopian. But John's message was quite concrete. When asked, "What shall we do?" John's answer is lapidary: "He who has two coats, let him share with him who has none" (Lk. 3:10).

How right he is. The world would be different on the spot if people acted the way John insists. The recipe is quite simple: No one should have more than he or she unconditionally needs; everyone should go halves with a neighbor in need. Naturally the haggling will begin at once over what one unconditionally needs. "One" absolutely needs a car. But do I really need it? "One" absolutely needs a home of one's own. But do I really need it? "One" absolutely needs tax-free life and health insurance. But do I really need it?

There are millions of people who when they get up in the morning have no more idea of what the day will bring than do stray dogs on the streets of a metropolis. In exchange for their uninsured and insecure condition there would only be the uneasiness and restlessness of our hearts. Those were the feelings John wanted to engender. There are millions of people in Calcutta, Madras, São Paulo, Manila — all over the world, who sleep under bridges and on the pavement. How shall we take them in, so that God may receive us into "eternal habitations," since all humans have the same right to a home (see Lk. 16:9)? There are millions of people so hungry and exhausted that they can scarcely drag themselves through life. Should the cultivation and cult of our comforts really be more important than the language of their wasted bodies and their souls, stifled in sorrow and help-lessness? Visitors to Auschwitz today are shown the impressions from the fingernails of the prisoners systematically murdered in concrete gas chambers. But what does it take to make an impression on us? Redistribute half the surplus, and there would be no more need on earth. Two thousand years after John we can only admit that the man at the Jordan was right.

Tax collectors come to John, and his directive to them is engagingly simple: Don't take in *more* than the regulations pre-scribe. There were many people in Israel who would have liked to put an end then and there to the whole tyranny of the Ro-mans — the quintessence of ungodliness. Even in Qumran they indulged in the idea of a holy war against the impious foreign conquerors. And naturally the fellow travelers, trimmers, and collaborators among the Jews were considered incomparably worse and more dangerous than their opponents themselves. Such fishy individuals smudged the clear battle lines, they de-fused the dynamics of polarization. In the forefront of this group were the tax collectors.

Thus a moral veto against them as a profession is the first thing one would expect from John. But he was no dreamer who would have forced people to destroy their existence so as to start all over on the wreckage of the past. If at least you could avoid need-lessly increasing the objective inhumanity of violence (when it can't be displaced without fresh violence) for your own profit — *that* would be doing a lot. Once again the world would look de-cidedly better if only there were enough people to follow these guidelines.

Soldiers come to John. Presumably they were Roman soldiers or mercenaries, because ever since Pompey marched into the holy city in 63 B.C.E. there had no longer been any legal Jew-ish armed forces. That might make it seem all the more divinely ordained for them to lay down their arms. How many teachers of pacifism hadn't history already seen trying to convince the world of the inhumanity of war and the necessity of peace![13] By contrast John once again merely wants what is possible for the time being. This is disappointingly little for principled thinkers, but for that very reason sufficiently binding *not* to be utopian: The soldiers were to be content with their wages and were not to rob and plunder defenseless civilians. If existing injustice could at least, insofar as the individual had any say, be pushed back more or less to the limits of the inevitable, that would be a major gain. First and foremost, it would create enough breathing place to reflect on whether existing injustice and violence really were unavoidable, or whether they weren't just as willful and grasping as the brutality of marauding militiamen. The soldiers' bravery had been spurred by handing over to them the population of conquered cities — women and children for the slave trade and their belongings for private booty, as if war dissolved all the boundary lines of humanity.[14]

One might object, of course, that here at least John was a fantasist in thinking he could change something in the world by changing the behavior of individuals. In point of fact, John stands in the tradition of the moralists who try to address the individual in his irreducible freedom and responsibility. Along with this tradition, John refuses to look upon human beings as fish wriggling in invisible nets, as victims of structures that they have unconsciously helped to create but that they certainly no longer have the power or will to change. Yet don't we have to agree with John on this point too? You have to begin with people, not with the complexities of politics and the economy. Otherwise you'll very quickly knock against the ever so rational logic of the "iron laws" of public life.

For example, anyone who feels outraged by the fact that more than two-thirds of the human race is living in misery will be very quickly informed that only a healthy national economy can "cope with" the additional burdens of foreign aid. And, in turn, a healthy economy presupposes a smoothly functioning internal market with a high level of productivity and consumption. In short, only the sum of the extended egoisms of all the good burghers, busy producers, and eager consumers can serve as the basis for the idea of general justice. In the face of this rational logic John the Baptist would have showed himself to be completely unteachable, a typical "fanatic." He would have refused to believe that "capital" represents a "personal relationship,"[15] as if people could be judged by how much they owned. Above all he would have refused to be hoodwinked into believing that only the well-to-do can be really useful. To that John would have objected that people who have what it takes to climb to the level of home- and car-owners in this world of need and misery will most certainly be of no use to anyone. Conversely, he would say, in this world the really helpful people will, of course, never make it. They will never be really reliable citizens: competent, successful, ambitious, responsible – and audacious enough to feel reassured, despite their status as "officials," on the matter of eternity.

These "pillars of society" are unsurpassably captured in Georg Grosz's *Eclipse of the Sun* (1926), which depicts the figures of a financier and a military man surrounded by their faceless "subalterns," consisting only of briefcases and suits.[16] Despite their big-mouthed watchwords and fat-bottomed certainties, these worthies are weak and impotent inside, blind donkeys eating paper like hay – the exact opposite of free and frank human beings. That's the only reason their characters turn out badly, becoming a mockery of their true nature. And for this very reason a man like John inevitably makes it clear by the manner of his appearance that he doesn't count as one of the "reeds shaken by the wind," as one of the "fine people" in "soft clothing" (Lk. 7:24–25). What he has to say is simple, as simple as the desert where he issues his call for conversion. It's as simple as the Israelites' time in the wilderness, when trusting in God alone they received each new day from the hands of the Almighty like manna falling from heaven, without knowing *"man hu"* ("What is it?" – Ex. 16:15).[17] "Give us this day our daily bread" (Lk. 11:3), Jesus will later teach his disciples to pray.

Why do people keep believing they'll be "more secure" if they have more? Squirrels may lay up food supplies for the winter, as instinct bids them,[18] to protect themselves from the danger of starvation. Humans might know that there is no protection against death (Lk. 12:16–21) and that the greatest danger lies not in the end of life but in the loss of meaningful life. "Where your treasure is, there will your heart be also" (Lk. 12:34), as Jesus will later tell the disciples.

If that's true, one must choose once and for all. John already sees the coming Messiah standing before him, as he will baptize with the Holy Spirit and with fire (Lk. 3:16). "His winnowing fork is in his hand, to clear his threshing floor, and to gather the wheat into his granary, but the chaff he will burn with unquenchable fire" (Lk. 3:17). Indeed, like a firestorm the wind is already blowing from John's mouth, and it will brook no delay. Anyone still defending his hackneyed, insubstantial, hollow, and sterile life as something he is entitled to, as his duty, as absolutely necessary, will come to grief on his own hollowness. The question can no longer be how something looks and strikes us from the outside. The question is who one really is and how one stands before God. John, who passionately hated the world of pretenses and deceiving surfaces, longed with all his heart that at long, long last God would restore his order, whatever it took.

Thus far John the Baptist, thus far his hope, thus far his threatening promise. In retrospect we have to say: He was right, and he was wrong. While the early Church believed Jesus as the Christ, it saw in him the prophecies of the Baptist fulfilled and confirmed. But against the background of John's preaching the figure of Jesus looks completely different from the one proclaimed by the Baptist. Instead of "winnowing" on the "threshing floor" and separating the wheat from the chaff, Jesus sees himself much rather as the "physician" who is sent to the "sick" (Mt. 2:17). The God of Jesus is far more concerned with the one lost sheep than with the ninety-nine others who have no need of conversion (Lk. 15:7).[19]

But how does one save a lost sheep?

We need only visualize the image in its external reality to realize how little the Baptist's notions corresponded to Jesus' attitude. In the rugged hill country of Palestine it often happens that a single animal will remain behind when the herd moves on through. Completely helpless, plaintively bleating, it will cower down and become a defenseless victim of birds of prey and wolves. Its situation is so serious that in Hebrew the word for "be destroyed," "perish" (*'abd*) is actually equivalent to "become isolated" (*bdd*), like a single thread (*bd*) from a rope. If the lost sheep should find its way back to the herd, then the shepherd has to attend to it and, if the animal is exhausted, carry it back on his shoulders. That is the manner of the "Good Shepherd," which the Egyptians already revered in the wind god Amun, but which on the thrones of the mighty was threatening to sound more like a caricature of their actual claims. In Jesus' mouth, at any rate, this image expressed his whole attitude toward his mission to the lost sheep of the house of Israel (Mt. 15:24). But it was exactly on this point that Jesus distinguished himself from the preaching of John. It is completely senseless to preach to people who are literally "lost" with moral appeals in the style of John. They are incapable of fulfilling any of them. This sort of feeling of "lostness" can be broken up not by new demands, but only by a deeper understanding, not by urgent commands, but at most by a more sympathetic "going after," not by a further strengthening through fear, but at most by a gradually ripening trust.

I. B. Singer writes in his novel *Shosha,*

> Each time I went into a library, I felt a spark of hope that perhaps in one of the books there might be some indication of how a person of my disposition and world outlook could make peace with himself. I couldn't find it ... not in Schopenhauer, not in the Scriptures. Certainly the Prophets preached a high morality, but their promises of plentiful harvests, of fruitful olive trees and vineyards, protection against one's enemies made no appeal to me. I knew that the world had been and always would remain as it was now. What the moralists called evil was actually the order of life.[20]

Obviously we have here an absolute frontier invisibly dividing people into two halves. In Jesus' view, the real decision for or against God takes place along this hidden line of demarcation. So long as people still have the impression that on the whole they can manage their lives quite capably, they will perceive everything that Jesus said and did as at best a lovable exaggeration, at worst a dangerous dissolution of all good behavior and tried-and-tested arrangements. In no way will they understand how essential to the individual is the feeling of being entitled and accepted. Such questions have never posed themselves to them, and in doubtful cases they know how to get what they need. They can't imagine that some issues might not be resolvable with intelligence and good will, with clear decisions and unequivocal stands. The "unconscious" that psychoanalysis speaks of is something they simply can't get any feeling for. For them it's an arbitrary assault on their personal security or just "an unproven and unprovable hypothesis of psychology." The whole of life, not one detail of it, life in its totality, presents itself differently, depending on whether or not we have already experienced by ourselves or with our intimates how helpless and driven people can be under the spell of anxiety.

For a while it may be possible to explain to an alcoholic that he has to pull himself together: Under all circumstances he has to avoid alcohol, since even a tiny quantity could conjure up the danger of a severe relapse. If he goes on this way, he is facing the threat of permanently ruining his health, of rapid social decline, irreparable damage to the brain, the heart, the liver, a speedy death, etc. All these threats will not have the least effect on him. At some point there will be no dodging the realization that this man doesn't drink too much from time to time out of carelessness or imprudence, but that he *is* a drinker, a *sick person.*

This insight changes everything, because from now on we know that the drunkenness is only a symptom. It can't be fought with moral reproaches; and it won't disappear until the underlying causes are discovered and overcome. But the more one begins to recognize the "causes," the clearer it becomes how the so-called sick person is internally bound up with the so-called healthy ones.

If we look closely, we will often notice that the apparently "healthy" people maintain their cheerfulness at the cost of those whom they claim the right to label first as "failures" and then as "sick." Behind every manifest neurotic stand people who solve their inner conflicts and problems with repression and "deputized wars." The eternally righteous, with their anxiety, with their well-adjusted lives, with their all-around guaranteed mediocrity, can in a certain sense commit a murder every day. But they don't notice it, and if they were told, they wouldn't have the faintest idea what you were talking about. If ever there was a perfect murder, it's with these magicians of death. They never sense all the life they are stifling in themselves and are trampling on all around with their steady stream of advice and their oh-so-reasonable reminders. At best they have an abstract knowledge of their share in the wretched existence of their fellow humans. For them all psychic disturbances are rated, as occasion demands, "medically" conditioned, as a matter for the experts, the right medication, and more "rational measures." It often takes a lifetime (or longer) before one of these thoroughly satisfied, morally upright, but psychologically monstrous characters understands that "compulsory neurosis" is only another name for "sadism of the superego," for "repressed aggressions," and for anal insurance of one's existence through owning and ordering. But it is just this sort of realization that Jesus in principle demanded of his contemporaries.

Characteristically both John and Jesus confirm their "kinship" in the fact that both die a violent death for their convictions. Meanwhile the difference between them is made unmistakable by the manner of their death. John dies by incurring the revenge of the mighty with his moral protest – he goes under in a dissolute collage of calculating rage and tremulous lust (Mk. 6:14–29). His last appearance at the *danse funèbre* of Salome,[21] challenges and summarizes what he himself has fought a life-or-death struggle against. But even in his death he changes nothing. It's enough that his disciples recover his body (to this day the head of the Baptist is venerated in the Grand Mosque in Damascus).

By contrast, the death of Jesus is positively not "arbitrary." It results inevitably from the eternal contradiction between kindness and law. The message of Jesus does not focus on *how* we should live, but *what* we can live *on,* the religious, not the ethical problems of life. The central insight of his most urgent parables is that *all* men and women without exception need *forgiveness* from God. Instead of, like John, primarily threatening his hearers with the judgment of God and calling for works of saving righteousness, in the wonderful story of the roguish servant Jesus describes (Mt. 18:23–35)[22] how hopelessly indebted we *all* are to God. It's a completely senseless, indeed a grotesque, promise when the indebted servant in the parable explains to his king that he will pay back everything. Even if he were to make good on all his assertions and really "buy" everything – his wife, his children, and himself – that wouldn't cover even a fraction of his debt. No sacrifice however great, no effort however strenuous, is capable of making up for human lostness before God. *This,* Jesus says, is our situation. Do what we can, it is utterly desolate.

There is no more radical way than Jesus' to question ethical optimism from the profoundest depths of religious experience. Despite the ultimate, stinging point of his message, John too shared this ethical optimism[23] – with the prophets of all times and cultures. All ethics is founded on the conviction that we ourselves can put our life in order and keep it that way. But Jesus' parable assumes and describes the exact opposite: We live, if at all, purely and simply on God's forgiveness. This is the same experience that Paul will later systematize theologically.[24]

Meanwhile it also corresponds to the experience of the Yahwist in the Old Testament: He introduces God's decision to annihilate the world by observing that "the wickedness of man was great in the earth, and that every imagination of his thoughts was only evil continually" (Gen. 6:5). But when the Flood is over, he has God use the same words (Gen. 8:21), in a strange mixture of resignation and kindness, as he promises never again to curse the ground because of man, "for the imagination of man's heart is evil from his youth" (i.e., in his whole nature).[25] If God were "just" in this sense, then in the face of human history he would have to "cry out" indignantly — together with the earth, which had to lap up the blood of Abel, when Cain, his brother, struck him down (Gen. 4:11). He would have to burst in ferocious and raging, as the prophets from Amos to John paint him doing, with powerful gestures. And he would have to determine, again and again, that there was no measure, no purpose, no end to the eradication and extirpation of his chastising judgment. Again and again, flood upon flood, he would have to wipe humanity out, generation upon generation, only to wind up refuting himself as Creator of such a human race.

That we live at all — this is the "logic" of the Yahwist — that we even exist, the way we are, can be explained only by the fact that God is not simply "just" and essentially "moral." If there can and will be a salvation and purification of human beings and human history, it is solely because God is ready to accompany them with incomprehensible patience and forbearance. Therefore there will be no second Flood, no "baptism of annihilation." That also happens to be the opinion of the person whom the Baptist, according to the Evangelists, points to as the "lamb of God." Jesus did *not* want to be the axe laid to the roots, but the living word of God's forgiveness and compassion, *not* the winnowing fork on the threshing floor, but the outstretched hand of brotherliness and mutual understanding. And even in prayer nothing seemed as important to Jesus as the request and the offer, "Forgive us our debts, as we forgive our debtors" (Mt. 6:12; Lk. 11:4). Conversely, nothing seems to have repelled Jesus as much as the attitude of unfeeling "righteousness" or a narrow-minded, sadistic arrogance.

Can we imagine, then, that the man in the parable of the roguish servant, for whom his king has remitted everything, the entire debt, out of pity, for nothing, should the next moment grab the first person he meets by the throat to arrest him and throw him in debtors' prison for a relatively trivial amount? This, Jesus says, is what we call our "perfect right." The only thing that remains left of our concepts of morality is the damning judgment of our incapacity and the absolute necessity for forgiveness of all we are and do.

Thus in Jesus' eyes the standpoint of "morality" seems to abolish itself. Obviously it is a necessary part of the moral thinking of society (and of the religious institutions that support it) to agree with the moral-universal principle in every case and to harness the individual to its service. Insofar as anyone doesn't agree with the general standing rules, he or she will be found guilty; and the transgression of social norms will automatically call for "just" punishment.[26] Everywhere in every society, this system of morality seems to function, and yet it does injustice every time, because it looks only at external behavior, not the inner attitude of the agent. It ignores the living connection that binds us all in guilt, the psychological interwovenness of all of us in good and evil. It does this by forging an abstract division into what is presumably good and what is presumably evil, while making its internal justification dependent on conformity to the status quo.

Jesus' attitude seems to be quite the reverse, when he demands forgiveness from everybody as a matter of principle, but also insists on free play for every individual, a place of unconditional acceptance and absoluteness. Only from this standpoint, which is not essentially moral but purely religious, does it become clear how sovereignly Jesus attacks the centers of social morality and puts them out of operation. He attacks, for example, the practice of swearing oaths – in his eyes it's nothing but legally organized lies and hypocrisy (Mt. 5:33)[27] – or the patriarchal form of marriage.

In marriage woman is considered an asset of male power (Ex. 20:17; Mk. 10:1, 12)[28] and in questions of love the iron law of "you belong to me" becomes the foundation of the moral code. Jesus disdains the absurd notions of honor and public status, which inevitably boil down to prostitution of character and self-betrayal (see, by contrast, Lk. 8:16–21). He rejects the arbitrariness of traditional ties with which men in their quality as "fathers" claim the right to play "authority": "But you are not to be called 'rabbi,' . . . and call no man your father on earth, . . . neither be called masters . . . " (Mt. 23:8–10). That's how much Jesus hated every kind of heteronomy, even and especially in bringing up children. What was only a symbol and sign in the image of the Pharaoh – the royal dignity of *every* person, his right to autonomy and self-determination in his life, his claim to "breadth of heart" as a living image of God on earth – all this in Jesus' approach becomes lived reality.

For this very reason, though, the confrontation with Jesus' standpoint reaches a much deeper point than in the case of John. The Baptist's opposition was aimed at specific individual rulers, and it failed mostly because of who they accidentally turned out to be. But we can really say of Jesus that his dying was unavoidable, in *every* society and under all circumstances. The questions raised by his humanity imply an overthrowing of *every* kind of social order and social morality: "He stirs up the people, teaching throughout all Judea, from Galilee even to this place" (Lk. 23:5): This accusation, the only real reason why he had to be done away with, runs down through the ages.

But *every* time and *every* culture will notice at the same time that with the condemnation of Jesus it is only signing its own death sentence. Unlike the death of John, the lethal challenge of Jesus touches the life of every person. It asks him to what extent he himself is living, to what extent he himself is a person, just how far he has allowed himself to be a human being. For all time to come it will no longer be possible to say, "I am a priest, hence I must sacrifice a person to God." Or: "I am a politician, so I have to betray so-and-so." Or: "I am – as official, mercenary, subject – obliged to obey, so I had to carry out the death sentence." The God of Jesus Christ demands *no sacrifices*. He would have us live, pervaded by happiness and capable of encounter. The "kingdom" of Jesus Christ exists in everyone's understanding and readiness to understand. It is based not on the interests of power, of money, and the egoism of certain individuals and groups. The rule for *obedience* will be what Peter will learn for himself from the disaster of Good Friday: "We must obey God rather than men" (Acts 5:29).

The life that came forth from Jesus' death is thus exactly as new, as original, as "virginal," and "divine" as the "beginning" of his life itself. The symbols of his descent into the underworld and his ascent into heaven are thus existentially the indispensable pendant of his emergence from the sphere of God and his birth from spirit and light, of which the annunciation by the angel Gabriel has already reported. From both ends, in other words from birth and death, the circle of closeness and kinship between Jesus and John ally with one another; and yet they both belong to fundamentally different worlds.

Thus, what does it mean when Luke tells us that just before his birth the mother of Jesus visits the mother of the Baptist, who joyfully leaps toward Jesus in his mother's womb as toward the goal and destiny of his life? What does it mean *religiously,* rather than for the *history of religion?*

If this treatment (necessarily very brief here) of the appearance of the Baptist and the figure of Jesus is basically on target, then it's clear that both in fact need one another. And so the word "precursor" has a much more profound and in no way merely temporal (or historical) meaning. Precisely because with his relentless clarity John demands that people show moral responsibility before God, he takes his message to the point at which it is blocked. If the weal or woe of a person is to be dependent on what that person actually does, then there is no longer any way to get rid of the hovering anxiety at the heart of human existence. On the contrary, the more people try to "do" the deciding thing in their life, the more they will slip away from themselves. Psychoanalysis has penetratingly described these tragedies of the unconditionally "good will," with all its mechanisms of repression, counter-cathexis, the prevailing, despite all, of the unconscious, and so on. As a result, any religious system in which the relationship of humankind to God is produced and represented essentially in terms of law and judgment, merit and moral lapses, or rewards and punishments, must be seen as pathological. There's no way to miss the Baptist's intimate ties with Qumran. All that should be added is that within "orthodox" Judaism probably only the Pharisees could rival the Essenes in strict, exact adherence to the Law. It is these same "scribes and

Pharisees" with whom we see Jesus in bitter confrontation.[29] No doubt about it: A man who could say, "The sabbath was made for man, not man for the sabbath" (Mk. 2:27) is miles apart from the mentality of the pious followers of the Law.[30]

And still Jesus' attitude unconditionally presupposes the Law, and hence the preaching of the Baptist. It can't be separated from the Law; it can be understood only as seen from John's perspective. Without the background of *despair over the Law* something like *forgiveness* would be completely superfluous. Only when the distinction between good and evil is presented as clearly and unequivocally as John does, with the full earnestness of a decision that must be made, will the dilemma existentially arise to which Jesus essentially can and did respond. Without John, metaphorically speaking, the servant in Jesus' parable wouldn't even notice how hopelessly in debt he was to his king. Every word of forgiveness is literally insubstantial when there is no guilt to be forgiven. No act of forgiveness can be life-saving, if guilt itself is not utterly lethal. Heinrich von Kleist's drama *The Prince of Homburg,*[31] for example, describes this situation with inimitable intensity: The prince has successfully led his troops into battle but contrary to orders. So the victor in the battle of Fehrbellin has to accept the just death sentence of his father with no prospect of being saved, before the elector can forgive him. Apart from the admission of guilt all talk about forgiveness would turn human life into an indiscriminate fog, into shapeless enervation or a warrant for every kind of anarchy.

In that sense the image of John's baptism of repentance fits even better than the Baptist himself might be able to realize: Immersion in the Jordan is really like dying, like being taken back into the womb of the world, and *without* hope for forgiveness. Any who understand John radically enough must be signing their own death sentences in the act at the Jordan. If they are to go on living after that, then it can only be out of grace. To that extent the baptism of John really happens only with "water": It washes away. Of itself it gives no support; it ends a life that is no life. But it does not renew. It calls attention to the untenability of the situation, but it doesn't transform it.

So basically the Baptist stands at the *end* of the history of religion. And instead of the punishing Messiah, as he may well have historically promised him, we must endorse the Gospel accounts when they describe the Baptist as pointing, despite all his fearful threats, to the God of compassion, to the lamb of God (Jn. 1:29–36).[32] That is, to the one who, when he stepped into the Jordan, saw the heavens open and the Spirit descending upon him like a dove (Mk. 1:10). Only when the confession of human guilt is no longer a "trick" designed to make us appear in a favorable light after all, only when it means a complete capitulation, a hopeless declaration of bankruptcy, can a voice from heaven say: "Thou art my beloved Son; with thee I am well pleased" (Mk. 1:11).

Only from this standpoint can we understand the great importance that the baptism of John acquires in the life of Jesus. To all appearances Jesus took the image of baptism, the vision of the Flood's drowning of sin, more seriously than everybody else, even than John himself. Ultimately this human symbol of purification, above and beyond its moral content, was condensed into a central religious experience. Its message is that despite all guilt there is an emergence from the depths, a new birth, a saving riverbank of forgiveness: The water bears you up, if you cross it trusting in God (Mk. 6:45–52).[33] This vision shaped Jesus' whole existence. Everything that he did later presupposed the revelation from the opened heavens, the voice of reconciliation. It all went back to John's baptism, to fill it with a completely different meaning.

Matthew, whose Gospel ends with the risen Jesus' command to baptize all nations (Mt. 28:19), very clearly recognized this change of meaning in the symbol of baptism. Whereas Mark writes: "John was baptizing in the wilderness, preaching a baptism of repentance for sins" (Mk. 1:4), as if God's forgiveness followed on the heels of human penance, the Evangelist of the "tax collectors and sinners" has stricken that phrase (Mt. 3:11). In his preaching the Baptist can only exhort to repentance. Matthew holds off the word of *forgiveness* for twenty-two chapters until the farewell scene at the Last Supper. With the words of the institution of the Eucharist, Jesus will tell his disciples that it is the *blood of his covenant* that will be shed for everyone "for the forgiveness of sins."[34]

Thus it is not the baptism of John, but the sign of the sacred meal, the sacrament of death and resurrection, that takes all guilt away. The image of the Eucharist is a thoroughly *matriarchal* symbol. It seeks to get rid of the crime of the forbidden fruit in Paradise, the saturation of all of life with feelings of fear and guilt in the face of a punishing God the Father. God himself turns himself into food, so that humans may live in a trust that gives them back to themselves.[35] So from now on the question of those who came to John ("What shall we do?") should no longer be the first question that people ask themselves. Under the aegis of the sacred meal the first question that may and must be asked is: "Who *are* we?" and "Who are we allowed to be?"

There's no need to fear that the wholly unearned and yet absolutely necessary gift of such an unconditional and perfect forgiveness, of such a general amnesty for our entire life, will lead to the comfortable nonchalance of all those who spend their lives in search of an alibi for their laziness. It's not true that laziness of soul and comfortableness represent something naturally given. Actually there lies hidden in every person a drive toward the unfolding and fulfillment of all the forces whose total image is given to him or her by nature.[36] And considerable energy has to be exerted to hold back the original driving forces and to block the desire to realize one's own being. Only when people have been so intimidated by the whip of fear that they do nothing at all except by command and compulsion, does there build up alongside the tyranny of duties a chaotic enervation and spiritless slackening. This condition does seem like a desideratum of nature, yet it only creates more anxiety. Jesus believed that people are capable of goodness from a spontaneous motion of the heart, that they positively have a need to communicate to others the happiness they feel at being saved. He trusted that gentleness and kindness could free up more energy than the power of anxiety, of threats, and all the cramps and seizures of ascetical virtue. Unlike the Baptist, Jesus wanted joy around him, not penitential laceration and self-suppression (Mk. 2:18–20).[37] People should meet God and one another with the bridal song of lovers, not with the complaining cry of the hopelessly damned. It seems to be this completely different basic attitude and mindset that made Jesus say so harshly and emphatically: "Unless your righteousness exceeds that of the scribes and Pharisees, you will never enter the kingdom of heaven" (Mt. 5:20).

Thus, *essentially,* John and Jesus need one another. So the legend is right and does well to show the Baptist and the Christ meeting even before they come into the world. It is and must be

Jesus who comes to John. But it is and must be John who in his very being needs Jesus' message to recognize that the name his father Zechariah gives him fits: "God [Yahweh] is gracious" (Lk. 1:60). But in the course of the meeting of the two there occurs what we live on: the reconciliation and union of freedom and duty, of law and grace, of truth and putting to the test. Only when Mary goes to her cousin Elizabeth does the divine child begin to take on the form of our human reality. But how the child comes into the world is the story of a new revelation, of a new *myth,* a new insight into in a domain full of mysteries.

3

The God of the Shining Light, or the Scene of the Holy Night (Lk. 2:1–20)

ଔଃ

T HE CHRISTMAS NARRATIVE aims neither to provide a historical record nor to serve as a warm-hearted edifying legend."[1] Most exegetes would subscribe to that proposition without any reservations. But how do we understand discourse that is neither a historical report nor a subjective representation? Currently historical-critical exegesis tries to solve the problem by retreating to the scheme of prophetic (Old Testament) promise and eschatological (New Testament) fulfillment. A number of observations do fit this scheme: The fact that Jesus is born in the city of David, Bethlehem (Lk. 2:1–7), evidently fulfills the well-known promise of the prophet Micah (5:2). And the announcement of the angel to the shepherds (Lk. 2:8–14), as well as its confirmation, may be considered an apocalyptic completion of the prophets' message. In the words of H. Schürmann: "The historical fact presents itself first as a revelatory event in the word-revelation, without which the event wouldn't be revealing and disclosed. Thus behind the simple story lies a profound understanding of how the 'revelation' comes about."[2]

But how does "revelation" come about if in Luke's presentation we are presumably dealing only with literary reflections,

"with devices of the haggadic-apocalyptic narrative art of the period, with the addition of . . . many biblical reminiscences . . . and
a meaning-laden narrative style that will open itself up . . . only
to a childlike faith"?[3]

Historical Criticism and the Vision of Faith

The historical-critical method of interpretation, with its fundamentally rationalistic thrust, never manages to open up the
"meanings" themselves to the "childlike" soul. Hence its "faith"
remains stuck in a pure positivism. One has to believe in Christ
in order to recognize the Christmas stories as "revelations." But
in reality no "revelations" take place that could ground this belief in the way that this story of the birth of the divine child
in Bethlehem tries to do. Instead, historical-critical exegesis continually loses itself (in principle contrary to its own findings) in
historicizing investigations. In the end it only finds in passage
after passage that things certainly did not occur the way the
narrative says they did.

To mention just a few points: *Jesus' birth in Bethlehem* is
contradicted by Jesus' roots in Nazareth.[4] The authors evidently
wanted to speak of the "city of David," Bethlehem, in order
to present the prophecy of Micah as fulfilled and Jesus as the
"son of David," the Messiah. To motivate *the journey to Bethlehem* Luke makes use of the emperor's command to register for
taxes. But then in the meantime Mary and Joseph would have
had to live together, because such a journey was forbidden to
engaged couples. But there is no mention of their getting married. Furthermore it is historically true that Augustus introduced
a new system of tax assessment, part of which involved a *new
registration on the tax rolls* every fourteen years.[5] But Flavius
Josephus reports that in this case a tax assessment wasn't carried
out until 6 c.e. by Quirinius (together with the first procurator
Coponius), when Judea was incorporated into the province of
Syria.[6]

The appearance of the angels to the shepherds presents a
completely autonomous Christmas story that in a way competes
with the appearance of the angel to Mary.[7] Indeed, *when the
shepherds report about their vision,* "all who heard it won-

dered" about their account, as if there had been no report in
the previous chapter about an apparition in Nazareth.[8] H. Schürmann correctly points out: "What the earliest apostolic kerygma
saw as realized with Jesus' entering upon his proclamation of the
Gospel . . . is now back-meditated and back-dated into the event
of his birth."[9] But then why bother studying the occupation
of shepherds in ancient Palestine, the custom of night watches
there, the "curious sign" (*sic*) — the Messiah in a manger[10] —
methods of swaddling infants, and so forth?

Those who wish to "meditate" and admit that the texts tell
their story entirely in the manner of meditative images may not
go jumping back and forth between (1) a "meaning" that is a
literary construct and hardly experiential, a purely theologica[
assertion, and (2) a history viewed purely as foreground. Insteac
such readers must do exactly what the images of the Christma:
story themselves do and what they invite us to do: They mus
paraphrase belief in Christ with symbolic pictures. They mus
condense it and let it work upon them as concentrated realit)
Only then will they be able to move beyond the historical puzzle
and theological positivism and become capable of an experienc‹
in which there is no contradiction between dream and realit)
between promise and fulfillment.

Only in this way will we notice that there are very fev
archetypally given and psychically *objective* symbols in whic
one can narrate the birth of the divine child and internally live it
out. Not until we acknowledge this will we acquire *dogmatically*
the right to celebrate *liturgically* the words of the Christmas
gospel as our own confession of faith. And only then will it be superfluous to file away *all of popular piety* as a fantastic historical
mistake. There would be a host of historical-critical reasons for
saying that if the shepherds are out in the fields, then naturally
it can't be cold and wintry, as the Christmas carols proclaim.[11]
Since he was a "carpenter," Joseph was certainly not poverty-
stricken. Rather he was a member of the middle classs.[12] The
text in fact says nothing about any "search for lodging" or any
hard-hearted innkeepers' turning anyone away.[13] In Palestine the
"manger" is never a box lying on the floor,[14] as countless pictures of Christmas show. The ox and the ass come from Isaiah
1:3. Luke himself attaches no importance whatsoever to them.
In summary the judgment of historical criticism can only be: "On

all these matters if pious fantasy would experiment with imag-
ining the opposite of what it does, it would more readily find
its way to everything that the text thinks really important and
worth mentioning in the event (if it was an event)."[15]

In truth, however, "popular fantasy" actually has an inimitable flair for the symbolic meaning of a scene. Its living
commentary on the Christmas story has retroactively completed
Luke's account, which is quite laconic and almost fragmentary,
with many details. In this way "fantasy" has for the first time
shown us the image in its original totality. It is always a herme-
neutically venturesome procedure to want to interpret a myth
against the grain of its own effective history. The decisive point,
though, is always the same: Those who as exegetes feel obliged
to understand the images "theologically" as carefully thought-out
constructs by individual scriptural experts necessarily attribute
their own mode of being and working to the biblical narrators.
But people of this sort see no angels and herd no sheep. Nor do
they imagine the visions and testimonies of sacred revelation that
the Bible abounds with. The poetry of the people, by contrast,
continually serves as the solid foundation of mythical and legendary narratives. Those who can't or won't acknowledge their
objective truth will end by willy-nilly having to exclude religion,
with a barrage of contempt, both sociological and (depth-) psychological, from the very realms of experience in which it is at
home.

There is scarcely a better formula for what mythical birth
narratives are and mean than H. Schürmann's "back-meditation
of faith." The essential point here is the insight that a certain
attitude of trust will necessarily release certain images and metaphors from the depths of the psyche, in order to complete and
communicate itself in them.[16] This *psychological process,* and
not literary dependencies, gives rise to the oft-noted closeness
of biblical narratives to the mythical traditions of the "pagans."
Meanwhile what "myth," what symbolic scenario is "appropri-
ate" to the biblical narrative depends, of course, on the stance
taken, or the question posed, by the text of each particular passage. Thus here, where the text is to speak of the birth of the Son
of God, of his entry into the world, only one image can be con-
jured up to mediate between heaven and earth, between dream
and daylight. This kind of image is not to be sought either in the

religion of Osiris, the god of the dead,[17] or in the bright world of the sun god Mithra.[18] Earlier scholars liked to make comparisons between these myths and the Christmas gospel; but the most eloquent parallel is to be found in the Greek myth of the birth of Asclepius, the god of healing. This story renders many details of the Lucan narrative visible and comprehensible above all in their *typicological* necessity.

Asclepius — the Savior
between Dream and Daylight

When the angels proclaim out in the fields of Bethlehem that "to you is born a ... *savior*" ("Heiland," or healer, in German), this word evidently reminds German readers of the healing and holy physician-gods of antiquity. Above all it recalls the preeminent healing god Asclepius, whose sign, the healing snake of the caduceus, doctors and pharmacists still use as a coat of arms. The symbolic kinship between this Greek god and the person of Christ is a deep one, especially in the story of their birth. And just as one must dream again the myth of the Pharaoh's birth to understand the scene of the annunciation in Nazareth, one must visualize the myths of Asclepius in order to understand the scene in Bethlehem with its images.

In his *Description of Greece* (2:26. 3–5) Pausanias tells how

> Phlegyas, a warlike king from Thessaly, and his daughter, Apollo's beloved, come to Epidauros when she is near to childbirth. Here she abandons the child Asclepios on a mountain, then known as the Mount of Myrtles, later on the mountain of the Teats. There the shepherd Aresthanas finds the child lying between a goat and a dog: the goat suckles the child and the dog guards him, all in a light so dazzling that the shepherd has to turn away as from a divine epiphany. At the same moment a voice is heard, proclaiming over land and sea that the newborn babe will discover every cure for the sick and awaken the dead.[19]

Here we immediately find a series of important parallels to Christmas: We see the mother of Asclepius as a bride of the god

Apollo. The child comes into the world when his mother is traveling. The child is exposed – his defenselessness, which is sharply stressed in Christian folk customs, is obviously a pertinent motif of the birth of the divine child.[20] The shepherd who finds the child sees an apparition of divine light. At the same time he hears an explanatory voice from heaven that reveals to him the saving meaning of the divine child. The child lies between a goat and dog. This too obviously represents an essential feature of the divine birth: The child, who is homeless among men, is peculiarly close to animals.[21] It is here, not in the arbitrary quotation from Isaiah 1:2, that in all probability we should look for the reason why the animals gather around the manger of the Christ child too. The "ox" and the "donkey" are in fact only a Christian stopgap measure. They really don't fit into the scene with the shepherds, since they presuppose farming country. In addition the animal has to be a female (a cow in the case of farmers, a nanny goat with shepherds, a she-wolf or she-bear with hunting cultures).

In the myth itself the "animals" are still parts of the divine, earlier than the humans and bearers of secret messages. They are the protectors of the person and the symbol of his nature. In a Yiddish song as sad as it is beautiful, this wisdom is preserved in the verses: "Hinter jedem Wiegele / steht ein klein weiss Ziegele" ("Behind every little cradle / stands a little white goat" – an angel of God, one would have to say in biblical terms).

To return to Asclepius: It is part of the mythic tradition of religious "events" that they exist in numerous variants, just as the birth story in Matthew differs from the text of Luke.[22] While from a historical standpoint it is never possible to "reconstruct" the "factual" history behind the stories, the different traditions appear to depth psychology as necessary completions of, and commentaries on, a theme that in principle is inexhaustible.[23] This theme can be communicated only in images with many levels of meaning, since it always defies conceptual comprehension. Hence we also have various mythical traditions concerning the birth of Asclepius.

Thus Isyllos of Epidauros, whose cultic poems were inscribed on the shrine of Asclepius in the city around 300 B.C.E.,[24] reports further details about the mother of Asclepius:

Malos, a primitive man whom Zeus bound in holy marriage with a virgin of Apollo, the muse Erato, becomes the father of a daughter likewise connected to the Muses, Kleophema, she who "proclaims fame." Phlegyas, a primeval dweller in Epidauros, takes Kleophema to wife."[25]

And then follow the words: "And begotten by Phlegyas — and her name was Aigla — her epithet was this — because of her beauty however she was given the epithet Koronis."[26] The beauty of Koronis ("curved," "crowlike") can have been based only on the raven black hair of Apollo's future beloved. Her name "Aigla" ("the bright one") gives her child his name: Asclepius. The transitional forms of both names and the phonetic change can be unequivocally documented under the influence of the ancient Mediterranean language that preceded Greek.[27] Thus (significantly) we learn something from the mother about the nature of her son: In keeping with his whole nature Asclepius is the brightly shining one. "According to these mythologems Asclepius is the procreative Apollo, flaring up from out of a mother both dark and bright."[28]

Meanwhile what this bright shining forth of Asclepius is and means cannot be understood simply from the angle of the sunrise. And once again animals configure the nature of the divine child. To this day the custom prevails among many "primitive peoples" of naming a child after the animal (or the natural event) that was most noticeable at the moment of birth. The dog that watches over the newborn Asclepius belongs, like the snake,[29] to the domain of the underworld goddess Hecate. But in mythology the dog can also be golden, thus attached to the light.[30] The nanny goat, however, was also considered the constellation of the rain[31] and its pelt a symbol of the clouds.[32] The latter perhaps plays a role in the strange Old Testament story of Gideon and the sign of the fleece on the threshing floor (Jg. 6:36–40). In any case Asclepius clearly occupies a middle position between above and below, day and night, life and death. And this twilight-condition constitutes his nature.[33] He himself is the Apollo who shines out of the dark, the Apollo Aigletes. And so we understand why he could appear in this form to the Argonauts on the Island of Anaphe, the island of "blazing up."[34]

The impression of the in-between nature of the god is further strengthened by the background landscape in which Asclepius comes into the world, as well as by the bright-dark double nature of his mother. The homeland of the Asclepius religion was undoubtedly Thessaly. "If Epidauros was in a sense the Rome of the religion of Asclepius, whence it spread through the ancient world of ancient culture, Trikka may be called its Bethlehem and Thessaly its Palestine."[35]

On the southeastern slope of the mountain of the ancient Acropolis excavators discovered the characteristic votive statues of Asclepius: the little hooded god Telesphoros (who as death, as completion "brings to the end," or who at the moment of death inaugurates the phase of new beginning – a dwarflike figure, who continues to live in a number of fairy tales), a rooster, the proclaimer of the day at the end of the night, at the end of earthly life,[36] as well as a child "wrapped in swaddling clothes" (Lk. 2:12).[37] Around the birthplace of the god flowed the River Lethe, the underworld river of forgetfulness and security. But beyond the mountains, in the sunrise of Trikka, lay the Lake of Boibeis, belonging to the moon goddess Boibe or Phoibe, who as the wife of the Titan Koios is the ancestress of the Apollonian line: The grandson of Koios is, according to Hesiod's genealogy,[38] Phoebus Apollo.[39]

Only from the nature of the moon goddess can we now understand the dark-light name of Asclepius's mother, Aigla-Koronis: She is the beloved of Apollo, the god of light, but at the same time she also maintains a secret kinship with the underworld goddess Persephone; and in other myths she is identical to Phoebe. For

> the goddess of Lake Boibeis was also called Brimo, like the great goddess of the nearby Thessalian city of Pherai, the northern Greek form of the mystery goddess Persephone.
> ... In the Mysteries of Eleusis, when the birth of the divine child was celebrated, the priest proclaimed the event with the words: "The queen has given birth to a sacred child: Brimo has borne Brimos."

The strong (f.) has borne the strong (m.). This "strong one," this Ischys,

> representing pristine virility ... loved the divine primordial woman, the moon goddess Phoibe, or Brimo, "The Strong,"

and begot the child invoked in Eleusis as Brimos. In Thessaly this child was said to be Koronis's son, Asclepius, who was worshipped at Trikka.

As Kerényi quite rightly observes,

> this is the way of the true mythological tales that are not literary inventions. They vary the same theme, employing different names and figures: in this case the theme of the birth of a divine child who – first dark, then bursting into light – springs from the union of the moon goddess with a strong god who dwells in the darkness.
>
> Some of the different names that were given to the goddess refer to the different phases of the moon. In mythology these phases appear side by side as sister figures. There are usually three of them, and their names signify: the waxing moon rising from the darkness; the moon between the two "half moons"; and finally the phase in which it again takes the form of a sickle and vanishes. Thus it is understandable that in Messenia, whither the myth of Asklepios' birth came from Thessaly, the mother should have been called Arsinoë, one of her two sisters Hilaeira, "the Gracious," an epithet of the mild full moon, and the other Phoibe. The first part of the Arsi-noë suggests the rising from the darkness and so indicates the moment when Asklepios was begotten: a time of darkness when the new moon had just appeared. And this also explains why the mother of Asklepios, according to Isyllos, may be called Aigla, "The Luminous," and yet in her role of Apollo's beloved is known as the "Crow Maiden," as Koronis the dark beauty.[40]

If these lines are read in the spirit of the usual theological hostility to myth, someone will no doubt heatedly object that this is exactly where the difference lies: Mary was a historical person, not a mythical creature. Her name does not swing back and forth between Aigla and Koronis, Phoebe and Arsinoë. She was never worshipped as a moon goddess. And in the biblical message, beginning with the Old Testament, the historicity of revelation has overcome myth. But this objection has long since been refuted: The birth of the Son of God does not occur on the level of history. It takes place on a level of reality that can be described only with mythic metaphors. The story of Jesus' birth in Bethlehem has to be read *symbolically*. We now see against the background of the Asclepius myth that even the historically clothed moments of Luke's narrative have to be understood in themselves as typical motifs. Only in this way do we get the frame of reference in which we have to place the individual images of biblical history too. Only from the perspective of the moon nature of the mother of God can we understand that the lying-in always occurs on her travels (across the heavens). Another part of the typos of the divine birth is broadly depicted in the Gospel of Matthew: the persecution of the child born of a virgin (Mt. 2:16-19). For example, the mother of Asclepius, according to one mythical version, is placed on a woodpile, and not until she dies burned at the stake (the moon being extinguished by the sun?) does Apollo save Asclepius, the "son born in the death of the mother."[41] Even Luke seems to reflect this sort of persecution motif, when he links the birth of the Savior to the tax decree of the Emperor Augustus (Lk. 2:1). It is true that in his Gospel Luke takes a rather conciliatory view of the Roman authorities,[42] when for example he largely downpedals Pilate's part in the condemnation of Jesus (Lk. 23:4, 14-15). But, in adopting the collection of sayings available to him, Luke also vehemently stresses the opposition *in principle* between the kingdom of God and the kingdoms of this world: For Luke it is the devil himself who gets to confer the power and "glory" of earthly regimes. The last words of Jesus in the upper room, as we have seen, are a harsh rejection of the "kings of the Gentiles" (Lk. 22:24). In addition as early as the infancy narrative the prophecy of Simeon (Lk. 2:34-35) makes it clear that even (and especially) in Luke the child Redeemer is destined to enter "into his glory" through "suffering," as the risen Jesus will definitively explain to the doubting disciples on the road to Emmaus (Lk. 24:26).

Furthermore, part of the *typos* of the birth of the divine child is the interpretation of the event by heavenly powers. Thus the schema of promise and fulfillment in no way constitutes a peculiar feature of biblical tradition. From the standpoint of form history that schema rather presupposes the structure of the narrative style mentioned above. Here it is merely illustrated and filled out with certain passages from the Old Testament that are now read as promises. Consequently the primary task must be to understand the symbolic sense of this schema itself, instead of taking refuge in the exterior of a theology of fulfilled promises, which only *seems* to formulate the story in a rational manner.

The images themselves say more than all the words and Scripture quotations. And if it were at all possible to communicate the mystery of the birth of the Son of God in "rational" concepts, two of the Evangelists would not have had to fall back upon existing materials from mythical traditions. But then it's all the more necessary, this time using the model figure of Asclepius, to name the psychic experiences that generate the various symbols and that in Christian faith are connected with the person of Jesus as the "Savior of the world."

In the radiance of the light shining out from Trikka we realize that in the biblical narratives much more is at stake than a biographical account of the birth of the child Jesus. With the birth of the divine child we are basically entering upon the domain of the primeval creation and first beginnings, the emergence of life from death, the renewal of the (moon)light out of the dark. We become witnesses to a marriage of light (Apollo) with darkness (Koronis), of heaven with earth, of the brightness of the sun with the darkness of the moon. In the language of depth psychology this is a wedding of consciousness and the unconscious, of spirit and instinct, of understanding and emotion.

Mediating between these opposites and reconciling them, a child comes into the world who shares in the nature of both spheres. The fact that this child, scarcely born, is relentlessly persecuted by the figure of a violent "king" is exactly what depth psychology would expect. Using Matthew's story of the slaughter of the innocents in Bethlehem I have elsewhere pointed out the huge contradiction we necessarily fall into when something really new shows up in our life that evades the control of consciousness and all our rational planning.[43] That is, tension arises when this novel element, however strange and uninvited it may be, nevertheless speaks to the deepest longings and expectations of our souls. Despite all our defensiveness we know that on this new arrival rests the promise and hope of our life.

Meanwhile from the perspective of the figure of Asclepius we can see something of the nature of a healing god, of a divine physician. From the outset it's important to get to know the figure of Christ under this aspect.[44] When Asclepius came into the world, the heavenly voice proclaimed that he would find a remedy for all diseases and for death. But we can't understand mythical birth stories until we see that the life task of a god, of a bringer of salvation, is already represented and realized in the way his arrival occurs.

The physicians in Epidauros knew how to draw the correct doctrinal conclusion from the nature of Asclepius by transforming his birth at night into a process of salvation. Two and a half millennia before the discovery of psychoanalysis, and still untouched by Christianity's one-sided emphasis on the standpoint of consciousness, the doctors of Asclepius received from the hands of the gods in the shrine at Epidauros the cure through dream therapy.

This god of the flaring light, begotten by the coupling of the darkness of night with the brightness of day, marks in his nature the border region between the unconscious and consciousness. He embodies in his whole person this transitional sphere between non-being and being, between essence and experience, between sleeping and waking. Thus *dreams* are the actual realm of this god, this late descendant of the ancient Egyptian sage Imhotep, who early on assumed the qualities of a living god and who in later times completely fused with Asclepius.[45] Asclepius is essentially the god who heals through the light of the spirit shining out in the darkness of the unconscious. The key is for men and women to let in the message of their dreams, so that this marriage between "Apollo" and "Koronis," this wedding which is in itself forbidden, apparently illegitimate, and at first seems worthy of being wiped out, can really take place.

Whenever it does, a journey will get under way, an inner process of heading off and coming back home, at the end of which lies the birth of one's true self. The physicians in Epidauros knew about this wonderful human capacity for perceiving our true selves in dreams and for receiving visions in the night as divine messages. They were confident that a person need only dream undisturbed in the sanctuary itself, under the god's protection, secure in the realm of a prelapsarian world,[46] stretched out on the ground of the sanctuary, in the most intimate contact with Mother Earth, in order to "wake up" changed inside.

And weren't they right about that?

How many diseases that impress us, the successors of Hippocrates, as "medical cases," as one or other purely physical or biochemical process, are actually, when seen with the awakening eyes of Asclepius, infirmities of the soul and not the body? In the religion of Asclepius sickness is at first not an object of scientific research, but an expression of the inner attitude toward life. It is the manifestation of a religious attitude that has to be overcome from the first with religious means, not with "medicine." It is religion itself that appears in Asclepius as a "remedy" against illness. Conversely the healing powers of the human soul cannot really unfold until we take the language of its dream images to be so essential that something divine can appear in it.

Only in this light can we grasp the attitude of the New Testament when it recognizes in suffering and disease the symptoms of a world fallen away from God. In the same vein it interprets Jesus' miracles as signs that God's power over the hearts of humans is growing stronger.[47] Basically Christianity heals the anxiety of existence that drives people into opposition to God and hence into discord with themselves.[48] Therefore it is one and the same thing to liberate persons from their anxiety through trust in God and to heal them from the psychosomatic pattern of mental and bodily ailments. Thus when he proclaims and brings the nearness of the "kingdom of God," Christ is essentially a physician, a figure from the experiential realm of the religion of Asclepius.

In this way it becomes supremely clear that the figure of Christ, the images of his birth, his nature, and his activities, must be dreamt along with in order to assimilate them deeply enough into ourselves. As the Son of God, who comes into the world in the night, beneath the radiance of the angel, he has power alive in him to touch our souls and fill them with healing dreams. He himself, the presence of his person, creates a space similar to the shrine of Epidauros, a zone where we become silent and secure, where we linger on. This is where the souls of men and women become transparent to themselves so that they come into contact with their origins. This is where, beneath the petrifaction of everyday consciousness, like the healing wellsprings of fairy tales and legends, a water of life gushes forth. As it does our youth is renewed (Ps. 103:5), and primeval dreams and wishes begin to flow again.

Only now too do we realize why shepherds had to get the

first news of the birth of the divine child. In more recent exegesis, in an effort to re-emphasize the "actuality" of the Bible in the historical-critical method, much ado has been made about the fact that the message of redemption is directed, in the figure of the shepherds, to the poor, the outsiders, the deprived and dispossessed, the "marginal existences," etc.[49] But paradoxically all this political move does is redrape the otherwise so despised "popular fantasy" over the poverty of the Holy Family. It doesn't make sense to bolster an important concern (such as liberation theology) with bad arguments. In the Palestine of Jesus' day shepherds were, socially speaking, by no means looked down upon. Economically speaking, they were even fairly prosperous.[50]

It's different when the "shepherds" are understood not as a social class but as a mythical typos. Then they designate the *border region between nature and culture* or the transition from the level of hunters and gatherers to the life of the sedentary farmers.[51] Like hunters, shepherds still belong to nomadism, and they too consume the flesh of animals. On the other hand they already live on the products of nature – in the form of milk, cheese, wool, etc.; and they raise animals as the farmer raises wheat and millet. Precisely as embodiments of transition, shepherds are proper recipients of the message from a God who himself personifies the pure transition, the ripening and fulfilling unity of opposites, the evolution of the inchoate developing essential form of the human psyche.

In the symbol of the "shepherds" the otherwise so fiercely divisive oppositions between instinct and intellect, feeling and understanding, the limbic system and the cerebral cortex are, physiologically expressed, posited as a living unity. In the "shepherds" as a *typos* dwells an openness and a possibility of development that has kept its original freshness and creative energy. But at the same time this natural and uncomplicated manner, which is psychologically associated with the shepherds' life, appears in a form that impresses us as neither frighteningly crude nor unreflectively primitive. Hence in this relatively undeveloped form of the "shepherd's" existence lives the promise of being able consciously to win back the unity of one's own being.

A similar pattern holds for the appearance of the animals. To be sure, "animals" are to be understood from the depth-psychological viewpoint as symbols of the world of the instincts. But with the birth of a divine child it is always domesticated or motherly-tame animals that warm, protect, or raise the newborn.[52] Thus in a certain sense the image of the beasts by the side of the divine child resembles a fulfillment of the paradisiacal prophecy of Isaiah (11:6–8) about the child who in the days of the Messiah will play unconcernedly by the hole of the asp, while bears and lions peacefully graze alongside sheep and lambs. This is a vision that Virgil too will pick up.[53] Evidently there is no other way to imagine it: Wherever there is an image of successful humanization, then the fear of the "animalistic" powers in one's own self must give way to a deeper trust in oneself. Often enough, therefore, fairy tales describe how animals become helpers of the hero, so long as the hero doesn't try to "kill" then or otherwise exclude them.[54] If one meets the "beasts" withou fear, they let themselves be tamed without any difficulty and the) do the ego priceless services that it could never achieve through its own reflection and will.

Thus the (paradisiacal) unity with the animals is an insepara ble part of the figure of the "Son of man," of the child Redeemer With just the right flair the Gospel of Mark shows us this tremen dous image at the beginning of the public activity of Jesus, when it describes how after the forty days in the "wilderness" he was "with the wild beasts" and "the angels ministered to him" (Mk. 1:13). In other words only in a mode that links the highest with the deepest and in which the world of pure spirit unites with the world of dark instincts, will Jesus face men and women. Only in this mode will he be able to speak credibly to people about God; and only as one who has reconciled the human contradictions of the "beast" and the "angel" in his own person will he also be able to liberate other human beings from the contradictions and inner strife of their souls.

What Mark describes with this short, but extremely important note on the definitive psychic maturation of the Redeemer, myths such as the story of the arrival of Asclepius shift to the birth narrative of the son of the god. Once again we have the opportunity to extol the sensitivity of "popular fantasy" when in its visions of the manger and Christmas carols it freely and with infallible accuracy adds the element missing from Luke's infancy narrative: the closeness of the animals. Hence the images of the angels rightly hover over the stable in Bethlehem, and the animals bend tenderly and gratefully over the Christ child. It's also just right *psychologically* when Isaiah reproaches the people of his day: "The ox knows its owner, and the ass its master's crib, but Israel does not know, my people does not understand" (1:3). Our unconscious, the world of the "animals" in us, always perceives the message of the divine more readily than does the sphere of our consciousness. In just the same way King Herod in Matthew may well know the truth, but he refuses all the more to recognize it, because it fatally calls into question the self-glorification of his claim to power.[55]

Such a "taming" of the beasts, however, requires the attitude of a downright playful and aimless familiarity. Researchers into cultural history continually assert that the taming of domestic animals took place mainly because of practical necessity.[56] But it can't have happened that way. It can't have been men who, for example, tamed the first wolf cubs and hence probably the first animals of any sort, in order to train them for the hunt or to put them to work as watchdogs. Before herds of goats and sheep were introduced, there was no milk to raise the young of animals. So it must have been *women* who along with their own children brought up wolf pups simply out of playfulness and joy in creaturely solidarity.

H. Zimen found this hypothesis confirmed among the African natives of Turkana, where the little dogs grow up side by side with the children, lick off their excrement, and in other ways take care to keep the huts clean.[57] The dogs don't have other "responsibilities," such as hunting or guarding the herds. They are simply the playmates of the women and children. Psychologically speaking, the "taming of the animals" can only be viewed as the result of an attitude both maternal and childlike on the part of human beings toward themselves and toward the natural world around them. This too is a wisdom that we have to learn from the birth myth of the religion of Asclepius, if we wish to get a deeper understanding of the message of Christmas. It would be more than a shame, it would be positively harmful if the purely masculine guild of theologians, with their one-sided intellectuality and hostility to myth, should manage to kill such truths. Even the child of Bethlehem doesn't come into the world without experiencing unity with the "beasts."

Only one promise made at the birth of Asclepius remained un-fulfilled, and this one is central to Christianity: *the victory over death.* The heavenly voice, heard by the shepherd Aresthanas in Trikka, proclaiming that the newborn child would call the dead back to life, could not, when all was said and done, "deliver."

It's true that Apollodorus reports (III, x, 3) that Asclepius, after being trained by the centaur Chiron,

> not only prevented some from dying, but even raised up the dead, for he had received from Athena the blood that flowed from the veins of the Gorgon, and while he used the blood that flowed from the veins on the left side for the bane of mankind, he used the blood that flowed from the right side for salvation, and by that means he raised the dead.[58]

In other words, as the religion of Asclepius sees it, human beings are basically "composed" of two halves, both of which have to form a unity for anything like life to be possible. In this system the left side (corresponding to the crossing of the neural paths[59]) is associated with the unconscious, the imagistic, the non-logical, while the right side of the body is bound up with consciousness, the speech centers in the left hemisphere of the brain, the realm of reason. From the "blood of Gorgon," i.e., from the victory over the fear that turns one to stone,[60] Asclepius gains the power, thanks to his becoming aware of the old "Gorgonic" portion in human beings, to cure diseases and to conquer death. Meanwhile unawareness of the animalistic, the "monstrous" in human beings is lethal.

Thus far this tradition also fits perfectly well into the familiar image of the transitional nature of Asclepius, just as in mythical traditions the inner coherence of all partial elements, however historically disparate they may be, constitutes a highly important pointer for the correct, organic understanding of the whole.[61] It has to come as a surprise that Asclepius's beneficial activity stirred up Zeus's resentment. The highest of the gods "fearing that men might acquire the healing art from him (Asclepius) and so come to the rescue of each other, smote him with a thunderbolt." One might, perhaps, interpret this strange con-clusion to the story to mean that Asclepius was in fact only a "physician," and so merely had the power to control the point in time when earthly death occurred. But humans, it seems, may not presume to wish for immortality on earth, unless that would only make them all the more painfully aware of their mortality.

This sort of connection is not in itself alien to fairy tales and myths, as the Grimms' story "Goodman Death" makes beautifully clear. It tells of a man who at his birth, since he is a child of poor parents, gets death for his godfather. Death makes his godchild a celebrated physician by giving him a herb by which he can cure even fatally stricken patients. But he is allowed to use it only if he sees death at the head of the sickbed. If death is standing at the foot of the bed, the man has to declare that his help is of no avail. For a long time the famous doctor follows this directive. But when the king of the country becomes mortally ill, he saves him, even though he sees Death standing at the foot of the bed.

For this one time Death lets grace prevail over justice. But shortly thereafter, when the king's daughter falls sick and the physician tries a second time to cheat Death of his share, Death pronounces the life of his godchild forfeit and with his ice-cold hand drags the terrified doctor down into a cave, in which many thousand lights of varying size are burning, some about to be extinguished, others just lit. These, Death explains, are the life-lights of human beings, of older people with their lives fading away and of still young ones who have just entered into life. He points inexorably to the doctor's light, which is on the point of going out. At the last moment the doctor asks Death to place a new, larger life on top of the first; and his godfather seemingly tries to grant this wish. But in fact he deliberately overturns the life-light of his godchild, and the doctor instantly slumps to the ground as if mowed down.

If we take the symbolism of this fairy tale literally, then doctors owe their power solely to a limited pact with Death, whose "godchildren" they are in a quite peculiar sense. Their whole activity depends upon the favor of Death. And the medicine they use is nothing but a gift from the hand of Death. Hence they may never presume to leave the "constellation" of Death out of account. Every act of autonomy vis-à-vis Death would be suicidal. All medical art is accordingly based on the recognition of the dependencies and conditions that Death places on our "poor" life. The "message" of the end of Asclepius, it seems, must be understood in a quite similar vein: The divine physician does not have power over death, only on the frontiers of death.

But thanks to this insight the activity of the physician returns to its ultimately religious point of departure. What actually is death for us, and what is life, if, in accordance with the phrase of Pindar quoted by that Lebanese woman in the museum of Beirut, our existence is nothing more than the "dream of a shadow"? Aren't we already dead in the midst of life? And isn't that true not only because of the "temporary" nature of our existence-unto-death,[62] but above all because of our incapacity, trapped as we are in the ghetto of anxiety, to fill our life with content and meaning? Between anxiety and death aren't we really already, in the midst of life, like the undead amid the shadows?

What is *real* about the things we do, about the events we attach importance to, about the opinions that we want to be true? The divine physician has an influence on the decisive change of existence from unlife to life, from transitoriness to duration, from nothingness to eternity, only if he gives himself up to the mystery of death and resurrection and climbs out of the underworld up to the light. The image of the rooster at the birth of Asclepius points to this sunrise of eternal light at the end of the shadows. In point of fact, however, it was not the religion of Asclepius, but the Eleusinian mysteries that provided this sort of insight into the mystery of the indestructibility of life.[63] Asclepius only overcame the portion of death that looms over life in the form of sickness. Meantime it was reserved to the mother goddess Demeter and her daughter, Persephone, to overcome the power of Hades. Thus the victory over death is not to be achieved through medical manipulation. And thus with every successful cure the physician-god Asclepius is only holding out a promise of life, one case at a time. This promise will not be kept for *all* of life until the priests of Eleusis make it come true in the cult of Demeter.

Hence, in keeping with the intermediary mode of his nature as the light shining out in darkness, Asclepius himself does not cross the threshold to the morning of the permanent truth of the sun. But even so at this point we see what the contrast between Luke's two annunciation scenes, in Nazareth and in Bethlehem, really means. From the historical-critical standpoint the scene in Bethlehem fundamentally reveals nothing that hasn't already been expressed in Luke 1:26–38. It is simply a competing doublet that at most could be viewed as a biographical vignette offering a little further development of the story of Jesus. But now against the symbolic background of the history of religion we can see that both narratives need each other for reciprocal completion. And this configuration itself, despite the alienness of the traditional material, has an Egyptian model.

In the annunciation in Nazareth, the commentary provided by the Egyptian myth of the birth of the Pharaoh (of the High House) dealt essentially with the question of how the spiritual potency of the wind, like the pure light of the sun, how Amun-Ra fashions himself an earthly body. His purpose, as we have seen, was to reveal the royal nature of humanity in the lowliness of the earthly, in the life of a mortal. Conversely in the annunciation scene in Bethlehem, the commentary provided by the *Greek* myth of the birth of the divine physician Asclepius takes a different tack. The story of Asclepius is essentially concerned with the question of how out of the darkness of night, on the shore of the "lake" of a sublunary world, the shimmer of the spirit, the light of Apollo irradiates human life with healing.

Thus the movement of both texts is from two opposite poles toward one another, like the geometrical lines within the two halves of one and the same sphere. What is thought from above in the world of the "sun" as a pure idea struggles and stretches from below in the world of the "moon" up to the sunlight. And only in the correspondence of both movements can the truth of the *rolling sphere,* as Thomas Mann called it,[64] be adequately expressed by means of myth. The truth is that the model becomes incarnate in reality, and reality itself is in accordance with the model. The reconciliation of opposites, the unity of the divine and the human, is the central theme of *all* traditions of a god becoming man. That unity couldn't be shown more splendidly than in the interrelationship of the two annunciation scenes in the Gospel of Luke.

In this process not only are heaven and earth coordinated, along with light and darkness, above and below, sun and moon. But above all so are birth and resurrection, essence and reality, being and fulfillment. We don't really understand the scene of the birth of God from the womb of the Virgin until we place it on the same level as the image of the opening of the tomb on Easter morning (Lk. 24:1-9). In both cases we have a victory over death, but with the birth of the divine Redeemer, as in the symbol of Asclepius, the power of death is conquered in the midst of life. By contrast Easter morning, corresponding to the mysteries of Eleusis, indicates the entrance into the sphere of eternity. The Egyptians expressed the polarity of this world and the next in this way: From the Fifth Dynasty onwards,[65] they correlated Osiris, the god of the underworld, with the sun god Ra, and placed both gods together in a a kind of identity as two "spaces," each conditioning the other, for experiencing the same reality:[66] Osiris became the night-sun in the underworld; in death the Pharaoh himself became Osiris.

With this the Egyptians bequeathed to Christianity a notion of human destiny that immediately had to result in another paradoxical doubling. The attempt was made to translate this teaching from the concreteness of the mythical view into the conceptual language of Greek philosophy. But as this was taking place, belief in the divine nature of humanity, in the immortality of the soul, in the divine sonship of Amun-Ra logically had to come into competition with the world of Osiris, with the doctrine of the resurrection of the body, and the resurrection of Christ in his triumph over the underworld. But both these halves of experience must form a single unit and must be left in their mythical unity in order to be comprehensible without contradiction.

This can be seen in one last look at Greek mythology, in the religion of Asclepius. We have already said that a lot of material from the ancient Egyptian sage Imhotep lives on in the son of the bright-dark Aigla-Koronis. Meanwhile in the Greek legends there is yet another "reincarnation" of Imhotep: the figure of the great artisan Daedalus, who united as it were two worlds in himself. He was the one who built the labyrinth in Crete, where the Minotaur, the son of Zeus in the form of a bull and the Cretan princess Pasiphaë, was imprisoned. But on the other hand he discovered the art of lifting off into the heavens with wings like a bird.[67] And isn't every human being *both:* a bull trapped in the dark, a child of the sun's generating force and the dreaming beauty of the moon, dull in its earthly servitude and yet capable of soaring beyond all barriers into the aether of freedom, in the heaven of light? When *both* truths about humankind come together and no longer conflict but are reconciled with one another, we can really say that God became man from the Virgin.

When the ancient Egyptians represented the human soul with their hieroglyphics, they could use a bull to indicate the *ka*-soul ("bull" and *ka* had the same sound). They saw in the *ka* the part of the (masculine) life force that flows through humans and connects them with the universal life of the cosmos.[68] But they could also depict the *ka*-soul as two hands that stretched out to heaven as if praying and pleading. Similarly they liked to draw the individual (personal) soul, the *ba* of humans, with a double sign: The Egyptians believed that when people died their *ba*-soul rose up like a bird to go back to the stars, back to their eternal home. Only at certain intervals would it visit the body of the dead person. This is a view that still survives in the Catholic Church's practice, in some parts of the world, of holding memorial services six weeks after death and the annual masses for the souls of the departed. But otherwise the soul was free for all possible transformations and different shapes,[69] just as the sun continually changes essential forms (its Cheperu) and nevertheless remains the same. But alongside the *ba*-bird the Egyptians drew the sign for "burning incense," which actually means, "what makes its way to God." Thus the Egyptians believed that the human soul is something that rises out of the dark like a pleasant aroma, like an evening sacrifice and, at the same time, something that came down from heaven and wants to go back there. Ra and Osiris, Amun and Asclepius — only *together* are they, and do they make possible, the truth of humans. This is the truth that Christianity believes in when it uses primeval images to say how close God is to humans and how close humans can be to God in the eternal symbol of God's incarnation.

"For the grace of God has appeared for the salvation of all men" (Tit. 2:11)

This book argues that the symbolism of the myths has to be read like expressionistic works of art in order to grasp their existential code language. One can say of myths somewhat as Edvard Munch said of his paintings, that he wasn't looking for photographic copies, but emotional symbols: "I don't paint 'after' nature. I take my motifs from her, or create out of her fullness. I don't paint what I see, but what I saw. The camera can't compete with paintbrush and palette – so long as it can't be used in hell or heaven."[70] Thus we have seen what a richly meaningful and sensual poetry lies hidden in the images of the Christmas gospel. And we are now well prepared to betake ourselves to the passage where these texts of old human traditions speak to us contemporaries *in the sign of Christ.*

Where actually is Bethlehem? Where can God be born?

The "Bethlehem" of the gospel is not the town south of Jerusalem. For, as we have seen, the gospel doesn't recount the beginning of Jesus' life. It recounts the beginning of our own humanized life, the history of our incarnation, as it has been made possible through the person of Jesus Christ. For that reason "Bethlehem" is everywhere that people can suffer from inhumanity and "hunger and thirst for God's righteousness" (Mt. 5:6). Only to *their* heart is God so close that he can live there. Hence two thousand years of Christian legends, drawing upon rich personal experiences, have simply managed to concentrate in the images of Christmas the conditions describing this miracle of the humanity and kindness of our God. Now we need only review all these encoded statements to test their meaning on ourselves and experience them in our lives.

Luke tells us that it was *night* in the hour of "Bethlehem." But do we really know what that is: "Night"? – when people see and have no prospects; when their dreams are dead, and the world is a yawning hole? Their hands grope for support and don't find it; and every morning begins not with a sunrise, but with a new solar eclipse.[71] The gospel tells these people of the night that Christ has appeared as a light shining in the darkness. On those who never knew God, "those who dwelt in a land of deep darkness, on them has light shined." This word of Isaiah's (9:2) has been fulfilled ever since the "night" in "Bethlehem."

Legends tell us that it was *cold* in the hour when the Redeemer appeared. But do we really know what that is: *cold?* – when the hearts of men and women freeze in the snow squall of words, and their feet stall in the drifts of superficialities; when their fingers tremble, frozen blue by the glacial masses of iced-over feelings? To these people of the cold Christ will say: "I came to cast fire on the earth; and would that it were already kindled!" (Lk. 12:49).

Legends tell us that Mary and Joseph were *lonely* and *outcast* in the hour of "Bethlehem." But do we really know what that is: *lonely?* — when people come into the world at a place where there is no shelter, only endless searching and longing outside people's doors? These are children not of parents, but of descendants of Mother Eve, the ancestress of all the banished, all who have been driven out into life, always having strange ground beneath their feet,[72] always running out of fear, with no rights, no place to stay, no home. Christ will say to these people of loneliness: "Foxes have holes, and birds of the air have nests; but the Son of man has nowhere to lay his head" (Lk. 9:58). Then he will say: "Come to me, all who labor and are heavy laden, and I will give you rest" (Mt. 11:28).

The legends tell us that the messianic king came into the world *in poverty*. But do we really know what that is: to be *poor?* When the soul of a person is as hollow as the mouth of a starving man and as empty as the hand of a beggar by the roadside? Or when the body is so exhausted that a woman no longer has enough strength to fan the flies from the eyes of her starving child? When in the morning you have to collect the newspapers off the curb if you want to shiver less from the cold at night, a life that is poorer than the beasts? To these people of poverty Christ will say, "You are close to God." And he will add in red-hot anger: "Woe to you that are rich" (Lk. 6:24).

All the gloomy, the freezing, the lonely, the outcasts, the poor will understand the "night" of "Bethlehem," because to all of them this child of God will promise: "Blessed are you that weep now, for you shall laugh" (Lk. 6:21). You who mourn are blessed; you who at least can still suffer are close to the kingdom of God.

The Bethlehem on the map lies twenty kilometers south of Jerusalem, but the real "Bethlehem" lies right next to "Jerusalem" in our own hearts. And where do we really live?

In "Jerusalem" different people inhabit the houses and the streets from those in "Bethlehem." In "Jerusalem" (or in "Rome," or wherever we mostly "stay") one meets the well-fed, the accomplished, the set-up, the powerful, the administrators and the manhandlers. It is the city of the "murderers," as the Gospel of Mark says (Mk. 12:8).[73] In that kind of "city" people expect nothing, because they fear change. There you cling to what you have: to the thoughts and imaginations you have learned, to the assets you've acquired, to the bastions and positions you've captured. You're afraid that some part of what has been finished and established might change. The walls of "Jerusalem" are broad and solid. But what if at the sound of the shofar, when the Lord comes to judge the earth (Ps. 98:6, 9), the walls no longer count?

To this day all the people are split up into separate camps, for the high and the low, the powerful and the powerless, the honorable and the contemptible, but then the walls will crumble. If the message of the "child" from "Bethlehem" adds up, then from now on there is no point of humiliation to which God has not descended, in order to abandon the fussily self-important to their ridiculousness, in order to overturn the seats of arrogance and to lift the lowly out of the dust (Lk. 1:51–52). What can happen to redeem us from our inhumanity, as we look at this "child" from "Bethlehem"?

Actually only this – that we give up our overbearing, presumptuous everyday life, get rid of the delusions of normalcy, and find the courage to believe unconditionally in the passion of love, in expansiveness of heart like the sun in the sky (as the Egyptians said), in the truth of compassion and the value of kindness. Then we will instantaneously know that we are all in truth "children." To be sure, none of us was really allowed to live when we were children; and we have all in our own way been forced to finish as quickly as possible and to become "grown-ups." For this very reason we find it hard to really stop being children – intimidated, anxious children, believing every authority, dependent on society, seeking recognition and currying favor.

That is why we can often barely remember the time of our childhood. And we run away from it through repression and denial, as if all we could do is flee like Lot from the flames of Sodom, the place where the divine is abused and raped (Gen. 19:5), where the punishment is enduring blindness (Gen. 19:11). For this very reason we feel as if we always have to stand there "grown-up," with our compulsions, our crazy drive for perfection, our useless "accomplishments," our ever-ready "information," our unquestioning phrases, and all the well-trained terror of our carefully memorized "knowledge."

If we look closely, they wanted us to be that way right from the start. All the people around us, in this merciless world, demand that we be good for something, that we be necessary and indispensable for something. But so long as we remain, to use Johannine language, "children of the flesh" (Jn. 1:13) we will destroy ourselves under the lash of these demands. We will never really get rid of the feeling that at bottom we are superfluous in this world. We will never really be able to believe that someone like us could be needed or even respected. We will always fear that at bottom we are only burdensome, inconvenient, unwanted, indeed a hindrance and harmful.

Who could ever prove the contrary?

But in this "night" we experience the contrary. In this "night" God became incarnate as a child and was nothing else but this sort of superfluous, inconvenient, homeless child. And *this child* is, was, and remains for all eternity God's own destiny between the manger and the gallows. Later on he will continue to be superfluous for all those who are at home in superfluity, to be inconvenient for all the pig-headed, to come at an awkward time for all the superior people, to strike all the pleasant people as extremely unpleasant, and seem absolutely uncomfortable for all the ever so comfortable people. But God wishes to identify himself with just this superfluousness, with this disturbing of the peace, with this inconvenience, with this unpleasantness and uncomfortableness.

Since that "night" the superfluousness of all people is justified. Grace to all the superfluous! is the message of this "night." Human kindness to all humans is God's gift to us.

Everybody around us demands that we know how to assert ourselves, that we be competent, that we achieve and succeed. For them success is what gives you the right to choose your means. Success itself justifies their right to live. But what happens to those who can't believe in their own success and at bottom don't even want it? What of those who are always getting the lowest grades from others for what they are and do? How can they, the eternal losers, the ones discarded as stupid and foolish, ever experience the opposite of failure?

But on this "night" they do experience the opposite. On this "night" God became incarnate as a child and was nothing more than such an underage, incompetent, helpless, powerless child. This child would also remain in the future without power or the ability to assert himself. Thirty years later he would come to grief in the eyes of everyone. And for the examination in what they consider life all the authorities would give him a grade of "Unsatisfactory." But God will himself become identical with this coming to grief, this shortcoming, this "unsatisfactory." It is God himself who will always have to come to grief in the world of success. Before God all men and women are failures, losers, deficient. But ever since that "night" we are justified even in our coming to grief. Grace to all the shipwrecked, to all the drowning, to all the born losers, is the message of that "night." That all people are allowed to be what in truth they are, without regard to success or results: This is the opportunity God grants us. On that "night" the wretchedness and impotence of all people have found their justification.

If ever men and women can find peace, then it will be in what begins in this image of "Bethlehem." Since that "night" when God became incarnate, we can leave off having to be like God. No person comes into this world without raising the question of to what extent he or she is and can be safe in the love of another. Only when this question is laid to rest will he or she dare to enter into life with his or her own person. For this very reason we look upon the mystery of the Holy Night as the beginning of our redemption: Since the days of Adam no one can take it for granted that in this world he or she is wanted, liked, and loved. But when it's no longer certain that we are *allowed* to be, we will try to prove that we *have* to be. And the more there is talk of Must and Should, the more the feeling will grow that all of life is like a burden, like a duty that we have to take care of. Only the "child" from "Bethlehem" will say that he is ready and willing to offer a yoke that is easy and a burden that is light (Mt. 11:30). Without such a chance for change we will never escape the atmosphere of mercilessness that we breathe. If one asks people — and oneself — *why* we actually live, almost always, once the superficial replies about enjoyment and amusement are eliminated, the depressing ones will remain: We live out of fear of death or out of responsibility for the weakness of others. It would be a cursed life if it stopped at that, born into and giving birth to unhappiness. But this cycle of woe can come to an end, and the evidence for that is the mystery of this holy night.

Thus the liturgy is right to place the celebration of the birth of the divine child in the season when the days are shortest and the nights are longest, as the light threatens to die. This is just the right moment to tell every person in particular and all people in general what they can really live on, apart from the cold, beyond the loneliness, within the poverty of existence, within the fullness of grace.

The light cannot die, so long as we ourselves maintain our longing for love; and even suffering is still like a reminder of this truth of the heart. Since that longest of nights this holy mystery has been busy growing, down through history. It increases with the life of every person who spreads a bit of warmth around, who makes other people's eyes a bit brighter, who makes their heart swell and their soul sing. Strictly considered, the mystery of this evening teaches us from now on to recognize in everyone an essential image of God and to encounter one another with the same reverence displayed by the faithful in the Eastern Church, who at the entrance to the sanctuary kiss and touch an icon, a sacred image. It's as if they wanted to brush all the dust off it and to keep bright and visible the purity of its gleaming gold background, fending off all the rust and filth with the tenderness of their hands and mouths.

All people, whether lofty or lowly, whether rich or poor, whether favored by fate or cast into a corner, are in themselves such a holy "image of the godhead," in their essence and evolution, in the beauty of their person. If we look into their eyes, we are gazing into the eyes of God. If we hear them talk, we sense in the exhalation of their words something of the breath-wind of God, which blows where it wills, everywhere in the world. And this mystery gives rise to a single command or, better, a newly granted capacity: For all time to come no child should or may ever come into the world without finding men and women to show it the way to heaven by reminding it that it is a child of God.

It is said that on the Holy Night God gave himself as *his Word*, that he himself entered into the tangible and vulnerable world of human life. But what does this mean for us? How can our hearts be seized by words that are worthy to express love? How can those words describe another's essence kindly enough to be valid? How can we teach children to speak a language that dares to express and give birth to feelings? How do we give them eyes with symbolic vision to transform this earthly world into a bridge to infinity – the walls transparent, gleaming with significance, a creation full of allusions, a living poem full of parables? How do we teach them the boldness to communicate the song in their hearts full of happiness and gratitude so that it turns into a spreading harmony?

In the heart of every person there are unheard, unheard-of Christmas songs. This inaudible music pervades the entire world, calling everyone to his or her beauty and breadth on the way back home to the stars. This earth will never be our homeland, but it is all the more familiar to us when it becomes our path leading over to the shores of eternity. We can accompany one another in growing humanization, in the struggles of gradual ripening, in a never-ending poetry of the heart. Ever since that night every man or woman is a living icon, a living shrine, waiting to be touched, to be spoken to with the signs and gestures of the love of God. God has chosen no other manger than our heart, in which he himself is and wishes to become human.

Ever since that "night" *everything* belongs to our God: *the body* of the human being; for in this night the "word" of God itself has become "flesh." It will have to bear in his body all the humiliations, tortures, and shamelessness with which humans can transform one of their own kind into no more than a prostrate, abandoned, frightened, trembling piece of flesh.[74] But ever since that "night" it is also true that human beings no longer live and are born from the human desire and longing of blood, but from God alone (Jn. 1:13). From now on no person is another's subject, product, or property. Since that "night" everyone is forever the property and child of the eternal king. And *our soul* too, that butterfly (one of the meanings of *psyché*) made of gold dust and yearning, is God's property. On this "night" God's tender hands, which formed the *ka* of our life from the potter's wheel of Chnum, caress the cares and the shame, the anxiety and guilt, away from its thin wings. On this "night" God's gentle fingers have captured the dreams of all people: God has made us humans into the image of his dream.

While the night with its silence spreads over this earth, the word of God begins to speak in us. And God's word is: Peace, peace to all men and women. From now on everyone's existence is the life of a child that belongs exclusively to God. But from now on we humans belong indissolubly together, because God is the father of us all.

The truth of Christmas is a mystery that only love can teach us. It reveals itself only to men and women who, like the shepherds in the fields of "Bethlehem," are still capable of visions of the heart.

How brightly must the eyes of people glow with happiness because they see the reflection of the heavens shine over them in the darkness of the night? But only the dream of love makes the eyes of a person radiant.

How filled with joy must the heart of a person be before it swings into the harmony of the universe, so that it hears the blowing of the wind as the song of angels? But only the dream of love makes the heart of a person sing.

How much happiness must dwell in our souls before we feel as if we had the power to bless the whole world and to experience it as a blessing, as a place of peace and questioning of the heart? But only the dream of love teaches us to take love as a gift and to look upon ourselves as something blessed by God. Yet we have this wonderful capacity to take one another into our hearts so that we are born anew into the world, so that everything originally put into our essence is admitted to life. When we humans become dreamers, we meet the magic of this new life on its deepest level. When the harshness of external reality in darkness and cold cruelly gives the lie to every sort of hope, God speaks most clearly in our hearts. It is as if since the first days of creation God had given our soul images to accompany us on the way, images strong and gentle and magical enough to draw us into their spell and to show us the right path — over to "Bethlehem." We have to see *this world* with the eyes of angels, that is, capable amid human suffering and wretchedness of recognizing the divine form and of perceiving its body, its growth, its ripening perfection.

Of course, the skeptics will ask whether the dream of the "shepherds" in the "dark" isn't *suspicious,* whether this Christmas message isn't too irenic and comforting. And how can you prove that angels were speaking, if immediately afterwards they withdraw into heaven? How can you show that it's possible to hear angels and to see this world through an angel's eyes? The Germans have even incorporated this cynicism into their everyday language. They say people can be clobbered so badly that they "hear the angels sing" (=see stars). That way they can be driven to the edge of death.

The skeptics find in external reality an infinite supply of arguments, hard to refute, proving how mean, how ugly, how wretched and messed-up human life is. On many details they are surely correct, up to the point where they are the only ones who see rightly "in the daylight," as "grown-ups" are accustomed to see. But as cutting as the voices of critical "reason" may sound, *dark* eyes see more truly in the dark. And it is possible to return from the edge of inhumanity into the deeper truth of a boundless sympathy. It is possible that out of loneliness can grow a peculiar empathy of the soul. Hence this gospel of Christmas proclaims that, yes, the host of divine messengers did return to the spheres of heaven — but simple shepherds replaced them as messengers of grace, and in a manger the radiance of heaven appeared to them as real.

The liturgy of Christmas day shows a wonderful delicacy in letting us take part at three different times in three different masses. This is designed to bring us together through the individual stages of the Christmas gospel as sites of personal experience and inner emotions. Thus along with the midnight mass the Church celebrates at dawn the "mass of the shepherds," in order that between night and day, at the hour of Asclepius, in the dawn of morning, it can hear the "Transeamus" of the shepherds. That is their "Let us go over to Bethlehem" (Lk. 2:15) as a personal song of the heart. The celebration of this mass at dawn applies to what is probably the most difficult thing in life, the transition from dream to reality, from vision to perception, from the angels' message to insight into life, from appearance to being.

In fact it requires the company of God to set out on this path. At this moment one must fear for the "shepherds," as for any people who try to follow their dreams and to find the path leading from the "shepherds' fields" to "Bethlehem." For at every step the so-called realists will follow after with their warnings. They'll say that dreams crash and crumble on the rocks of reality. They'll explain that visions are just imaginings of the heart that must shatter against the bitter experiences of the real world. They'll claim that "one" may not follow illusions, that we don't have a shred of evidence for the possibility of our view of the world, and that we'll only make ourselves ridiculous: We can *see* what the photos show — a crying child, wrapped in swaddling clothes, lying in a manger! How many people have lost their dreams on the way to "Bethlehem," as they learned the terrible lessons that forced them to become "realists"! Finally we have been taught since our childhood that even love can become routine. Indeed we're told that it must turn into something "ordinary," in order to be "reliable" and "sure," and that it supports us only so long as it bores us and keeps us waiting. It's as if all the poetry and magic of a person automatically had to fall away once we start to get to know that person.

There are skeptics about the human domain who when we have scarcely "grown up" expect us to believe that truth is fundamentally dirty, bloody, or repulsive, as if that were its trademark. How much courage it takes to go over to "Bethlehem" with the image of the angel before one's eyes, to go to the stable and the manger! But in the dawn of the holy night aren't those people the ones who are fooling themselves with their skepticism or "realism," the ones who always know what "has to be done"? They are the people without dreams, without vision, without song, without angels, without the dancing nights in which the stars glow for happiness?

Every narrowness of our heart brings with it the danger of constricting other people. Every dream of our being that we don't dare to live will destroy the dreams in the hearts of others. Every hope that we ourselves deny will rob other people of hope. Every person bears within himself or herself at least the longing that the human form should for once disclose itself as pure and genuine. At some point somewhere in the world it must be possible for the children of humankind to be allowed to live as God intended them to — without God's work being continually overwhelmed by a multitude of seemingly rational reasons, and gradually buried alive in the maelstrom of habit.

Ever since that Christmas morning it's not a different world that lies before our eyes. It's the same world as before, with its old powerlessness and misery, as urgent as ever. In an external sense it's not true that, as the legend sings, everywhere the Madonna placed her foot, the thorns began to blossom and the world of Paradise returned.[75] Externally the world continues to be the way it was. Apparently nothing has changed in it until we come to this group of "shepherds" who follow undeterred the message of their dreams, who dare to recognize their dreams in the wretchedness of the stable and manger. Amid the tiny beginnings and in the face of the insignificant-looking exterior one has to see the extraordinary side, the hidden royalty of a person.

Without the courage to bind our visions to what must continually run aground on the judgment of the senses we will never get to faith. Without the humility to bow before what looks so slight, without the patience to find value in what has yet to unfold, there will be no chance on this earth for the figure of our Redeemer. The whole art of the incipient incarnation is to recognize amid reality the shimmer of our own dreams. This gospel of the "going over" of the "shepherds" says that we don't really begin to live as human beings until we succeed in looking upon reality with the same eyes that just saw the angels. Not until we are capable of this all-transforming poetry of the world and of discovering its hidden beauty and truth will we be able to recognize and adore God in a newborn child.

This too counts as one of the insights of Christmas morning: *that the dreams of human beings are true.* They are sent from God, they are part of the person as God made him or her. That is exactly how the image-loving ancient Egyptians thought, the people to whom, as we have seen, we owe the first part of the Christmas narratives. They believed that it must be possible for one person to perceive another as a "living image of God (on earth)." For that is what we *are,* if only we look deeply enough within us. In every person God is waiting for people to open their eyes afresh. And this wonder can succeed when eyes that look on the person can see the divine element in that person.

In this sense we may now recall the code name of "Bethlehem." Anyone who hears "Bethlehem" mentioned in the Bible thinks of the time when David was still a boy and guarding his father's flocks out in the fields of Bethlehem. It's worthwhile to take another look at the wonderful scene when Samuel is sent from God to Bethlehem to anoint the youngest son of Jesse — in place of Saul, who in God's eyes has already been rejected. An ancient fairy tale, a recurrent popular tradition, tells that somewhere amid his siblings there is the youngest child, despised and misunderstood, who year-in, year-out waits to be discovered. Then one day the call does come, and suddenly he turns out to be the secret king of a hitherto unknown kingdom. Such stories are told all over the world, so we have to assume that the world is full of people in whom some special quality is alive, though hidden and withdrawn. But in the end this quality alone is worthy of calling them to the rank and office of "king." With fairy tales of this type we have a motif that seems designed to give us a deeper understanding of the scenery of Christmas. It certainly can't be accidental that for the calling of David (a central episode in the history of Israel)[76] the Bible should pick up precisely this old fairy tale (1 Sam 16:1-13). Evidently the eternal question of how to see what is most valuable in a person and at the same time what is most veiled can be answered only in the form of a fairy tale.

The Bible describes this sort of perceptual miracle with a statement that at first glance looks patched on for the sake of its moral and furthermore seems to be in contradiction with the context. The Lord, we are told, spoke to Samuel when he went on his errand to Bethlehem and saw Eliab, the oldest son of Jesse: "Do not look on his appearance or on the height of his stature, because I have rejected him; for the Lord sees not as man sees; man looks on the outward appearance, but the Lord looks on the heart" (1 Sam. 16:7). This astonishing remark doesn't hesitate to assert that whenever we begin to perceive the other *internally,* we are learning to make God's eyes our own. And whenever this happens, a dream, a fairy tale comes to be the actual reality of our history. Indeed what we call history doesn't realize itself until such dreams are fulfilled. That is accomplished not by the deeds of supposed heroes, but by such fairy tale moments when someone manages to discover another person in his or her inner truth and greatness.

Upon closer inspection there are *two* kinds of "seeing." The first is the usual sort: We are sitting in a café or on the veranda of our apartment and see people passing by at a distance. At first we see them entirely in the way Samuel observed the sons of Jesse: We see their exterior, their stature, their gait, the superficial impression they make. With this sort of observation a man like Eliab, the eldest, or Abinadab, the second eldest, or Samma, the third eldest of Jesse's sons, is likely to appear quite "princely." But there is another kind of seeing, and often enough it will captivate us from the first instant without our being able

to say what has enchanted us. In such a moment the outside becomes a perfect mirror for the inside. It's as if the body, the
language, the movement of the other person struck us as only
a manifestation of that person's essence. Everything that the
other does or says seems to us in this case to be just an expressive form of a communication from the soul. In this process of
inner seeing what reveals itself is at bottom *love* for the other.
For how else should love be characterized than as a movement of
the soul which makes that soul transparent to us in everything
the other does? At the same time love awakens the impulse in us
to learn more about the other, to get to know and to understand
him or her more deeply in every way. Thus seeing *internally*
means perceiving the meaning of each communication behind
the "facts" and understanding each impression of the other *as
the expression* of the person.

At this point the way the Bible "defines" the presuppositions
of such "seeing" with the eyes of the soul must be called altogether brilliant. For the Bible the function of Samuel, the *prophet*
and *priest,* is to be able to recognize the future king of Israel
in the simple shepherd boy from the fields of Bethlehem. This
integration of two roles in the figure of Samuel is extremely unusual. In the classical sense priest and prophet behave altogether
contrary to each other.[77] We generally associate with "prophet"
the sort of person who breaks up the established order, who
tears down institutions and unmasks false compromises. By contrast we associate with "priest" the idea of something statutory,
anchored in tradition, ritually consolidated. In truth such opposition exists. In and of itself, however, it ought not, it wouldn't
have to, exist.

Basically someone becomes a *priest* through the capacity to
perceive internally the soul of another person, and to help unfold, by blessing and sanctifying, what God has built into him
or her. Anyone with this ability, whether man or woman, has
essentially a priestly nature.

The *prophet,* by contrast, has the capacity to take everything
that has been internally sanctified, as it projects into the present,
and to open it up to a vision of all the powers and possibilities in
a person that want to be called forth. Anyone who can speak to
people on the strength of this vision of their person, in order to
elicit their best energies into the future, is essentially a prophetic

person. A prophet doesn't *predict* the future; instead, a prophet creates in the present, in the heart of others, the conditions that are pregnant with the future and will shape it.

This is exactly what Samuel does when he chooses Jesse's youngest son to be king. But then, after such an inner view of his nature, there is absolutely no contradiction when the narrator of David's royal calling freely praises the *outer* appearance of Jesse's son: How handsome he was! Reddish blond with wonderful eyes. Now, after the fact, all this has a place; it reflects and reveals the soul. Any who begin looking in this way on their *own* existence, as a priest and prophet like Samuel sees it, so deeply, so kindly, so expectantly and bravely, such persons, this Old Testament fairy tale tells us, enter with their life into the field of force of God's truth.

But we mustn't let an all-too-ready familiarity with the Christmas gospel make us overlook the surprising point of the narrative. Usually when we hear the text of this story, we presuppose the annunciation in Nazareth as something already known and done with. But, as we have already seen from the myth of the birth of Asclepius, it is a *typical* motif of such tales that others (the shepherds) disclose to the mother of the god the meaning of what she has just brought into the world. There must have been a stratum of tradition in Luke that knew only the one annunciation in Bethlehem and that thought of it as the only valid form of a Christmas gospel. Then we are almost dismayed to hear that in the stable at Bethlehem Mary is surprised and full of wonder at the shepherds' message.[78] Not angels, but human beings have to tell the Madonna how beautiful she is in the birth of her "firstborn" child. To authenticate their message the shepherds have nothing more than the vision of their heart in the darkness of the night. But that's just it: This gospel believes that it's possible for us to communicate our dreams to another so convincingly as to touch with them the deeper truth of her being.

Conversely it's altogether possible for us to produce something decisive in our life. Yet we won't know what it really is until others announce its meaning to us. According to this gospel, people have such a wonderful ability thanks to the indestructible dream-poetry of love: To see the brow of another person as a treasure chest of heaven, adorned with a diadem of gold from the sun and with the silvery gleam of the moon and all the starry jewels of his or her royal power.

Which miracle, then, is actually greater: that of midnight, when the Madonna bore the Redeemer to the world, or that of the morning hour, when she gave credit to the words of human beings that they saw in the visions of the night as a revelation from angels? Faith is stronger than the destruction of fear, and dreams win out over the seeming omnipotence of circumstances – *this miracle of our soul* saves us as human beings. It is the only thing that lets us live the way Christ was: as wanderers between two worlds, between night and morning, between dreams and daylight, between this world and the next, pilgrims all of us in this roadside inn that we call life.

Yet if we include Simeon's warning about the sword of sorrow (Lk. 2:35) and think besides of the tradition in Matthew about the persecution of the counter-king Herod, the fledgling hope of the Christmas message could quickly slip away from us. What is Mary to say? "But Mary kept all these things, pondering them in her heart," says the Gospel of Luke (2:19). "Oh, yes, Mary, pay close attention to the words of the shepherds! Very shortly there'll be nobody left to testify that you have brought something holy into the world. On the contrary. Soon people will be saying that your son is the child of a whore.[79] Soon they'll claim that he is an agitator (Lk. 23:5), a blasphemer against God (Mk. 14:64; Lk. 22:71), possessed by the devil (Mk. 3:30; Lk. 11:15), insane (Mk. 3:21). The mill wheels of throne and temple, palace and altar stand ready to receive your child and grind him like wheat.

They'll explain that you were wrong, when you believed the shepherds, and for proof they will give him back to you – dead, lifeless, disfigured, *annihilated*, as they think. Don't you hear the tramp of the horses, the pounding of the hooves, the crying of the women in the streets of Bethlehem? Flee, child Jesus, flee to a country whose language you don't know and that nevertheless dreamed you sooner and more worthily than any other nation in the world. Hide yourself from people, conceal yourself in the woods,[80] hide yourself in the mountains. The human bloodhounds are already lying in wait for every word from your mouth. They are afraid, these children of darkness (Jn. 1:5; 3:19), of every explanation and clarification. They tremble before the breath-wind of your freedom. Yes, if all that counted was the slogan, "Peace to the huts, and war to the palaces."[81] But one mustn't call up the storm wind. You, child of Bethlehem, will bring the most frightful thing that this world of iced-over feelings knows: You will come with the power of the south wind; and everything will melt in a sea of tears. You will teach the people to pray for those who persecute them (Mt. 5:44; Lk. 6:28); and even on the cross you will plead with God, your Father, to forgive your executioners – because they didn't know what they were doing (Lk. 23:34).

But do we really not know what we are doing? On this "night" of cold, loneliness, exposure, and poverty in the glowing of the heavens above the fields of Bethlehem, what of those whose eyes have still not opened, whose heart is still not warm? Such people, one must fear, will keep their eyes closed forever; their heart will remain forever frozen. And no hand of God can open those eyes or warm that heart anymore. God could do no more than be a light in the darkness of the world (Jn. 1:3,4). *We know what we're doing;* we *would have to* to do it. We may well continue to say: "But we're still powerless, we're too small, we can't make any headway against the world." Yet must we first know who we *are* before we can know what we must do? Ever since that night it's enough that God is working in virgin territory. And God completes all beginnings, even the smallest, if only we believe God's goodness and hold our hearts in readiness as the place at which God can come into the world. Because "Bethlehem" is our heart, or there would never have been a Bethlehem.

For this very reason we have to *choose* between the "kingdoms of this world" and the one kingdom of God (Lk. 4:5–6). "Emperor Augustus" in Luke is the history we are used to, *big* history. Anyone who wants to study *that* need only read what Nicolaus Damascenus, chancellor and court scrivener of King Herod, had to say around 23 B.C.E. about the Roman emperor:

> Men have conferred on this man the honorary name Augustus and they honor him with temples and sacrifices here and there in the cities and nations . . . out of gratitude for his splendid life work and the benefactions he has done for them. For he is the man who has reached the summit of human power and wisdom. Under him the boundaries of

the Roman empire have reached their greatest extension. He has united the greatest host of people known to history under his dominion. He has won over not just the peoples, but the hearts of all men once and for all, at first with weapon in hand, but then entirely without arms as well. He has made tribes whose name no man had even heard of into civilized nations. Nations who in human memory have not tolerated any ruler over them voluntarily pay him allegiance for the sake of the kind humanity that is revealed ever more radiantly in him.[82]

That was Augustus, the "august," the "divine." "This, / this is the man you heard so often promised," writes the poet Virgil, "Augustus Caesar, son of a god, who will / renew a golden age."[83] And in fact the dictated *Pax Romana* ruled with the power of an empire spanning the whole known world, from Scotland to Mesopotamia, from Romania to North Africa. The gates to the temple of the war god Mars were solemnly closed. If ever power achieved what it wanted and was destined for, then it was under and through Augustus.

But for that very reason it is startling and frightening when at the same time, far from Rome, in the province of Judea, the "savior" is proclaimed by the angels, the true prince of peace, the religious realization of the ancient Egyptian vision of the divine king. There is no clearer way of saying: Augustus is *not* the savior; his peace is no peace. The peace of Bethlehem is an absolutely challenging declaration of war. "Glory to *God* in the highest" positively means the end of that earthly divinization of power and violence.

From the time around 120 C.E. we have a handbill directed against the Roman cult of the emperor, which very clearly connects the profession of faith in God with the rejection of Rome:

Only God is worthy to receive renown and power and glory and victory and dominion. If a man as king makes his entrance into a city, all those before him praise him: He is strong; but he is weak. He is rich; but he is poor. He is wise; but he is a fool. He is compassionate; but he is cruel. He is righteous and faithful; but he has none of all those heroic virtues. But everybody flatters him. God is not like that,

God who spoke and the world was made. Whatever man
may praise him for, He is more than his renown.[84]

This Christmas message must be understood as a similar rejection of *every* "emperor," of the principle of power altogether.
Because even the "good" that people do only gets continually
perverted, in the cycle of authority, into its opposite. That is the
reason why Thomas Müntzer's understanding of Luke 1:51–53
("he has put down the mighty from their thrones") will always remain a misunderstanding. Though he has been much maligned,
Müntzer was a prophet of tragic greatness. He took the words
to refer to a democratic theocracy that had to be brought about
with all the instruments of war.[85]

Only fifty years after Virgil hailed Augustus quite different
verses were being written about his successor Tiberius: "Emperor, you have thoroughly transformed the Golden Age; for, as
long as you are still alive, it will be an Iron one."[86] Anyone who
really wants peace must not succumb to the seductive undertow
of power, but must exercise and learn the "fearful power of gentleness" (Dostoyevsky).[87] Augustus was the poverty of a human
being in the splendor of an emperor. Christ is the power of God
in the poverty of a human being.

As far back as the birth legend of the *Buddha* (see p. 23), we
are told that the newborn son of the king will have to choose:
Either he will be a great ruler, or a great sage. He will either
conquer people through the power of his word, or through the
power of his kindness. He will win either through the strength
of his armies, or through the liberating persuasive power of his
words.[88] Meanwhile the really chosen individuals can't "choose"
on this point — they believe only in the power of the goodness
that God has sunk into our heart. To be sure, Pindar is right:
"Creatures of a day, what is any one, what is he not? Man is but
a dream of a shadow." But Pindar himself goes on: "But when
a gleam of sunshine cometh as a gift of heaven, a radiant light
resteth on me, aye and a gentle life."[89] Christianity says that this
gleam has appeared, as God's grace, in the figure of Jesus Christ
to the salvation of all men and women.

4

"Lord, Now Thou Lettest Thy Servant Depart in Peace, According to Thy Word" (Lk. 2:21–40)

℘

I N THE LUCAN INFANCY NARRATIVE, as the story progresses there appears a simple biographical notice that the Church's liturgy quite rightly commemorates with a special feast of the Holy Name of Jesus. The fact that the man from Nazareth bore the name "Jesus" was nothing special in itself. But the New Testament story is following a primeval mythical typos here, when it reports that the newborn Son of God receives the very name that heaven has sought out for him and proclaimed in advance.

"He was called Jesus, the name given by the angel" (Lk. 2:21)

Once again an Egyptian story suggests itself as a comparison piece for the biblical text. Admittedly it wasn't recorded in demotic writing until the second half of the first century. But it is surely based on a much older model: the famous story of Si-Osire

(= the son of Osiris).[1] Si-Osire came into the world as the son of Setom (high priest) Chaemwese (= who appeared in Thebes), the son of Ramses II. As in the birth legend of Samuel (1 Sam. 1:1–18), the mother of Si-Osire prayed in the temple for the favor of bearing a child. And thus one night she dreamed,

> That she was told: "Are you not Meh-usechet, the wife of Setom, she who lies (in the temple) in order to receive a blessing (from the hands of the god? When the morning) comes (tomorrow), go into the bathroom of Setom, your husband. There you will find that a melon shoot has grown. (Break a branch off it) together with its gourds and grind them to powder, make a medicine out of it, put it in water, and drink it. Then you will conceive a child from it that same night.
>
> Meh-usechet awoke from the dream when she had seen this; and she did everything as she had been told in the dream. She lay down alongside Setom, her husband, and she conceived a child from him.
>
> When the time of her purification had come, she had the symptoms of a woman who has conceived. Setom immediately informed the Pharaoh of this, because his heart was very, very glad about the news. He hung an amulet around her and read a saying over her.
>
> One night Setom lay down and dreamed in a dream that someone was speaking with him and told him: "Meh-usechet, your wife, conceived a child from you on that night. The child who is to be born, his name shall be Si-Osire (son of Osiris). Many will be the wonders that he will do for the Egyptians."
>
> Setom awoke from his dream when he had seen this, and his heart was very, very glad.
>
> During the months of her pregnancy she [Meh-usechet] felt the signs of the child's wondrous nature. And when the time of her lying-in came, she bore a male child. Setom was told of this, and he called him Si-Osire, as he had been bidden in the dream. Then he took him into his arms; he was rocked in the cradle and nursed.

As a matter of fact, Meh-usechet is right about her feelings during pregnancy; and her dream is just as true as her husband's:

Si-Osire really is the son of a god. In truth he is Horus, the son of Pa-nesche, who as a wise man in days of yore, with the help of his unconquerable magical power, had already protected Pharaoh Mench-ra-Pe (actually the transmogrification of a name of Thutmose III [1504–1450], meaning "of lasting essence [like] Ra")[2] from the evil plots of an Ethiopian magician. Now, Si-Osire explains at the end of the fairy tale, he has again returned to save the Pharaoh from another severe humiliation at the hands of the "gum-eaters" (the Negroid population of Ethiopia). Thus he has begged Osiris, lord of the kingdom of the dead, to be allowed to go out onto the earth, since at the time there was no good scribe or sage in Egypt to cope with the magic wiles of the Ethiopian enemy. And so he grew up in the form of that melon gourd with the intention of returning into the body of a human being.

This "oral conception" by Meh-usechet is an authentic expression for the *virginal* conception of the divine child — a motif, by the way, that is found all over the world in the myths of various peoples.[3] Only when Si-Osire, his mission complete, withdraws as a shadow from the eyes of the living, will Meh-usechet conceive another boy from her husband, the priest Chaemwese, in the natural fashion. By contrast, Si-Osire shows himself both in birth and death to be a real "son of god"; and his naming *must* take place in accordance with a divine message, since only the gods can know about his name, his true essence.

In fact in the period that follows, Si-Osire does all honor to his name, "son of (the god of the dead) Osiris." It is just this part of the fairy tale that proves how widespread, even in Palestine, the story of Setom Chaemwese and his divine son must have been. Jesus himself picks up a parallel situation in his famous parable of Lazarus and Dives (Lk. 16:19–31).[4] The Egyptian version of this story tells how one day Chaemwese is happily praising a rich man who has been given a sumptuous funeral, as opposed to the pitiful burial of a poor man. Then Si-Osire takes his father into the underworld and shows him in images that anticipate Dante's Inferno the places in the kingdom of the dead. Chaemwese has to acknowledge that divine judgment sets no store whatsoever by external splendor and wealth; it delivers just retribution for whatever men and women have done. "Those who are good on earth are treated well in the kingdom of the dead. But those who are bad on earth are also treated badly there."[5] Hence that rich man is horribly punished by having the hinge pin from the gate of the kingdom of the dead driven into his eyes and screwed in and out. By contrast the poor man, clothed in royal linen, is throned as a man of God near the place of Osiris and now calls his own all the possessions of the kingdom.

This is similar to what Jesus promises the disciples shortly before his death: They will be at his table in the kingdom of heaven, eating and drinking; and they will sit on twelve thrones to judge the tribes of Israel (Lk. 22:30). The Egyptian fairy tale shows how much the ancient Egyptians' way of thinking had already become internalized long before Christianity came into existence. It likewise shows how far people had come from the external display of luxury in the (magical) attempt to assure an afterlife for the Pharaohs. Even the cosmic balance on the scales of Maat had now become a moral works-righteousness in the sense of the Roman *Justitia*. But unlike in Luke 16:27–28 the return of a dead person from the underworld seems to have struck the Egyptians as warning enough to make a corresponding adjustment in their actions and get ready for the judgment of Maat. Here as in many other many points of its teaching, Christianity needed only to connect with the already existing position worked out by Egyptian popular piety.

As for the prophetic announcement of the holy name of a child Redeemer, it is quite possible that, given the many points of comparison between the Gospel of Luke and the Egyptian fairy tale of Si-Osire, the motif of the divine promise of the right name was something Luke was familiar with. In any case we are not concerned with the reconstruction of traditional or even literary dependencies. The question is rather what a specific motif means *in itself,* because a mere discussion about the (presumed) origin of certain motifs in the historical sense has as little to do with their real content as the postmark on an envelope has with the letter inside. What does it mean when fairy tales and myths *continually* recount how the name of a divine child is announced to the parents by an angel, by a dream, by an oracle, or by other forms of divine communication before his birth — *that* is the question.

Evidently the widespread mythical idea of the divine name-giving is a truth that has been almost completely lost in our thinking. The ancient Romans were prosaic enough to name their children not after the sun or the mysteries of the gods, but after their rank order in the family reproductive process: Primus, Secundus, Tertius . . . Sextus . . . Decimus. This brutal sobriety was, of course, sufficiently free of illusion to destroy any faith that naming a person expresses anything of his or her personality. It's different when in today's generation we have long since stopped naming our children after this or that saint, preferring instead the names of rock stars and other glamorous "personalities." Without realizing it we are acting as if our "eagerly awaited children" came into the world only to fulfill our notions of recognition, advancement, and success.[6] Names of this sort characterize not the essence of a person, but at most the role expectations parents have of their children.

By contrast, if we want to know what the ancient myths meant by the divine (dream-) revelation of a name, we have to cast our thoughts back to the days of Eden when Adam was in search of a partner. First he gives a name to all the animals around him and then finally, awakened out of a long sleep, to the woman of his dreams (Gen. 2:23).[7] Such names of love always come into being out of an interior dialogue of tenderness, just as lovers at all times have enjoyed inventing certain private names for one another that remain their most personal and strictly guarded secret. In the paradise of love we are poetic enough to dream of one another day and night and to speak out the name of the other "in Egyptian," as a kind of magic spell that transforms the entire world. In love it's true that we need only hear or whisper the name of the beloved to relate all things to an invisible center in which the person we love is at home. To speak or hear the name of such a person gives us all the joy and happiness on earth. Above all it makes us for the first time want to live with all our heart. The name of the beloved is in fact for us "like the taste of life."

This whispering of endearments between longing and fulfillment can go up to the limit of unconsciousness, because in love we are with ourselves only when we are with the other. And we don't find our way back to ourselves until we find our way to him or her. In love we feel quite clearly that the "name" of the other is given to us as an inspiration from heaven. His or her whole existence strikes us as a unique grace. While all other things in the world seem quite arbitrary – they might be and again they might not – in love we sense with all our powers that the other unconditionally *must* be.

To be sure one may readily object that we ought not to prize the other so highly. Love always inclines to a nearsighted, maniacal overvaluation of the person of the beloved.[8] Indeed, the gainsayers continue, the whole romantic notion of love might just be a false ideal cultivated by frustrated bourgeois.[9]

But lovers don't think with such critical "rationality." They feel very clearly that their love does not overvalue the beloved, that it contributes first and foremost to recognizing his or her true value or at least to getting an approximate sense of it. The person of someone we love from the heart becomes for us the decisive "place" of our life. From this "place" we experience how the whole world exists thanks only to the overflowing profusion of a love that lies at the bottom of everything, and for which there is simply nothing trivial or non-essential. Only love leads us to the point where the world comes forth from the hand of its creator. Only love opens heaven to us and lets us carry out within ourselves the process similar to the god Chnum's shaping on the potter's wheel the beauty of the body and the beauty of a human soul as a perfect work of art. Only love lets us hear the name with which God from all eternity has called a person into existence.

In the paradise of love lies the capacity of every person to feel, to think, to see, to hear – and to live in the manner of this sort of "seeing a work of art," of natural poetry of the heart. On the other hand, in "life," as we are usually familiar with it, contact with the divine seems mostly like something unknown and exceptional, like something separate or downright peculiar. That is why if we ever become aware of a person's real name, it's at most during special psychic states, in a dream or vision, or under special circumstances, in holy temples or at holy times. What is normal in love we consider almost abnormal. We find anything with pathos in it pathological, everything effusive we see as overstrained. We are frightened of invasions from this different, wonderful world of happiness, of beauty and poetry.

Yet love alone schools us to name a person "rightly." To be sure, only heaven knows a person's name completely; but en route to heaven only love teaches us to see the other with the eyes of heaven. Only love looks upon the other in his or her absolute self-worth; and yet love at the same time shows us most enduringly his or her absolute value for ourselves. It reveals to us that without the other we would scarcely know how to live. In love the other appears to us as the summary and fulfillment of all longings and dreams, indeed as the revelation and confirmation of everything that we could ever hope and wish for ourselves. The happiness of every deep love consists in this sort of return to the lost paradise where God spoke (speaks) to the heart of us humans face to face.

Hence there is no more profound interpretation of the feast of the Holy Name of Jesus then the Jesus-prayer of the Eastern Church, in which "Jesus" is continually repeated in a low tone of voice with great feeling. Those who pronounce the name of Jesus in this manner to themselves, as the quintessence of all their hope and yearning, know that such a name has to be revealed by angels: Yeshua-Savior. This is a form of prayer that resembles the one that, as I. B. Singer tells us, was used by Israel ben Eliezer (the Baal Shem Tov):

> Israel didn't pray like other people. He sang his prayers, each one to a different tune. The melodies streamed straight into his soul from the house of songs. This wasn't the psalmody of a cantor, but of one whose soul was at once down here on earth and off in other worlds. The Levites in the holy Temple had sung in just this way. In his prayers Israel held a discussion with the Almighty in song, as if he were complaining to Him; and his listeners thought they heard the Almighty answering him, defending Himself to Reb Israel, and asking him to be patient and trust Him that everything He did would turn out for the best.[10]

It is the name of Jesus with which, according to the Bible, God tried to respond to all the hardships of our life and the troubles of our souls. "For there is no name under heaven given among men by which we must be saved" (Acts 4:12). All the love of God is concentrated in him — again and again. Those who feel this within themselves know that only an angel could reveal Jesus' name, as the greatest wonder of this world.

In his little poem "The Savior," Hermann Hesse has given voice to this eternal experience of Christmas when he writes of Christ:

Again and again he is born a man,
Speaks to pious ears, speaks to the deaf,
Comes close to us, then we lose him once again.

Again and again he must tower in loneliness,
Bear all his brothers' neediness and longing,
And be nailed once more to the cross.

Again and again God will proclaim himself,
Bringing down heaven to the valley of sin,
Everlasting spirit flowing into flesh.

Again and again, even in our time
The Savior is coming, coming to bless,
To meet our fears, tears, questions, cries
With a perfectly silent look,
Which we don't dare to return,
For only the eyes of a child could bear it.[11]

"For mine eyes have seen thy salvation" — The Prophecy in the Temple (Lk. 2:22–40)

The image of the "prophetic"[12] announcement of Jesus' call by the aged Simeon as well as by the widow Anna offers a typical motif from the birth of a divine child. And once again an Egyptian story provides the first parallels. Plutarch[13] tells of the birth of Osiris: On the first of the five intercalary days (added to the 360-day Egyptian calendar) the god of resurrection was born:

And at the hour of his birth a voice issued forth saying, "The Lord of All advances to the light." But some relate that a certain Pamyles, while he was drawing water in Thebes, heard a voice issuing from the shrine of Zeus, which bade him proclaim with a loud voice that a mighty and beneficent king, Osiris, had been born; and for this Cronus entrusted to him the child Osiris, whom he brought up. It is in his honor that the festival of Pamylia is celebrated.

The Christian feast of Candlemass (February 2) must owe its origin to the background of a liturgy such as this one.

Formally speaking, the closest thing to the Lucan presentation of the aged Simeon is surely the Buddhist legend that begins by stressing the virginity of his mother before, during, and after the birth of the Redeemer of the world: "When the future Buddha descended into the womb [i.e., from the heaven of the Tusita-gods], the future mother of the Buddha had no thoughts of men which had anything to do with sensuality, and she was inaccessible to any man's passion." Like the Christian Mother of God the mother of the Buddha is "immaculate" in body and soul, without sickness, free from physical infirmities. "Only in a standing position does the mother of the future Buddha bear the future Buddha.... Four sons of the gods receive him and present him to his mother: 'Be blessed, O lady! A mighty one has been born to you as a son.'" Undirtied by amniotic fluid, blood, or mucus, perfectly clean, the future Buddha immediately steps forward in seven long strides, "looks towards all the points of the compass and speaks the weighty word: 'I am the most excellent on this earth. I am first in this world.'"

"When the future Buddha comes forth from his mother's womb, there appears in the world...an immeasurably exalted radiance, surpassing even the gods' divine splendor." "But when ...Prince Vipassi [the future Buddha] was born, they reported it to King Bandhuma in this way: 'Blessed, O King, art thou! A great man, O King, has been born to you as a son!...For this prince, O King, is gifted with the thirty-three distinguishing marks of the great man, and to such a gifted great man only two paths are open:'" Either he will chose domestic life and be a world-ruling king of law whose sway will extend to the edge of the world sea in righteousness, or he will head off into homelessness and as a fully enlightened one overcome the cycle of suffering, the law of karma.[14]

As we see, this Buddhist text contains, along with the virgin birth, the shining light from heaven and the reception by the gods (similar to the Egyptian myth of the birth of the Pharaoh or to the angel's song in the Bible). It also has the motif of the sunlike[15] rapid growth and moving about of the divine child (see below, p. 159). Above all it has the feature often found in legends, that the future destiny of the newly born divine king under the influence of heavenly powers is announced in advance. This is paralleled exactly by the prophecies of Simeon and Anna in the Gospel of Luke. The one striking difference in the Buddhist text is the sharp stress laid on the choice between world dominion and divine dominion at the very beginning of the Buddha's life. In the New Testament, however, even the words of the Magnificat (Lk. 1:46-55) have in themselves a broad interpretive latitude about the nature of the messianic rule. Even after the death of Jesus (Lk. 24:21), indeed even after his resurrection, immediately before his ascension (Acts 1:6) the disciples managed to remain entangled in their earthly expectations of the Messiah. The motif of the annunciation sheds no further light on this matter.[16] At bottom Simeon and Anna do nothing more in the Temple of Jerusalem than the shepherds in Jerusalem have done already: They proclaim the meaning of the divine child Redeemer.

Nevertheless, it seems worth noting how much Luke's account emphasizes the advanced age of the two "prophets." The figure of Anna, whose career we learn in detail (Lk. 2:36-37), after the manner of a personal legend, is highly interesting in its own right. The description of Simeon (Lk. 2:25-26) likewise calls attention to the person of this man. Hence in evaluating the scene in the Temple we can't stick to the usual method of elaborating, as it were, only the immanent "Christology" of the passage. Instead, in keeping with the ethos of the personal legend, we have to ask how to imagine Simeon and Anna as *people.*

The crucial point here is that despite their advanced age neither of them has ever stopped hoping and waiting. *That* seems to be the actual question posed by the legendary motif of Simeon and Anna: How does the fact of ageing relate to the dynamic and passion of our yearning for fulfillment? In the context of Luke's infancy narrative how does the Christmas message work itself out in our life? Does it literally come too late, because we may have already outlived ourselves? Or has the magical power of longing kept us young enough to incorporate into ourselves the reality of the "divine child"? *"What may I hope for?"*

This human question is crystallized in the two old people, Simeon and Anna, who are on the verge of bodily death. What is left to wait for when life draws near its end? Isn't death, the finitude of existence, the end of everything, including hope? The primeval questions of Asclepius won't let go. If the message of Christmas morning was proclaimed in the rays of the rising sun, now the question is posed of how we can "see" that message, how we can "grasp" it as fulfilled in the face of the lengthening shadows of sunset.

When the Roman Emperor Marcus Aurelius (161–80) came to speak about the end of human life in his *Meditations,* he suggested that humans think in the following manner about themselves and their fate:

> How tiny a fragment of boundless and abysmal Time has been appointed to each man! For in a moment it is lost in eternity. And how tiny a part of the Universal Substance! And on how tiny a clod of the whole Earth thou dost crawl! Keeping all these things in mind, think nothing of moment what thy nature leads thee to do, and to bear what the Universal Nature brings thee. . . . Man, thou hast been a citizen in this World-City, what matters it to thee if for five years or for a hundred? . . . What hardship then is there in being banished from the city, not by a tyrant or an unjust judge but by Nature who settled thee in it? So might a praetor who commissions a comic actor, dismiss him from the stage. *But I have not played my five acts, but only three.* Very possibly, but in life three acts count as a full play. For he, that is responsible for thy composition originally and thy dissolution now, decides when it is complete. But thou art responsible for neither. Depart then with a good grace, for he also that dismisses thee is gracious.[17]

Marcus Aurelius, the last great Stoic, thus advises equanimity toward impenetrable fate, the peace of resignation, and an enlightened wisdom that no longer wonders at anything.

It takes a lot of strength to think the way Marcus Aurelius does: Follow your own nature. But what sort of hope lies in the courage of resignation and in this patient holding out unshakably to the end? Is it supposed to be human nature to hope for nothing and wait for nothing, simply out of anxiety over the lethal disappointments of life and the definitive disappointment of death, which may come at any moment? This same question finds its answer in the figures of Simeon and Anna, who in their advanced age seem like counter-images to the elderly sounding wisdom of the Roman emperor. Luke sums up the essentials in a single sentence when he says of Simeon: "And it had been revealed to him by the Holy Spirit that he should not see death before he had seen the Lord's Christ" (Lk. 2:26). Luke is undoubtedly right in this accentuation. If there is anything thoroughly characteristic and crucial to be said about a person, it is this: He was someone who till the end of his days never ceased to believe that he himself, with his own eyes, would see salvation. For it must be added that *only* people of this sort can discover something like "salvation."

People like Simeon and Anna may catch the eyes of other readers by the fact that they are absolutely not satisfied with what those around them would call happiness. They also presumably don't know what they should actually wait for instead of that. But, as a man like Simeon shows, they only know that it must be more than what the others believe in. For his part he too must have scarcely known what to say about how his life was supposed to be put in order. He just emphatically refused to say that what was untenable and wrong in his life was right.

He too, like Emperor Marcus Aurelius, probably strove again and again to understand why all the intolerable things, all the things in his life that had gone awry, should be the way they were. In the end he may have even begun to understand all this better than many others who had resigned themselves early on. But that's the strange thing about him: A man like Simeon, early and late, will continue to call what is monstrous and horrible, without mincing words, monstrous and horrible, precisely because he understands it. He won't find it normal; he won't put up with it; he won't resign himself to it, even if he can't change it. Despite everything that contradicts him, he won't lose the sense of longing that in his and in other people's lives something *can* be changed after all. Indeed he will cling unconditionally to the notion that his life was designed for the sole purpose of being made whole. He stakes his life on this faith. Because *not* to believe this would mean the same thing to him as death. And though it may take an entire life – though contrary to his hopes one year may have slipped away after another – he won't tire of holding on: "He would not die until he had seen the Lord's Christ."

The same has to be said of Anna, the daughter of Phanuel. In the ancient world a woman's life ended, properly speaking, when her husband died. Sociologically and legally she was nothing but an appendix to the man. Accordingly Anna's life ought to have been over with the early death of her husband. Or at least she should have made every effort to be taken into the house of another husband. She didn't do either, and yet she is neither desperate nor dependent. Rather she found the strength to direct all her expectations of life toward God and to hope for this, her earthly life, in a different way.

Surely the greatest puzzle of a human life is this paradoxical fact: People often enough seem crushed by suffering, degradation, and shame, and yet they don't lose hope. A hundred reasons, which they themselves are aware of, seem to show every thinking person that in all probability things will have to go on this way their whole life long. These people actually tell themselves that. Nor can they refute all the arguments against their hope. They have to admit that from a purely human standpoint there is no hope. And yet, and yet, and yet. They don't lose their tough, crazy faith that the purpose of their life is not to go under in a sea of filth, slowly sinking by the same law of gravity that governs all things.[18] They believe in salvation: They think it means *their* life, that *they* will get to touch it with their life. This keeps them awake and lets them live. This *is* their whole life: to wait and to wait and to hope for *more*, rather than being content with what is cheap and superficial and being satisfied according to the standards of the "normal" people.

Where do men and women like this get the strength for it? From nothing on earth that can be humanly grasped and explained. Whenever one runs into people like Simeon and Anna, one stands there moved and amazed; and at bottom one can only think as Luke does: This attitude must be from God. Something has taken effect here that can't be put in one's head by other people or sheer will power – something that the Spirit of God himself must have planted in the heart of a person. All the others "put down" such faith, and what *they're* doing would throttle that faith immediately. And yet it can't be killed. Instead it supports one's whole life, and a life that would otherwise have to lead straight to despair. Whenever we find such people of hope against all hope, we can only thank heaven for the fact that they exist, and that God has kept the longing and faith awake in them. People of this sort never let themselves be put off or appeased with anything that is not God.

It's not hard to see this fundamental principle in the figure of Simeon. He is a man who doesn't give up his faith in the salvation of his people, despite all the unfreedom and servitude that have been visited upon them from the outside. And despite all what is externally quite inevitable, he doesn't resign himself to it. Unswervingly and independently he goes on believing: He, Simeon, will see salvation, the consolation of Israel. This belief is the essential thing that has to be connected to his person. This *is* his whole person, because this faith alone has made Simeon remain true to himself, never abandoning the idea that his life was called to be made whole. Only this Spirit of God could stop him from going along with all possible forms of alienation and self-deception; and thus he has managed to carry on till the end, "doing his thing" before God.

Of course, we could also say that Simeon expected too much, that it was simply naive to dream his way past reality. As a grown-up – and at his age he should at least be considered that – one would have finally had to get used to the rough edges of reality. Isn't Simeon's faith in fact a dream and childish wishful thinking?

To be sure, we can call a wish or a dream *childish* just because it expresses a longing that is fundamentally built into all of us from our very origins. We can call it *dreamy* just because here someone is simply following what is alive in him, because it constitutes the only goal worth striving for in his whole life: that at some point our existence can open up to its real, perfect form. However, in this sense all of Christianity is "childish wishful thinking." Anyone who takes this formula critically, thinking to direct it *against* Christianity, might want to reflect that even if Christianity was never anything more than wish fulfillment, then this sort of illusion would still be a thousand times better than so-called reality. For only this dream lets people live and guards them from despair.[19]

No doubt what Simeon proclaims and promises in the Temple scene is thoroughly unprovable to outsiders. It lives only in him, and the vision of its fulfillment can't be demonstrated to an indifferent observer. Indeed, objectively considered, it appears just as childish and naive as the lifelong hope of Simeon himself. What does this old man already have in hand that makes him so jubilant? Basically it's only what lives in him: *a child*. We have to say that he himself, with his faith, has remained a wonderful child. For only children's eyes, which Simeon has always had, can see in this world something like salvation: Under the tangled mess of guilt the primal form of innocence, under the disfigured face of shame the true features of what strictly speaking cannot be dishonored, under the mask of conformity the beauty of the original creature.

This part that has remained whole and indestructible, this image of the "child" that dwells in every person, is henceforth Simeon's certainty. His existence does not end in stoic resignation, with the heroic swan song of fatalism on his lips. For him life closes in calm confidence. His end will be a completion in salvation and peace. God now releases his servant. And this child whom he bears in his arms will, once he grows up, one day prove with his very life that no one can ever be content with anything less than God, with anything smaller than what "intends" him in his whole existence and lets him live. A person lives only as a person in this holy longing and boundless unfulfillment, which is satisfied with nothing less than God.

5

The Twelve-Year-Old Jesus in the Temple, or Growing Up Means Standing before God (Lk. 2:41–52)

CB

TO SOME READERS, even without a more detailed examination of the text, it must seem inherently plausible that the appearance of angels, the virgin birth of the Son of God, and the "prophetic" announcement of his coming destiny are all archetypal symbols derived from myth. But it's not clear — until we once again compare it with the tradition of other religions — that even such an "unsuspicious," "normal" incident as the story of the twelve-year-old Jesus in the Temple has an archetypal model. And once again this episode must be understood not biographically, but symbolically.

For one last time the already mentioned story of Si-Osire, the son of Osiris, can serve as an example. Immediately after the virginal birth of this savior of Egypt the fairy tale reports about the rapid growth of the child:

> When the boy Si-Osire was one year old, people said of him: "He is two years old." And when he was two years old, they said: "He is three years old." Setom [his father] never let an hour pass without looking after the boy Si-Osire, for his love for him was great beyond all measure.

The boy grew up, and when he was strong enough, he was sent to school. After a short time he knew everything better than the teacher to whom he was entrusted. The boy Si-Osire began to recite the sacred texts, together with the scribes of the house of life in the temple of Ptah. And all who heard him considered him the wonder of the country. Setom wanted nothing more than to present him to Pharaoh at the feast, so that he would come face to face with all the sages of the country.[1]

When the boy Si-Osire was twelve years old, there was no scribe or learned man in Memphis who could be compared to him in reading and writing of magical formulas.[2]

Thus he did get to be taken before the Pharaoh. He was badly needed to read a sealed letter from the prince of Ethiopia, without opening it, through the outside of the papyrus. In so doing he would proclaim the superiority of the king of Egypt and the wisdom of his servants before the eyes of the world.

Such stories are certainly designed to demonstrate, first of all, the incomparable greatness of the growing son of the god vis-à-vis his contemporaries. But in the foreground of apparently biographical legends like this one we may not forget the ancient mythical origin of the motif itself. Originally in the myths of the sun[3] or the moon[4] we are told how soon after their birth (in the skies) they grew up to their full size. Only from this perspective does this myth become comprehensible in the legends of the childhood of divine persons.

But in the stories they tell the myths don't simply aim to describe natural processes. Instead they assign psychic contents to nature.[5] If we turn these mythic projections of the psyche onto nature upside down, we shall have to see in the rapid growth of the celestial light a symbol for the unfolding power of *consciousness.* In the figure of the "redeemer," of a person's true ego, this power dispels the night of unconsciousness and streams through the psychic world with spiritual clarity.

In the meantime we can't be satisfied with this (mythic) interpretive approach all by itself, not if we are to do justice to the *legendary* formations of this motif. We should note that in the transition to adulthood the nature of the spirit of the divine child must be demonstrated. Hence we must ask what this proof actually consists in. The "son of Osiris" proved the power of his mind by preserving the king of his fatherland from the ridicule threatening him from the inhabitants of the "negro country." He had the magical power to reveal what was hidden and to look behind the outside of a written document. But how is the motif of the superior growth of the Son of God presented in Luke's story of the twelve-year-old Jesus in the Temple? How does Christ prove the superiority of his mind? The answer is in a certain sense revolutionary.

In the Catholic Church when the faithful hear the gospel account of the twelve-year-old Jesus in the Temple given special emphasis on the feast of the Holy Family, there is no way to miss the authoritarian, moralizing intent in the reading. It's obviously the last lines of the pericope that give the text such a high rank in the Church: "And he . . . was obedient to them" (Lk. 2:51) and "Jesus increased . . . in favor with God and man" (Lk. 2:52).

To all appearances this is exactly how the Church would like us to imagine the relationships in Nazareth. Evidently it would like to turn the story into a regulation: the "Holy Family" ir the style of Nazarene painting,[6] featuring the adorable Chris child, the little lamb with a blissful Madonna in the background and haloes around everyone's head. But if *this* gospel really ha something to say on the subject of the "family," then it's exactl reversed. It shows that there is no such idyll, and indeed for the sake of the holy there may not be.

Some people may find this disappointing.

Shouldn't one think that at least one time on earth there actually was a "holy" family, in which people got along without conflicts, without disagreements, without misunderstandings? Isn't this the constant wish to present the figure of the saint as a star witness for a world made whole? In truth there is no idyll, at any rate not when a person has to deal with God, in other words not in the New Testament, whose sole concern is to show what happens when a person stands before God. On the contrary. This gospel of the twelve-year-old Jesus in the Temple is the only legendary snapshot that we have of Jesus' "family biography." It shows a picture full of contradictions, tensions, and human incompatibility. This, admittedly, is not done with the intention of presenting us with some purely accidental or exceptional conflicts (the one broken board, as it were, in the holy family's white picket fence). Rather the episode shows in a concentrated image what holds true for the life of anyone who wants to become grown-up. And it shows what in particular was the central determining theme of Jesus' life.

We have to ask how these two things belong together at all: growing up and standing before God? The connection between finding oneself and finding God seems to be the actual point of this story, but what does that connection consist of? Of course, we can say: It was a late Jewish custom for a twelve-year-old boy to go to the Temple and be declared a "son of the Law," a *bar mitzvah*, a grown-up member of the Jewish people. We can say that all peoples have some kind of rite of initiation in which the adolescent boy is led before the God of the tribe, in order to be made a full-fledged member.[7] But if this is so, if this is the custom for all peoples on earth, what does it mean, and what sort of experience lies behind the fact, that someone becomes a grown-up only before the face of God?

One level of the story is made up by Jesus' parents.

For their part, they would like to see the parent-child relationship described roughly like this: As a father and mother one invests one's best energies and capacities in taking care of the children, who in turn owe their parents the duty of grateful obedience. Everything that the directives of *morality* can say on the subject of the family boils down to a bond of loving care and obedience. We can test this with the example of what happens when a family goes through a crisis. What morality always says then is just this: "One" "has to" rediscover the children as a "value," that is, as a "gift and a task." "One" "must" accept responsibility for the coming generation. "One" "must" realize that a child is more important than, say, a trip to the Caribbean, etc.

Undeniably there are cases where problems are located at a sufficiently superficial level that they can be solved by moral means. But the actual, universal human problem does not consist in people's wishing to have no children or too few children or no responsibility for their children. The real problem is rather that parents let their children live only when they learn to relativize their own responsibility before God. Further, they will never be capable of relativizing their responsibility in this way until they learn, as the Gospel puts it, to hate their children for the sake of the kingdom of heaven (Lk. 16:24).

From the standpoint of religion the whole position of morality looks utterly ambiguous. And in any event it has value in human life only to the extent that the parents have religiously anchored their own existence in God. For even the respect for the freedom and personality of the other, which is required as the fundamental ethical stance, will be possible only if the *anxiety* of responsibility is eased. We can release our own child only when we hand it over to another absolute freedom that the child henceforth willingly takes upon itself. Morality always comes too late to solve the basic problems of anxiety in the depths of the human soul and human relations.

Nowadays it seems mostly a pious, meaningless custom for a child to be taken shortly after birth to the temple, to the church, to the spirit house,[8] in order to be given a name, or to be changed "from a beast to a human" (as they still say in Italy) through baptism, circumcision, or an ancestral ritual. In truth the old legend of the "seven sorrows of Mary," which relies on the story of Simeon's promise, is quite right to think that one of those sorrows was having to offer up her child to God in the Temple right after his birth. Yet this pain of offering up one's own child is ultimately the unique and essential pain that every mother and father suffers in respect to their child. Parents will never be able to say: *my* son, or *my* daughter.

To be sure, everyone is tempted to do just that. There is probably no mother in the world who hasn't for a long time completely identified with her child.[9] Indeed, a large part of maternal care consists in exactly this identification, where the mother lives her life in her child and considers him or her a part, even the proudest and most important part, of her self. But here is the point on which all morality and all good will have to come to grief: From a certain point in time onwards it is crucially necessary to reverse this natural identification and to give the child away, to let it out of one's own life.

It is evidently to prevent parents from forgetting this that the lesson is impressed on them right from the beginning. With the wisdom of all ancient peoples the Church, borrowing the practice of the synagogue, insists on offering up the child right away, if possible, in the first few weeks after birth. The idea is that just at the time of the parents' strongest identification with their child this truth and task may serve as a constant counterweight: Your child is never your property.[10] We can't for a moment deceive ourselves about the challenging fact that an eminently religious question is at issue here. For in no way is it simply innate motherly or fatherly feelings that cause a woman or man to fuse indissolubly their own life with the life of their child, at least for a time. What often makes the sacrifice of one's own child so difficult, indeed, often enough totally unbearable, is the inability to lead a meaningful life of one's own.[11]

Whenever a woman doesn't know how she can go on, she is liable to feel the temptation of getting pregnant. Whenever she seems to herself unloved and forsaken, she will want a child who "has to" love her because she is its one and all. The less people can live for themselves, the more they are paradoxically driven for a while to pass life on, to live in each other — one of the main reasons why the most unhappy families often produce the most children.

To see how things go on for such a child as a substitute-life for its mother or father, we can look up the Grimms' fairy tale of Rapunzel.[12] The story concerns a woman who never wanted anything more ardently than a child, so much so that she thinks she can no longer live without it. She looks upon the child as if it were the salad in her garden (*Rapunzel* means "lamb's lettuce" in German): She devours it as if it were an elixir of life. The fairy tale obviously wants to say that the woman's love for "Rapunzel" has to be thought of in just this way: The woman "could eat her all up." The girl is the content, the substance, the filling of her hollow life. But for that very reason a girl like this will be incapable of living by her mother's side. Then try coming to such a woman as Rapunzel's mother with moral lessons and impressing upon her duties as a mother: Impossible. It would be hard to find a more morally excellent, caring, well-meaning mother than this one. Yet the fairy tale explains that deep down she is a witch, a monster of sorcery and foul play, a real jailer.

And rightly so. Because scarcely does her daughter turn twelve years old when the (step)mother locks her beloved Rapunzel in a tower, placing her daughter so high above her that she literally hoists herself up every day on the golden tresses that Rapunzel lets down. This woman does *not* offer up her daughter. Instead when she learns one day about Rapunzel's secret love for the son of a king, she angrily disowns and gives up for lost the daughter she supposedly loves above all things. But from that moment on the mother ceases to exist, i.e., she falls back once more on the unlife she has lived from the beginning. The fairy tale says that she is dead, and never mentions her again. You only "keep" what you offer up – the old rituals knew this paradoxical truth, which is so supremely important to human beings.

The gospel of the twelve-year-old Jesus in the Temple agrees completely with this paradoxical truth. Indeed it even gives it special emphasis by the way Mary finds her son exactly where she has already "lost" him as a child. The so-called joyful mysteries of the rosary summarize these two contradictory aspects quite rightly and with extraordinary density in two phrases that must be prayed and lived: "Whom Thou, O Virgin, hast offered up in the Temple," and "Whom Thou, O Virgin, hast found again in the Temple."

Externally the gospel describes this crucial *double movement*[13] of sacrifice and rediscovery as a mere "custom," as if Jesus' parents (Lk. 2:21ff.) were just obediently following in the footsteps of tradition and cultic practice. But at the time the episode seemed to take its course only as an impersonal and purely collective ritual, following custom and rules. It was just something to get out of the way. But now when Jesus is twelve years old, the story breaks out of every ritual routine and unexpectedly demands that its meaning be acknowledged. Year after year Jesus' parents may have gone to Jerusalem within the framework of Passover. That would hardly be reason for surprise. *Now,* at this moment, where the actual meaning of their ritual action is revealed and realized, "they do not understand." Now when they can notice – when they *have* to notice – that all dealings with their child in the final analysis have been and can be only a kind of death, an escorting of Jesus down the road to "Jerusalem," in the sense of Luke's Gospel,[14] now they are "astonished" (Lk. 2:48).

Year in, year out they performed the ritual sacrifices in the Temple, where in a certain sense they had already "presented" the boy Jesus a dozen times. But now when what they let happen posits itself as truth, it seems to them a tragic loss. And this loss seems to have happened, as it were, solely out of negligence and a failure to do their duty as supervisors of their son. Just when "their" Jesus is definitively moving out of their lives, they voice the most vehement reproaches of themselves and him.

This sort of thing is likely to happen to any father and mother when the time comes for "losing" their child once and for all. At first they always try, metaphorically speaking, to find him or her among their own "kinsfolk" and "acquaintances." There always remains the hope that their question, "Where are you?" will be answered, if not in their own house, then at least in the circuit of what is one way or another still familiar and part of their world. By contrast the scene in the gospel strikes us as brusque: To Mary's question, "Why?" Jesus gives an answer that can be understood only as a blunt rejection: "Did you not know? ... " This sort of answer implies a complete break with his home. From his parents' point of view it comes down to the definitive and incomprehensible loss of their child. If the boy Jesus hitherto seemed only accidentally and externally "lost," his separation now proves to be intentional and internally consistent. And now everything depends upon how Jesus' parents will deal with this "astonishing" realization.

At bottom there is only one way to "rediscover" the "lost" child. One must integrate the event into one's own heart, into one's own "memory" (Lk. 2:50). Thank God, Jesus' parents had long been ready to take that step. What Jesus is doing does at first seem to be a provocation that one would hardly approve of. Yet this is precisely the point toward which his parents too have been slowly moving all their lives: Didn't they want their son to stand before God one day with his own life? Didn't they know that their son's standing before God would ultimately mean that they, his parents, had to stand back? But it can be hard to admit this: The autonomy of one's child before God, one's own responsibility and immediate ties to one's creator, one's own irreducible independence and sovereignty vis-à-vis other people — one can have wanted that all one's life and intended to honor it.

It may still be ever so hard to accept the realization of one's own wishes. But if we do, we should be able finally to rediscover ourselves and the other in the fact that from now on we stand together before the eyes of one and the same Creator. We should see that what Jesus would later say to the disciples is simply true: "Call no man your father on earth, for you have one Father, who is in heaven" (Mt. 23:9). The wisdom of the ancients is profoundly religious: A "beast" doesn't become a "human," until, like Jesus in this scene in the Temple, he can say of himself: "Did you not know that I must be in my Father's house?" (Lk. 2:49).

Of course, there is an attitude that prevents people from accepting this truth. And once again the attempt at a moral answer to the problems of human life proves to be an extremely ambiguous kind of regulation. Morality elevates care and concern to the highest duty of parents to "their" child. But it is precisely this care, with its anxiety and feelings of responsibility, that makes parents resist accepting the necessary release of the child. "Your father and I have been looking for you anxiously" (Lk. 2:48), says Mary, wounded and reproachful, as if it was the duty of a good child, indeed the commandment of simple considerateness, never to do anything like that to his parents.

It is so hard when the day comes to renounce even the duty of responsibility, even the anxiety of caring, and to recognize what hitherto could only be considered a "loss": The other has a different living space, which is as holy as the Temple itself. From now on the other will have to risk his own life, and for all the understandable anxiety this may cause, the rule here has to be, as Psalm 121:4 puts it, "He who keeps Israel will neither slumber nor sleep." From now on *God* will assume the parents' task of watching over the child.

If we go along with this, in the end the improbable and unexpected will occur: Precisely because of the "loss" everyone winds up returning home together and goes on belonging together in one and the same family. It is now been settled that no one "belongs" to, or "has to obey," the other any more. Now everybody wants and promotes the freedom of the other.

What we basically have here is an attitude that could be called "the teaching of the pigeon-breeder." Anyone who has raised a pigeon and has paid every possible attention to it will one day find that the pigeon is pressing to be free. The keeper's anxiety will tell him that the pigeon can lead a life without danger only within the protected confines of the dovecote. Outside there are high-tension lines, poisoned fields, buzzards and hawks. But the pigeon *has* to be able to fly through the sky. Indeed it *has* to be the pride and joy of the pigeon-keeper to see his pigeon risk its freedom as it soars in great circles. The pigeon has the built-in capacity to fly hundreds of miles over land and, following the invisible lines of force of the earth's magnetic field, find its way back to the dovecote. The pigeon-keeper will never understand how this is possible. He can't teach the pigeon this most important of skills, but he can trust that his pigeon will find its way if only he leaves it to its internal compass. He's done all he can. The pigeon has ceased to be his property.

That's one side of the problems in the story of the twelve-year-old Jesus: the parents' perspective.

But alongside it there is another, fundamentally more important, perspective: that of the child who has to take the first steps into its own life. As the child sees things, it's not a matter of "losing" one's parents. The child simply lets them go and finds a standpoint of its own. Still, this step toward freedom is likewise profoundly religious, as can be seen in the story of the twelve-year-old Jesus.

We may assume that Jesus never took the religious legacy of his people more seriously than when as a twelve-year-old he was placed for the first time under the Law of Israel. If ever he felt in the Temple that he was in his father's house, then it would have been at this point. But this was obviously the moment that most distanced him from his parents. A new principle, a new discovery dawns on him at this juncture and flings him with infinite force out of the human context. Later Jesus will express this experience by saying that one must "hate" father and mother for God's sake (Lk. 14:26). This inner strife and antagonism is something he must have experienced for the first time at this moment.

The paradoxical opposition between morality and religion, already mentioned several times, can't loom larger in the experience of an adolescent than here. Now as ever ethical duty enjoins obedience, but he feels now that the only important demand of his life is to follow the commandment of ancient Israel: You shall love the Lord your God with your strength and obey only him (Lk. 10:27). Convention holds out to him the prospect of being safe and secure as he was before with his parents at home. But now he already feels the infinite loneliness that he will later put this way: "The Son of man has nowhere to lay his head" (Lk. 9:58). Human feeling and piety find him guilty for having stayed behind in Jerusalem, without explanation or apology, literally forgetting his parents. But he senses in himself a new and absolute necessity that makes him forget all the demands of social morality.

Two different principles of life slam into one another. The moral-universal principle demands that he define himself by what all others are and think. Meanwhile the basic religious attitude insists on his individuality and demands that he no longer rely on what others, even his own parents, have told him.[15] It's a moment of complete separation from all other people, an unrelenting absoluteness, and above all a total inability to make himself understood by others.

For all that, this is also a moment of perfect happiness. No one awakening to himself can avoid this moment. And no one who enters this zone can bear it without the guarantee of a new security and stability in God. Looking outwards at this moment of breakaway everything is open to question. What's certain is the sense of being called into action, to live one's own life, and of having to be on guard for any interference from strangers. This is a time when nothing can be accepted uncritically just because it has been handed down and said this way or that.

A time of personal searching and questioning begins, a time of thinking and deciding for oneself. This new need not only lets one's parents go their own way; it continues on *its* way in the holy halls of the Temple. It's not frightened by the authority of the theologians and scribes. Nor does it shrink from unheard-of and surprising insights, from truths that stun other people and leave them beside themselves, but that are nonetheless right there in Scripture, word for word. It seizes with a special passion ideas that none but the young, it seems, are really capable of handling. At any rate these are the kinds of truth that old age would always seek to protect itself from, if youth didn't keep having these provoking outbursts of enthusiasm. Such flare-ups literally force the "old ones" at long last to believe what they say.

In this scene one can't help seeing the faces of so many young people — with a power to think that works twice as fast as the physical energy of a forty-year-old. These young people have an unconditional idealism, not yet corrupted by doubts, a scintillating intelligence that thinks with all the more logical sharpness and abstract verve since it has only a disorderly beginner's knowledge of life. And yet, what enormous drive to know the truth, cost what it may!

Friedrich Nietzsche was a great critic and enlightener of the moralistic self-assurance of the Philistines, both the religious and bourgeois variety. In moving, eternally valid pages Nietzsche has described this moment, as blissful as it is tragic, when freedom breaks through. He writes in *Human, All-Too-Human:*

One may suppose that a spirit in which the type "free spirit" is to become fully mature and sweet, has had its decisive event in a *great emancipation,* and that it was all the more fettered previously and apparently bound forever to its corner and pillar. What is it that binds it most strongly? What cords are most unrendable? In men of a lofty and select type it will be their duties; the reverence which is suitable to youth, respect and tenderness for all that is time-honoured and worthy, gratitude to the hand which led them, to the sanctuary where they learnt to adore, — their most exalted moments themselves will bind them most effectively, will lay upon them the most enduring obligations. For those who are thus bound the great emancipation comes suddenly, like an earthquake; the young soul is all at once convulsed, unloosed and extricated — it does not itself know what is happening. An impulsion and compulsion sway and overmaster it like a command; a will and a wish awaken, to go forth on their course, anywhere, at any cost; a violent, dangerous curiosity about an undiscovered world flames and flares on every sense. "Better die than live *here*" — says the imperious voice and seduction, and this "here," this "at home" is all that the soul has hitherto loved! A sudden fear and suspicion of that which it loved, a flash of disdain for what was called its "duty," a rebellious, arbitrary, volcanically throbbing longing for travel, foreignness, estrangement, coldness, disenchantment, glaciation, a hatred of love, perhaps a sacrilegious clutch and look *backwards,* to where it hitherto adored and loved, perhaps a glow of shame at what it was just doing, and at the same time a rejoicing *that* it was doing it, an intoxicated, internal, exulting thrill which betrays a triumph — a triumph? Over what? Over whom? An enigmatical, questionable, doubtful triumph, but the *first* triumph nevertheless; — such evil and painful incidents be-

long to the history of the great emancipation. It is, at the
same time, a disease which may destroy the man, this first
outbreak of power and will to self-decision, self-valuation,
this will to *free* will; and how much disease is manifested
in the wild attempts and eccentricities by which the liber-
ated and emancipated one now seeks to demonstrate his
mastery over things! He roves about raging with unsatis-
fied longing; whatever he captures has to suffer for the
dangerous tension of his pride; he tears to pieces whatever attracts him. With a malicious laugh he twirls round
whatever he finds veiled or guarded by a sense of shame;
he tries how these things look when turned upside down.
It is a matter of arbitrariness with him, and pleasure in arbitrariness, if he now perhaps bestows his favour on what
had hitherto a bad repute, — if he inquisitively and tempt-
ingly haunts what is specially forbidden. In the background
of his activities and wanderings — for he is restless and aimless in his course as in a desert — stands the question mark
of an increasingly dangerous curiosity. "Cannot *all* valua-
tions be reversed? And is good perhaps evil? And God only
an invention and artifice of the devil? Is everything, perhaps radically false? And if we are the deceived, are we not
thereby also deceivers? *Must* we not also be deceivers?" —
Such thoughts lead and mislead him more and more, on-
ward and away. Solitude encircles and engirds him, always
more threatening, more throttling, more heart-oppressing,
that terrible goddess and *mater saeva cupidinum* [cruel
mother of passions] — but nowadays who knows what
solitude is?[16]

It is exactly in this sense, as the experience of a spiritual
breakthrough to freedom, that we have to understand the scene
of the twelve-year-old Jesus in the Temple. For this sort of poetic description of Jesus' "youth" even to be conceived means
that the man from Nazareth must have evoked the idea of an
unheard-of spiritual independence. This connection must have
been just as Nietzsche has so masterfully described it, with all
its dangers and loneliness, its testing and trials, its penetrating
challenges and moral dubiousness, its pain in separation and its
internal consistency.

If we spoke earlier of the royal appointment of a person to freedom and sovereignty, here we have before us, in the form of a legend, the document of a similar accession to the throne by Christ. If bishops making their confirmation rounds through the parishes ever need sermon texts, if they can summon up a little bit of courage vis-à-vis young people's desire for independence and self-determination, they will find a telling passage in this story.

It's not hard to imagine all the questions already in the mouth of the twelve-year-old Jesus in the Temple of Jerusalem. Perhaps they were the questions that he would later, but with the inexorability of a life-and-death decision, direct at the scribes and Pharisees. Those were the questions that had to, and have to, strike every new generation of "theologians" and scribes like an annihilating judgment: "And if you had known what this means, 'I desire mercy and not sacrifice [Hos. 6:6],' you would not have condemned the guiltless" (Mt. 12:7; see 9:13). Or: "They [the scribes and Pharisees] bind heavy burdens, hard to bear, and they lay them on men's shoulders; but they themselves will not move them with their finger" (Mt. 23:4). "White-washed tombs," "full of hypocrisy" (Mt. 23:27).

Those were the last words that Jesus had left for this guild of theologians. To gain such freedom from *all* ruling authorities, from the favor of the mob as well as from the support of superiors, it takes a dizzying high-wire self-assurance, an unwearying spiritual alertness. Psychologically speaking, such an attitude implies specific experiences that go back to early childhood and youth.

From the standpoint of history, this episode must be labeled a legend. But read symbolically, its guiding spirit appears at every turn in the New Testament as the best possible and absolutely credible description of the inner reality in the life and experience of Jesus.

Of course, we could always fall back on theological jargon and say that in this Temple scene Jesus is revealing his "Messiahship." We could say that Luke simply used a typical legendary motif to make that point. But if such stories of youth are really "typical" of a future teacher of wisdom, don't we have to say that here is the psychic truth about such people: Very early on they take the greatest risk — the risk to be internally free, independent in their thinking, autonomous in their judging, and continually surprising in their outward action. "For writers," Graham Greene remarks in his novel *The Comedians*, "it is always said that the first twenty years of life contain the whole of experience, — the rest is observation." "But," he adds, "I think it is equally true of us all."[17]

In fact to gain freedom, as Jesus later proved, you must upon entering puberty (at the latest) complete something that could be called — by contrast with the "teaching of the pigeon-breeder" — the "leap of the guillemots." Every year in the month of July a strange spectacle takes place on the rock walls of the western shore of the island of Helgoland in the North Sea. In the sandstone galleries hollowed out by storms in the sheer cliffs more than a thousand pairs of guillemots, penguin-like birds, lay their variously colored eggs. For weeks the monogamous parents feed their clamoring hungry chicks, clean the brood-niche, and defend themselves against the incursions of kittiwakes. But as soon as the chick is big enough, the parents lure it out of the sheltering niche to plunge over the cliffs more than thirty to forty meters down into the water.[18] In taking their dramatic plunge into autonomy not a few of the guillemots lose their lives, depending on the ebb and flow of the waves that pound against the island. But they have no choice, because as the young birds grow it's impossible to feed them adequately; and the summer is short, so there is a race against time. When they leave the brood ledge the young guillemots have reached just a fifth of the body weight of the mature birds, but now they swim with their parents into the open sea, "moult into the first year's plumage and become capable of flight."

Entrance into freedom involves a similar dive into insecurity, a similar leap into a different element. And surely there is no real insight later in life not already contained embryonically in this launching out into a new existence.

But above all, aren't all Jesus' later words marked by an unspoiled youthfulness, an unbelievable freshness and carefree spirit? Doesn't his "Messiahship," his "royal" capacity to drive out "demons" and to teach as one with authority — and not as the scribes (Mk. 1:22) — essentially consist in recognizing as his father and king none other than God himself? Later on even his enemies will say of him that he is a teacher who doesn't care what people think (Mk. 12:14). They admit that he is concerned only with God.

But if that's true, then this very scene in the Temple of Jerusalem shows the twelve-year-old Jesus for the first time in his true "Messiahship." And his answer already has the authority and power of the Messiah: "Did you not know that I must be in my Father's house?" (Lk. 2:49). Later on Jesus will do nothing except — as he does here — remind people about what they could actually long have known in God's presence. *Externally* his appearance on the scene will violently shock and provoke people. But internally every one of them could know quite clearly that their anxieties and fears of God were unjustified.

As he does here, Jesus will continually learn that he is not understood. And yet the most astonishing thing will be to see how great the power of anxiety in humans must be, to make them fail to understand things that are so obvious. The scene of the twelve-year-old boy in the Temple, read this way, is the summary anticipated portrait of his whole later public career. And from a depth-psychological point of view we have to say: Things *must* have begun like this, and they must have remained that way throughout Jesus' life.

In particular we see in this passage — as we continue to see later on — that from the perspective of an adolescent it was quite unnecessary to postpone, out of pure anxiety, the moment of loneliness and personal awakening under the pretext of piety and doing one's duty. If you were to miss the call to freedom at the critical moment, then you could, to stick with our metaphor, quietly return with your parents to Nazareth. But in a certain sense you would never get back home. If you avoid the step leading to a life of your own, you may admittedly remain "innocent" in the moral sense. Under certain circumstances you may continue to look well-behaved and obedient, but you will thereby fail to hear God's actual demand. This is what God demands of us, as his property, in the Temple, on his property. If we fail to hear the call, we exclude ourselves from God and ultimately put human beings in God's place. As far as the word of the Law goes, there might not be any visible difference at all. But in our own lives everything depends on whether or not we perpetuate obedience to our mother and father (and their successors) in the name of God. If we do, then we are basically refusing to become a human being out of sheer anxiety. The other option is to defend God's call to a life of our own even *against* the claims of father and mother and to undertake to see the world with our own eyes.

In the first case we remain, psychically speaking, children all our lives, and in the religious sense we worship idols. In the second case we mature psychically and grow up, precisely by becoming, in the religious sense, a child in the presence of God.

We can't really choose between the two possibilities, because in the long run it's impossible to persist in the absolutizing of parental authority without locking ourselves up in Rapunzel's tower. Granted, living in unbroken dependence upon our parents we may appear lofty in the eyes of others and morally superior to the world. But if we do this, we remain narrowed and gnomish, and we don't even fulfill the most primitive presuppositions of truly "moral" behavior. And to make the tragedy of the infantile life complete, if we divinize our parents, they turn into witches and evil spirits. Just when we pretend to love them most faithfully, we actually fear and hate them most.

Then we no longer inhabit our parents' home, rather we live in an unsevered (neurotic) connection to our parents. Inwardly and outwardly we live with members of our family like a prisoner in a jail from which there is no escape.

Conversely, we find the way back home with our parents only when we reject their claim to absolute control. As we have seen, it is nothing like an act of private pride when Jesus separates from his parents. Rather it is a necessary process of rediscovering himself in everything that his parents thought and wanted when they led the child into the Temple and taught him the prayers of Israel. *We literally find the way back home only if we have found ourselves in the Temple.*[19] Only then does the truth of our own parental home reveal itself, and we begin from our own point of view to learn everything that hitherto we seemed to have heard from strangers.

The Gospel of Luke says that long years passed in which Jesus was "obedient." But this "obedience" was no longer the obedience of a child to its parents, but a kind of inner listening. To be sure, nothing changed outwardly in the life of Jesus of Nazareth. Everything seemed to take its old course. But in fact the whole world had been transformed. It is a risky, a divine form of obedience that, as soon as it presses outward, will strike everyone involved as uncanny, as it already did in this first scene in the Temple of Jerusalem. Was it really a time of "favor with God and man" (Lk. 2:52)? With God surely, but with man surely not always. Most likely the freedom of God could live for a short while among humans without being immediately stifled. But that's just it: The longest segment of this time remained hidden.

Coda

∞

WITH THE STORY of the twelve-year-old Jesus in the Temple the Lucan infancy narrative comes to an end. With this reading of what is probably the most poetic tale in all the New Testament I hope to have made audible something of the mysterious music that, echoing ancient mystical traditions, rings through the souls of men and women of all times and regions of the earth. "All true blessedness," thought Johannes Tauler, "lies in right serenity, in will-lessness. All that is born out of the ground of littleness. Then our own will is lost, for the will is like a column in which all disorder dwells. If we could knock it down, then all the walls would fall down with it. The smaller (in humility), the lesser the will."[1]

What else should the story of the virgin birth of the Son of God teach us? Only when we begin to listen again to the inner song of our soul will we leave the world in which people are "born" or, better, *made* from (or according to) the "will of man" (Jn. 1:13). Only when we rediscover dreaming will we be able to encounter the God of the light that shines forth at the end of the night. And only when we get the courage to release ourselves internally from the ghetto of heteronomy will we achieve the humanity that derives from the royal dignity of our freedom. That heteronomy has been compelling us ever since childhood to behave like "grown-ups," while in reality remaining infantilely dependent on every pressure from our environment.

All our *willing,* however morally upright it may be, can only lead us to the point of foundering, where the question no longer is, "What must we do?" but who we really are. The life-and-death question is not the integrity of our will, but the integration of our self. And the preaching of John the Baptist doesn't have the answer.

No doubt someone could be considered a man of perfect honor in terms of bourgeois morality while remaining, humanly speaking, a monster: Tolstoy's Alexei Karenin,[2] for example, or Theodor Fontane's Baron von Instetten.[3] *La médiocrité fonda l'autorité*. It's the same everywhere. But the nature of this divine child, whom we revere in the figure of Jesus Christ, surely reveals itself most powerfully in this: All the ratings of the "big people," which divide men and women according to the cast-iron categories of the eternally righteous into competent and incompetent, good and evil, successful and failures, count for nothing with him.

Yet what living theologian could be said to be a friend of harlots and "tax collectors"? Where in contemporary theology do they teach us to understand and stand up for, instead of judging and condemning, the other? And where in the Church today is there room for people who are breaking down under the laws of both society and the Church, yet are still infinitely close to God just because of their need? If "shepherds" were the first to praise the newborn Son of God, where do we stand between Jerusalem and Bethlehem?

As the foundational document of the Church, on the morning of Pentecost (Acts 2:17 — 18) Luke chose the passage from Joel (2:28) where the prophet predicts that in the last days, "Your sons and your daughters shall prophesy, your old men shall dream dreams, and your young men shall see visions." Should we think that such a world has become possible since "Christmas"? A world, that is, in which the children conquer the future, in which a generation of young people grows up without letting its dreams be destroyed by the disillusioning rationality of "grown-ups." A world where old people can see their lives as proceeding from a "great vision," as the Oglala Sioux shaman Black Elk could still call it?[4] How else is our humanization to succeed except by following the eternal images that God has placed in our soul long before the capacity for words, far stronger than the power of concepts? Even the message of Christmas can be used solely to identify all the heretics and heterodox — the Homousians or the Homoiousians, the Monophysites or the Adoptionists, the supporters of Cyril or of Nestorius.

But if we do this, how far have we removed ourselves from ourselves — and from the one thing that really matters: the mysteries of God, which can be expressed only in images because they are in principle incomprehensible to conceptual thinking?

Still, something of the Christmas experience can shine out amid both inner and outer hopelessness. I shall never forget the account of a man who had the crucial experience of his life after the Second World War while a prisoner of the French. Even before the war, as an eighteen-year-old idealist, he had fallen into the hands of the Nazis. He had worked his way up in the ranks, and during the war he had not wavered from his convictions. Only after the collapse of the war effort did the light dawn on his insanity. "I can see that morning quite clearly before me," he told me, still visibly shaken after all the years.

A large snow-covered field, on which about a hundred hungry, freezing people were crowded together, surrounded by barbed wire fences. For days I had felt so empty and exhausted that there was scarcely any distance now between myself and the things around me. My old self had totally broken down. I was walking along the hated fence, and suddenly it was as if the perspective had completely shifted, as if I weren't in a prison camp. The posts and the fence seemed to become a sort of playpen for a child. I was seized by an enormous joy, so that for a moment I felt I was losing my mind. I was alive! Although I hadn't deserved it, I had stayed alive! I would have the chance to begin my life all over again, to speak in a new way, to think in a new way. I would have to learn everything all over again, from eating to dressing. At twenty-five I was a child who for the first time was really beginning to live. This camp with its barbed wire was my nursery, and I knew that there would never again be any wires and fences for me. In the middle of imprisonment I was absolutely free. Ever since then I have believed in God. I know he exists. We are all children, and there are no barriers under heaven. Of course, there are differences between nations, languages, and religions, but the world is so rich. I would like to live forever and learn every day.

As I write this, I think of the woman archeologist from Beirut. *This* incarnation of God is something she would have understood. She would have most definitely understood it.

And there is yet another story that I can't get out of my head when I think of Christmas. I owe it to a man who had spent the decisive years of his life as a Russian prisoner of war. For some reason we had come to speak of Russian women: "Is it true," I asked him, "when in Dostoyevksy or Gorki the men are so often presented as drunkards and brutes who beat and bully the women just as they were beaten, while the women are described as incarnations of Mother Earth?" "Yes, they often really are that way," he said with a smile.

> The strongest impression I ever had was an experience while we were laying railroad tracks. The work was very hard, especially in the beginning. About a tenth of the prisoners died of physical or mental exhaustion. During work near a village one morning somebody collapsed, and a Russian overseer brutally hit the motionless prisoner with the butt of his rifle. Then a woman screamed — or rather something inside her cried out furiously: "*U kázhdogo mat* — Everybody has a mother."

These words echo Leo Tolstoy's "What Men Live By,"[5] and they raise to universal level the theme that runs through a person's entire life, first as the experience of a child but later as an enduring truth that embraces all of existence. Even in a religion as masculine as Islam such a Christmas message would be understood. "Everybody has a mother." This phrase from an unknown Russian woman about an unknown "war criminal" lying on the ground is something that that car dealer from Mersin would have understood. He would most definitely have understood it.

Nowadays there are many theologians who cling to the rationalism of their dogmas by looking on the truths of Christianity in a "more nuanced" fashion. For example, the story of the virgin birth is nothing more to them than a time-bound metaphor that may not be taken literally, any more than the Priestly account of the creation of the world in six days. Nevertheless they consider the divine sonship of Christ to be non-mythical, historical, reasonable, capable of being formulated in Greek concepts, the exclusive property of Christianity.

But in truth this attitude, which has become quite widespread, only shows how far and wide the inner split between experience and doctrine, feeling and thought, vision and abstraction has flourished. A myth is not a mode of expression that can be historically relativized, any more than a sacrament is a mere gesture that could be replaced by others. In the images of myths lives a truth that can be communicated only in them and whose sole power to convince is based on the fact that it resists every attempt at conceptual interpretation. It is not possible to distill the concept "Son of God" from the wonderful metaphors of the Holy Night merely to announce in the end that this concentrate of mythical traditions frozen into lifelessness is itself no longer a myth. As soon as we try to understand "concepts" like this, we inevitably have to translate them out of theological language and back into the metaphorical world of myth that they come from. Only by redreaming these images for their own sake can the infinite richness of their experiences be opened up. There are images that have absolute validity in themselves and that cannot be replaced. That Indian in the museum of Calcutta would have understood that. He would most definitely have understood it.

And would it have been possible any other way?

Only in a language that touches the hearts of *all* men and women can it be said that God has become a human being. Only in images that are universal enough for the incarnation (humanization) of every individual to take place in them can a message be preached that will bring salvation to the world: the incarnation of God, our Redeemer. When the early Church discovered that in keeping with the will of God it could no longer remain a Jewish sect and that "the gift of the Holy Spirit had been poured out even on the Gentiles" (Acts 10:45), it ceased to abide by the Law as a prerequisite for belief in Christ. If the Church today wants to uphold the command of the risen Jesus to go to *all* nations of the earth (Mt. 28:9), it may no longer remain a European sect. It must finally renounce the habit of looking on the Western intellectual tradition as a prerequisite for faith in Christ.

It is neither necessary nor possible to assault and shatter whole cultures before the sun of Christianity can rise over the fields of a scorched earth, to protect mighty conquerors and feudal investors. If there is to be a universal human religion of the incarnate God it has to be grounded where God himself prepared it: in the eternal dreams of our soul. There God dreams himself as a human being, so that we can look upon him as the sole ground of our humanity: as the God "made man," born of the "virgin," proclaimed to the "shepherds." What the Egyptians said to the god Amun, who came into the world from the womb of a king as a Son of God, can be the experience of all men and women who rediscover God in themselves and themselves in God:

"Your name is like the taste of life."

Notes

⁊

The Text

1. Following Joachim Jeremias, *Die Sprache des Lukasevangeliums: Redaktion und Tradition im Nicht-Markusstoff des dritten Evangelium* (Göttingen, 1980).

2. "You *will* conceive" is a "futurum instans," the event occurs in the announcement itself. The "*and* you shall call him Jesus" should be read as a relativistic "and," instead of retaining the Semitic parataxis in translation. See F. Blass and A. Debrunner, *Grammatik des neutestamentlichen Griechisch* (Göttingen, 1965), §297.

3. The "and he will rule" is to be translated as final. See ibid., §442, 3.

4. Instead of the false but customary: "For with God nothing will be impossible."

5. "But" is of itself adversative. Here, however, there is obviously no opposition, and it has to be understood responsorily or dialogically.

6. The Semitic "behold" refers to the event that has already taken place. It is interchangeable with "it happened." See Blass and Debrunner, *Grammatik des neutestamentlichen Griechisch*, §441, 7.

7. "Then" instead of "in those days." The text is speaking of a holy time, and the "in illo tempore" of the liturgical reading points up that "then" is *today* and keeps reoccurring.

8. "In a town of Judea" is false translation by a Greek source that Luke adopts. "In Palestinian Aramaic *medina* designates (a) a province and (b) a metropolis. The tradition on which Luke 1:39 is based spoke originally of the "province of Judea" (see Ezra 5:8), *lihud medinta* to the province of Judea (Jeremias, *Die Sprache des Lukasevangeliums*, 56).

9. The Hebrew "behold" roughly corresponds to the English, "you know."

10. Here the "behold" calls for a change of Mary's attitude from anxiety to trust. The point is to abandon the immediate reaction of fear and to see what message the angel is *"really"* bringing.

11. The aorist is best understood here as intensive: The receivers of the announcement themselves become announcers.

12. Instead of "weighing." The Greek word *symballousa* literally means something like "thinking symbolically" – that is, about a truth that can be perceived only in *signs* (Lk. 2:12).

13. The "And behold" is used here to characterize the unexpected, the not-yet-seen. In Luke 2:34 the "behold" serves as reassurance and so must be translated differently.

14. The "and" has a causal meaning here. God's grace is no mere addition to human development, but its foundation. On the epexegetical *"And"* see Blass and Debrunner, *Grammatik des neutestamentlichen Griechisch*, §442.

15. The "and" followed by the imperfect is evidently supposed to render a habit that is only now presented as an intrinsically recognized fact.

16. Here the "but" renders not an intellectual opposition but the matter-of-fact way with which things unwind on the level of the action.

17. Here the imperfect indicates the duration of the search.

18. E. Schweizer, *Das Evangelium nach Lukas* (Göttingen, 1982), in the section dealing with this verse, sees Jesus' parents as beside themselves with "terror." Now there is absolutely no reason for "terror," but rather for irritation at Jesus' apparently brazen mischievousness.

19. The "behold" is supposed to object to a self-evident fact that might have been thought about earlier.

20. The imperfect refers again to the (involuntary) length of the search.

21. The first "and" is to be translated as adversative, the second as final (see note 3).

Interpretation: Tuning into and Reflecting on the Reality of Myth

1. Stefan Zweig, *Sternstunden der Menschheit: Zwölf historische Miniaturen* (Frankfurt: Fischer, 1964), 49–65 ("Georg Friedrich Händels Auferstehung"), 57.

2. R. Goldwater, *Paul Gaugin* (Cologne, 1957), 84.

3. Ibid.

4. H. Renner, *Reklams Konzertführer: Orchestermusik* (Stuttgart, 1967), 33: "Music as a world language! That is what Händel unconsciously achieved. . . . Händel's language is universally understood in the exact sense of the word. . . . He deliberately turns to the widest public. . . . He doesn't shy away from picking up popular motifs."

5. On the meaning of this fairy tale see E. Drewermann, *Tiefenpsychologie und Exegese* (Olten, 1984), 1:141–46.

6. Franz Cumont, *Die Mysterien des Mithra*, trans. G. Gehrlich (Darmstadt, 1981), 154–55, points to December 25 as the day of the rebirth of the sun (*Natalis invicti*) in the liturgy of the Mithra cult. There, quite similarly to the Christian feast of Easter, the ceremonies of initiation took place around the beginning of spring, just as the Christians admitted their catechumens to baptism around Easter time.

7. See H. Usener, *Das Weihnachtsfest: Religionsgeschichtliche Untersuchungen*, part 1 (Bonn, 1911), 196. Usener shifts the origin of the Christian feast of the Epiphany to Easter.

8. See ibid., 348ff.

9. On the meaning of the zodiac in ancient fertility symbols within the framework of the cyclical rebirth of the sun, see the popular presentation of H. Haber in *Unser Sternhimmel: Sagen, Märchen, Deutungen* (Munich, 1981), 71–107.

10. The hermeneutical presupposition is that mythical birth stories have to be understood as portraits of the hero's essence. See E. Drewermann, *Tiefenpsychologie und Exegese*, 1:310–21.

11. One comparison is provided by the Mithra legend that tells how light, embodied as the magician Mithra, is born from a rock (*petra genetrix*), which gives him life and protection by the banks of a river, in the shadow of a sacred tree. Only shepherds, hidden on a neighboring mountain range, observed the wonder of his arrival. "They had seen how he struggled out of the mass of the rock, his head covered by a Phrygian cap, already armed with a knife and carrying a torch that lit up the darkness. Then the shepherds came to adore the divine child and to present him with the first fruits of their flocks and their harvests. But the young hero was naked and exposed to the wind, which was blowing violently. Thus he got up to hide in the branches of a fig tree. Then with his knife he cut off the fruits of the tree to nourish himself. Finally he stripped the tree of its leaves to make himself clothes out of them" (Cumont, *Die Mysterien des Mithra*, 118–19).

12. Even if the Christmas legend's "search for lodgings" belongs to popular fantasy, the "child in the manger" nonetheless remains a "paradox." See H. Schürmann, *Das Lukasevangelium* (Freiburg-Basel-Vienna, 1984), 1:107. The search for shelter itself, as a typos of the birth of a divine child, is widely developed in the Egyptian story of Isis's search for lodging. See E. Brunner-Traut, *Altägyptische Märchen* (Düsseldorf-Cologne, 1963), 107–9.

13. Dante, *Inferno*, trans. John D. Sinclair (New York: Oxford University Press, 1961), XXXII, 22ff., 395–97; XXXIII, 91 ff., 409–11.

14. The condition of psychological icing-over is described by the Norwegian author I. Vesaas in *Das Eisschloss* (Zurich-Cologne, 1965), 40–68, in the case of a (homosexually tinged) friendship of two girls that out of fear of the violence of their own feelings ends in flight and an emotional frigidity.

15. See M. Oesterreicher-Mollwo, ed., *Herder-Lexikon* (Freiburg-Basel-Vienna, 1978), "Symbole," 180.

16. See J. Brinktrine, *Die Lehre von der Menschwerdung und Erlösung* (Paderborn, 1959), 59.

17. I. B. Singer, *The Reaches of Heaven.* German trans., *Die Gefilde des Himmels: Eine Geschichte vom Baalschen Tow*, trans. H. Neves (Munich: dtv, 1984), 53.

18. The compulsory-neurotic violence of Christian dogmatic theology has been explored most notably by Theodore Reik, *Dogma und Zwangsidee* (Cologne-Berlin-Mainz: Urban, 1973).

19. W. Orthmann, *Der alte Orient* (Berlin, 1975), illustration n. 416, 484.

20. See M. Lurker, *Götter und Symbole der Alten Ägypter* (Munich: Goldmann, n.d.), 41–42.

21. On the figure of Inanna, see D. O. Edzard, "Mesopotamien," in H. W. Haussig, ed., *Wörterbuch der Mythologie* (Stuttgart, 1965), 1:81–89.

22. On the cult of Cybele see F. Cumont, *Die orientalischen Religionen im römischen Heidentum*, trans. G. Gehrich (Leipzig-Berlin, 1914), 56–86.

23. On the figure of Isis see H. Kees, *Die Götterglauben im Alten Ägypten* (Leipzig, 1956), 256–57, 406–10.

24. *Pindar*, trans. J. E. Sandys, Loeb Classical Library (Cambridge: Harvard University Press, 1968), Pythian Odes VIII, 95, 269.

25. See the description in P. Scholl-Latour, *Allah ist mit den Standhaften* (Frankfurt-Berlin: Ullstein, 1986), 368-435.
26. See E. Harder and R. Paret, *Kleine Arabische Sprachlehre* (Heidelberg, 1956), 155.
27. J. G. Frazer, *The Golden Bough* (New York: Macmillan, 1985).
28. E. Akurgal and M. Hirmer, *Die Kunst der Hethiter* (Munich, 1976), 104, illustration 150.
29. Ibid., 7.
30. See the Qur'an, Sura XIX (Mary), 36: "It beseemeth not God to beget a son. Glory be to Him! when He decreeth a thing, He only saith to it, Be, and it Is." At the same this Sura shows how distant Muhammad's real familiarity with the Bible is: In verse 29 he confuses Mary, the mother of Jesus, with the sister of Moses and Aaron. On the other hand he reports with surprising accuracy about the sending of the Holy Spirit (in the form of a "perfect man") to Mary. See *The Koran*, trans. J. M. Rodwell (London: Dent, 1963), 120.
31. On the Indus civilization around 2500 B.C.E. see Sir M. Wheeler, *Alt-Indian und Pakistan*, trans. G. Pfeiffer (Cologne: Du Mont, n.d.), 81-102.
32. On the sacred rivers of India see Heinrich Zimmer, *Indische Mythen und Symbole*, trans. E. W. Eschmann (Düsseldorf-Cologne, 1951), 123-36.
33. See the picture of Maya's dream and her copulation with the sacred elephant and the picture of the birth of the Buddha: R. P. Mookerjee, ed., *Buddha Jayanti Exhibition: Catalogue of Exhibition of Buddhist Art* (Calcutta: Indian Museum, Archeological Section, 1956), table 2, 4.
34. On the Christian doctrine of Mary's virginity before, during, and after the birth of Jesus, see E. Buonaiuti, "Maria und die jungfräuliche Geburt Jesu," in O. Fröbe-Kapteyn, ed., *Eranos Jahrbuch* (1938), vol. 6, *Gestalt und Kult der Gross en Mutter* (1939), 325-63.
35. See E. Waldschmidt, *Die Legende vom Leben des Buddha* (Graz, 1982), 39-45: "Without being touched, musical instruments rang out (at the birth of the Buddha) in heaven and earth" (44). A celestial radiance appears, and all sick people are cured.
36. See E. Drewermann, *Tiefenpsychologie und Exegese*, 2:46-64, 760-62.
37. Albert Schweitzer, *Aus meinem Leben und Denken* (Frankfurt: Fischer, 1982), 30-37, 45-52.
38. David F. Strauss, *Das Leben Jesu: Kritisch bearbeitet*, 2 vols. (Tübingen, 1835-36).
39. See H. Schürmann, *Das Lukasevangelium*, 1:161.
40. One need only consider that in the meantime a whole generation of young people has been born whose picture of the world is based on science and is incompatible, externally speaking, with the Bible's view of life.
41. On the early Church's hostility to myth see Eugen Drewermann, *Strukturen des Bösen* (Paderborn, 1981), 3:514-33.
42. Thus Auguste Comte in *Die Soziologie: Die positive Philosophie im Auszug*, ed. F. Blaschke (Stuttgart: Kröner, 1974), 137-319.
43. J. P. Mackey, *Jesus, the Man and the Myth* (London, 1979), 39.
44. Schalom Ben-Chorin, *Mutter Mirjam* (Munich, 1977), 41.
45. On the interpretation of Genesis 6:1-4, see Eugen Drewermann, *Strukturen des Bösen*, 1:171-90; 2:332-54; 3:310-24.
46. A point quite rightly made by E. Schweizer, *Das Evangelium nach Lukas* (Göttingen, 1982), 18. Schweizer reminds us of the Old Testament and Essene notions of how the spirit of God goes to work.
47. Schalom Ben-Chorin, *Mutter Mirjam*, 46.
48. Ibid., 47.

49. E. Schweizer, *Das Evangelium nach Lukas*, 20.

50. On the concept of "virgin" (*alma*), see Schalom Ben-Chorin, *Mutter Mirjam*, 43. Ben-Chorin refutes the interpretation of the Hebrew *alma* (young girl) as "virgin" by citing Proverbs 30:18–19: "Three things are too wonderful for me; four I do not understand: the way of an eagle in the sky, the way of a serpent on a rock, the way of a ship of the high seas, and the way of a man with a maiden (*alma*)." Ben-Chorin argues unanswerably: "The eagle leaves no trace behind in the sky, nor the snake on the rock; while the wake of the ship becomes immediately invisible. And the way of a man with a maiden can no longer be ascertained afterwards.... This comparison would make no sense, if *alma* meant virgin."

51. Especially R. Schneider, *Verhüllter Tag* (Freiburg-Basel-Vienna: Herder, 1959), 81.

52. Thus the liturgy of the Canaanite New Year festival with its central theme, the successful kingdom of God, was adapted to Hebrew religion and thereby the influence of the God of Israel was extended to the realm of external nature.

53. In keeping with this notion the king is the only mediator between God and the community, as attested to by the fasting liturgy in Psalms 80 and 89.

54. Schalom Ben-Chorin rightly point out in *Mutter Mirjam*, 40–41: "In the coronation Psalm [Ps. 2:7] the text speaks of a second begetting.... The essential feature of our phrase from the Psalm is '*Today* I have begotten you' on the day of accession to the throne or anointing."

55. See Eugen Drewermann, *Der Krieg und das Christentum* (Regensburg, 1982), 284–337.

56. The dilemma is always the same: First historical-critical exegesis destroys the objective validity of a specific symbol through historical reduction. Then it regrets that the dogmatic tradition seems to have arisen from misunderstandings of the corresponding passages in the Bible. To close the gap between exegesis and dogmatic theology it is indispensable to re-establish the archetypal validity of certain images from the perspective of depth psychology. That way a hermeneutics can be worked out that once again opens up the rationalism and historical relativism of contemporary exegesis to religious belief.

57. E. Schweizer, *Das Evangelium nach Lukas*, 20.

58. Thus Muhammad could quote the Christian legend of Jesus' birth to defend the purity of Mary against the charge of fornication and to emphasize Jesus' vocation as a prophet. "And she made a sign to them [the people who have just told Mary that her mother was not a harlot] pointing towards the babe. They said, 'O Mary, How shall we speak with him who is in the cradle, an infant?' It [the child Jesus] said 'Verily, I am the servant of God; He hath given me the Book, and He hath made me a prophet; / And He hath made me blessed wherever I may be, and hath enjoined me prayer and almsgiving so long as I shall live; / And to be duteous to her that bore me; and he hath not made me proud, depraved. / And the peace of God was on me the day I was born, and will be the day I shall die, and the day I shall be raised to life" (Sura XIX, 30–34, *The Koran*, 119–20).

59. Schalom Ben-Chorin, *Mutter Mirjam*, 49.

60. Ibid., 152.

61. See H. Fritsch, *Vom Urknall zum Zerfall* (Munich-Zurich, 1983), 223, 228, 268.

62. See E. Drewermann, *Tiefenpsychologie und Exegese*, 2:320–46.

63. Ibid., 1:302–10.

64. See ibid., 1:310–21.

65. On the so-called screen memories as private childhood myths see especially E. Drewermann, *Tiefenpsychologie und Exegese*, 1:350-74.

66. This always happens when in historical-critical exegesis the archetypal codes of the Bible degenerate into mere expressive tools, historically conditioned and reduced to being just one more item from the history of literature. From the standpoint of religion what is at stake here is not the historical origin of a symbol but its claims to enduring truth.

67. Friedrich Nietzsche, *The Birth of Tragedy* (with *The Case of Wagner*), trans. Walter Kaufmann (New York: Random House, 1967).

68. W. F. Otto, *Die Musen und der göttliche Ursprung des Singens und Sagens* (Düsseldorf-Cologne, 1955), 33-35.

69. On Orphic experience and its therapeutic effectiveness, see E. Drewermann, *Tiefenpsychologie und Exegese*, 2:169-74.

70. Ibid., 2:192, 345, where religion is described as the overcoming of the subject-object split.

71. See E. Drewermann, *Die Strukturen des Bösen*, 3:1-72.

72. See E. Drewermann, *Tiefenpsychologie und Exegese*, 1:218-30.

73. K. Hübner, *Die Wahrheit des Mythos* (Munich, 1985), 60.

74. Bertolt Brecht, *Galileo*, trans. Charles Laughton, ed. Eric Bentley (New York: Grove Press, 1978), scene 7, 82-86.

75. On Descartes's epistemology see E. Drewermann, *Tiefenpsychologie und Exegese*, 2:52-56.

76. René Descartes, *Discourse on Method*, trans. F. E. Sutcliffe (Harmondsworth: Penguin, 1968), chap. 4, 53-60.

77. On the teachings of the Deists see E. Drewermann, *Tiefenpsychologie und Exegese*, 2:46, note 4. M. Tindal's *A Christianity as Old as Creation* (1730) is particularly worthy of mention.

78. O. Keel, *Die Welt der altorientalischen Bildsymbolik und das alte Testament* (Zurich-Einsiedeln-Cologne, 1972), 332.

1. "She Awoke from the Fragrance of God," or the Egyptian Myth of the Birth of the Pharaoh and the Scene of the Annunciation (Lk. 1:26-38)

1. Thus in the Symbolum Constantinopolitanum (Denzinger, Schönmetzer, *Enchiridion Symbolorum: Definitionum et Declarationum de Rebus Fidei et Morum* [Freiburg, 1973], n. 150, 66), which professes faith in Jesus Christ as "light from light, true God from true God, of one substance with the Father, who for us men and for our salvation came down from heaven and became flesh by the Holy Spirit and the Virgin Mary." In particular the phrases "light from light" and "begotten" are, as we shall see, in the tradition of the ancient Egyptian sun-theology of the Pharaoh.

2. On the religious history of these concepts in the ancient Orient see J. Gray, *Near Eastern Mythology* (London, 1969), 129-35.

3. On the birth of Plato see H. Usener, *Das Weihnachtsfest: Religionsgeschichtliche Untersuchungen,* part 1 (Bonn, 1911), 72.

4. On Alexander the Great see *Plutarch's Lives,* trans. John Dryden, rev. Arthur Hugh Clough (New York: Modern Library, n.d.), 801-53.

5. On the birth of Augustus, see Suetonius, *The Twelve Caesars,* trans. Robert Graves (Baltimore: Penguin, 1957), "Augustus," chap. 94, 100-103.

6. On the figure of Empedocles, see E. Drewermann, *Tiefenpsychologie und Exegese* (Olten, 1984), 2:158–69.

7. On the birth of Asclepius, see below pp. 108–125.

8. On the birth of Romulus and Remus from the love of the vestal Rhea Silvia and the war god Mars, see Livy, *Roman History*, 1:4.

9. Plutarch reports on the march of Alexander to the Egyptian oracles of Amun (*Plutarch's Lives*, "Alexander," 820–21).

10. *Plutarch's Lives*, "Numa Pompilius," 77.

11. Athanasius, *Against the Arians*, Third Discourse, 4.

12. See Cyril's Second and Third Letter against Nestorius, Denzinger, Schönmetzer, *Enchiridion Symbolorum*, n. 250–64.

13. See E. Brunner-Traut, *Die Kopten: Leben und Lehre der früheren Christen in Ägypten* (Cologne, 1982), 52–56.

14. On Hegel's philosophy of history see E. Drewermann, *Strukturen des Bösen* (Paderborn, 1981), 3:64–70.

15. On Hegel's philosophy of religion see ibid., 71–75.

16. From the standpoint of depth psychology the poet Virgil characterizes the essence of Rome most clearly when he describes in the *Aeneid* (4:612–29) how Aeneas has to flee from the love of Dido in order to remain faithful to his destiny, while the proud Carthaginian seeks death from disappointed love, with curses for her fleeing lover on her lips.

17. On the "principle" of Rome as depicted in Revelation 12:17, see E. Drewermann, *Tiefenpsychologie und Exegese*, 2:548, 580–89.

18. Quite rightly E. Brunner-Traut, "Pharao und Jesus als Söhne Gottes," in *Gelebte Mythen: Beiträge zum altägyptischen Mythos* (Darmstadt, 1981), 36: "If we...wish to understand the ancient Egyptian notion of the Son of God, we must realize first of all that the religion of the people of the Nile was not a dogmatic, but a mythic one."

19. See K. Földes-Papp, *Vom Felsbild zum Alphabet* (Stuttgart, 1966), 101–19.

20. See, for example, Karl Rahner, *Kirche und Sacrament* (Freiburg-Basel-Vienna, 1960), 15: "In his historical existence Christ is at once the fact and the sign...of the redeeming grace of God."

21. See ibid., 73, where with logical consistency Rahner considers the Eucharist from the basic approach of incarnational theology "as the source of the other sacraments."

22. See ibid., 13, where Rahner develops the doctrine of the Church as the "primeval sacrament" from the incarnation of the Logos.

23. Thus Teilhard de Chardin, for example, understood Christianity as the inner axis of an evolution in which liturgy and secular piety form an inseparable unity. See "Christentum und Evolution," in *Mein Glaube*, trans. K. Schmitz-Moorman (Olten, 1972), 207–23.

24. E. Dondelinger, in *Papyrus Ani. BM 10.470* (Graz, 1978), 10–11, rightly refers to the matriarchal background of ancient Egyptian religion.

25. See E. Drewermann, *Strukturen des Bösen*, afterword to the third edition, 1:356–413.

26. On the mentality of patriarchal systems, see E. Drewermann, *Der Krieg und das Christentum* (Regensburg, 1982), 232–82.

27. On the sky goddess Nut see W. Barta, *Untersuchungen zum Götterkreis der Neunheit*, ed. H. W. Müller (Berlin, 1973), 100–104.

28. On the figure of the serpent see E. Drewermann, *Strukturen des Bösen*, 1:lxv–lxxi, 38–42; 2:236–37; 3:69–101.

29. On the nightly struggle of Ra with the Apophis serpent, see E. Drewermann, *Tiefenpsychologie und Exegese*, 2:534.

30. See J. Assmann, *Liturgische Lieder an den Sonnengott: Untersuchungen zur altägyptischen Hymnik*, ed. H. W. Müller (Berlin, 1969), 1:271-75, 333-52, 361ff.

31. Ibid., 1:241.

32. J. Settgast, ed., *Nofretete-Echnaton* (Berlin: Ägyptisches Museum, 1976), n. 47.

33. On the role of the monkeys of the sun see J. Assmann, *Liturgische Lieder an den Sonnengott*, 1:207-14.

34. On the figure of the baboon as the incarnation of Thot, see G. Posener, *Lexikon der ägyptischen Kultur*, trans. J. and I. von Beckerath (Wiesbaden: Löwit, n.d.), 11-13.

35. On the significance of the moon, see M. Lurker, *Götter und Symbole der Alten Ägypter* (Munich: Goldmann, n.d.), 127-28.

36. J. Assmann, *Ägyptische Hymnen und Gebete* (Zurich-Munich, 1975), 155-57.

37. See Blaise Pascal, *Pensées*, trans. A. J. Krailsheimer (Harmondsworth: Penguin, 1966), 67, n. 137. "Sometimes, when I set to thinking about the various activities of men, the dangers and troubles which they face at Court, or in war, giving rise to so many quarrels and passions, daring and often wicked enterprises and so on, I have often said that the sole cause of man's unhappiness is that he does not know how to stay quietly in his room."

38. Rainer Maria Rilke, *Duino Elegies*, trans. J. B. Leishman and Stephen Spender (New York: Norton, 1939), 29.

39. On the figure of the angel see E. Drewermann, *Voller Erbarmen rettet er uns: Die Tobit-Legende tiefenpsychologisch gedeutet* (Freiburg-Basel-Vienna, 1984), 35-46.

40. On the journeys of the soul into the world of angels see P. L. Wilson, *Engel*, trans. L. Mickel (Stuttgart-Berlin-Cologne-Mainz, 1981), 107-61.

41. According to Daniel 8:16 and Enoch 10:3, 54:6 Gabriel is the protector of Israel, "the avenging arm of God."

42. See J. Brinktrine, *Die Lehre von den letzten Dingen: Die Lehre von der Kirche* (Paderborn, 1963), 26-37.

43. Charles Seeber, *Untersuchungen zur Darstellung des Totengerichts im Alten Ägypten* (Munich-Berlin, 1976), 147-54.

44. On the figure of the eater of the dead, see ibid., 163-86.

45. E. Hornung, *Das Totenbuch der Ägypter* (Zurich-Munich, 1979), saying 30 B, 96.

46. On the Christian dogmas concerning the existence and structure of Hell see J. Brinktrine, *The Lehre von den letzten Dingen*, 140-64.

47. A. Erlande-Brandenburg, *Gotische Kunst*, trans. H. Adkins and H. Wischermann (Freiburg-Basel-Vienna, 1984), illustration 109.

48. See E. Dondelinger, *Papyrus Ani*, 31, 33.

49. On the one-sided ethicization of Christian theology see E. Drewermann, "Das Tragische und das Christliche," in *Psychoanalyse und Moraltheologie* (Mainz, 1982-84), 1:19-78.

50. On the problematic nature of lying see Eugen Drewermann, "Ein Plädoyer für die Lüge, oder vom Unvermögen zur Wahrheit," in *Psychoanalyse und Moraltheologie*, 3:199-236.

51. E. Dondelinger, *Der Jenseitsweg der Nofretari* (Graz, 1977), panels 21, 22.

52. On the goddess Mut see W. Helck, "Die Mythologie der alten Ägypter," in H. W. Haussig, ed., *Wörterbuch der Mythologie* (Stuttgart, 1965), 1:378.

53. E. Dondelinger, *Der Jenseitsweg der Nofretari*, 13.

54. Ibid., 10.

55. The cherubim of the ark of the covenant are usually understood as "mixed creatures," "best known in Mesopotamia as the protective genii at the entrances of temples and palaces" (Martin Noth, *Das zweite Buch Mose* [Göttingen, 1961], 166). But the Western representations of angels with their essentially feminine features and their human forms point much more to Egypt than to Mesopotamia. In Israel too Egyptian influence was likely stronger than the relatively late Assyrian-Babylonian style.

56. Contrast this with the theriopmorphic flying bulls in the palace of Ashurnasipal II (883–859 B.C.E.) in Nimrud or of Sargon II (721–705 B.C.E.) in Chorsabad. W. Orthmann, *Der alte Orient* (Berlin, 1975), illustrations 175, 176, p. 297.

57. The double function of Maat in the judgment of the dead is described by C. Seeber in *Untersuchungen zur Darstellung des Totengerichts im Alten Ägypten*, 144–45.

58. See the depth-psychological interpretation of the passage in M. Kassel, *Biblische Urbilder* (Munich, 1980), 258–79.

59. The story has a famous parallel in the tale of the fisherman and the demon from *The Arabian Nights*. See *Tales from the Thousand and One Nights*, trans. N. J. Dawood (Harmondsworth: Penguin, 1972), 79–105.

60. On the quest for perfection in compulsory neuroses see E. Drewermann, "Sünde und Neurose," in *Psychoanalyse und Moraltheologie* 1:129–62.

61. See, for example, in the Bible Genesis 18:1–16; Judges 13:1–25.

62. See P. Schwarzenau, *Das göttliche Kind: Der Mythos vom Neubeginn* (Stuttgart, 1984), 8–14, 101–44.

63. See A. Waiblinger, *Gross e Mutter und göttliches Kind: Das Wunder in Wiege und Seele* (Stuttgart, 1986), 157–62.

64. On the unity of, and the difference between, finding God and finding oneself in the confrontation with C. G. Jung, see E. Drewermann, *Strukturen des Bösen*, 3:417–30 (the example of the Flood); 3:123–48 (the example of the Fall).

65. See Paul Tillich, *Wesen und Wandel des Glaubens* (Frankfurt-Berlin: Ullstein, 1969), 9–12, where he defines faith as "being grasped by what unconditionally concerns us."

66. See Schalom Ben-Chorin, *Mutter Mirjam* (Munich, 1977), 45, who points out that the name of Jesus became unusual only because of the Jewish protest against Christianity.

67. On the category of the "beginning" in myth see E. Drewermann, *Tiefenpsychologie und Exegese*, 1:350–74.

68. On the figure of the "royal child" in both the religion and literature of Romanticism see the interpretation of Saint-Exupéry's *The Little Prince* in E. Drewermann, *Das eigentliche ist unsichtbar* (Freiburg, 1984), 15–20.

69. See Karl Rahner, "Zur Theologie der Menschwerdung," in *Schriften zur Theologie* (Zurich-Cologne-Einsiedeln, 1962), 4:137–55.

70. See Karl Kerényi (and C. G. Jung), *Das göttliche Kind in mythologischer und psychologischer Beleuchtung* (Amsterdam-Leipzig, 1940), 21–24.

71. See Fyodor Dostoyevsky, *The Idiot*, trans. Eva M. Martin (London: Dent, 1970), part 1, chap. 6, pp. 63–73. This is the impressive episode of Prince Myshkin with Marie, a girl who is mocked and despised by all the grown-ups

of the village, while the prince teaches the children to understand her distress and to love her nature.

72. Georges Bernanos, *Diary of a Country Priest*, trans. Pamela Morris (Chicago: Thomas More, 1983), 147-81, describes the conversation of the priest with Madame de Chantal.

73. See M. Ende, *Momo* (Stuttgart, 1973), 111-21.

74. Lao-tzu, *The Way of Lao-tzu* (Tao-te Ching), trans. Wing-Tsit Chan (Indianapolis: Bobbs Merrill, 1963), 126, n. 15.

75. On "poverty" in the New Testament, see E. Drewermann, *Tiefenpsychologie und Exegese*, 2:462, 688, 697-99, 708-10.

76. According to A. Erman, *Die Religion der Ägypter: Ihr Werden und Vergehen in vier Jahrtausenden* (Berlin-Leipzig, 1934), 52-53. See E. Brunner-Traut, *Altägyptische Märchen* (Düsseldorf-Cologne, 1963), 11-24.

77. On the names of the Pharaoh see J. von Beckerath, *Handbuch der ägyptischen Königsnamen*, 52-53.

78. On the figure of Mes-chenet see W. Helck, "Die Mythologie der Alten Ägypter," in H. Haussig, ed., *Wörterbuch der Mythologie*, 1:313-406.

79. On the figure of Heket see ibid., 358.

80. A. Erman, *Die Religion der Ägypter*, 52.

81. J. von Beckerath, *Handbuch der ägyptischen Königsnamen*, 54, 181.

82. Ibid.

83. Ibid., 30, 54, 181.

84. A. Erman, *Die Religion der Ägypter*, 53-54.

85. See E. Brunner-Traut, *Altägyptische Märchen*, 76-87.

86. J. von Beckerath, *Handbuch der ägyptischen Königsnamen*, 84, 226; A. Erman, *Die Religion der Ägypter*, 53-54.

87. J. von Beckerath, *Handbuch der ägyptischen Königsnamen*, 82, 224.

88. S. Schott, trans., *Altägyptische Märchen*, 78-80.

89. E. Brunner-Traut, *Altägyptische Märchen*, 78-80.

90. Ibid., 81.

91. Ibid., 82.

92. Ibid.

93. Ibid., 84.

94. A. Erman, *Die Religion der Ägypter*, 54-55.

95. E. Brunner-Traut, "Pharao und Jesus als Söhne Gottes," in *Gelebte Mythen*, 34-54.

96. Ibid., 47-48. See E. Drewermann, "Religionsgeschichtliche und tiefenpsychologische Bemerkungen zur Trinitätslehre," in W. Breunig, ed., *Trinität: Aktuelle Perspektiven der Theologie* (Freiburg-Basel-Vienna, 1984), 115-42.

97. Athanasius, *Against the Arians*, First Address, chap. 25; Second Address, chap. 28.

98. See Athanasius, *Against the Arians*, First Address, chap. 36.

99. See E. Drewermann, *Der Krieg und das Christentum*, 287-337.

100. J. von Beckerath, *Handbuch der ägyptischen Königsnamen*, 7.

101. Ibid., 4.

102. E. Brunner-Traut, "Pharao und Jesus als Söhne Gottes," in *Gelebte Mythen*, 48.

103. Ibid.

104. On the essentially priestly position of the Pharaoh see J. Assmann, *Der König als Sonnenpriester* (Deutsches Archäologisches Institut Kairo, 1970), 58-70. The echoes of the theology of the Letter to the Hebrews are unmistakable (see Heb. 8:1-5).

105. J. von Beckerath, *Handbuch der ägyptischen Königsnamen*, 24.

106. Ibid., 34.
107. W. Seipel, "Staat und Gesellschaft," in A. Eggebrecht, ed., *Das alte Ägypten* (Munich, 1984), 117–95.
108. Ibid., 125.
109. The notion of a struggle fought by two hostile brothers, as incarnations of both cosmic and psychic forces, is an archetypal theme found all over the world. On the Cain and Abel motif see E. Drewermann, *Strukturen des Bösen*, 1:111–14; 2:247–56; 3:263–99.
110. See E. Drewermann, *Tiefenpsychologie und Exegese*, 1:250–374.
111. J. von Beckerath, *Handbuch der ägyptischen Königsnamen*, 14.
112. On the figure of the sky goddess Nut, see H. Kees, *Der Götterglaube im Alten Ägypten* (Leipzig, 1956), 226–27.
113. J. Assmann, *Der König als Sonnenpriester*, 22.
114. Ibid., 38.
115. See Plotinus, *The Enneads*, IV 8 (6), 5, 29.
116. Joseph Roth, *Die Flucht ohne Ende* (Munich: dtv, 1978), 77.
117. Ibid., 78–79.
118. See J. G. Fichte, *Grundlage der gesamten Wissenschaftlehre* (Hamburg, 1956), part 1, §1, p. 11.
119. See Ernest Jones, "Die Empfängnis der Jungfrau Maria durch das Ohr," in *Jahrbuch der Psychoanalyse* (1914), 4:135–204.
120. On the concept of the "family romance" and its importance for the interpretation of myths and legends see E. Drewermann, *Tiefenpsychologie und Exegese*, 1:212–13.
121. See E. Brunner-Traut, *Altägyptische Märchen*, 78.
122. In "Die Umweltlehre des Paracelsus," *Paläoanthropologie* (Frankfurt, 1971), 1:240, R. Bilz makes the case for the following as an "elementary thought" in the sense of A. Bastian, "that in the final analysis God begets our children.... The lover takes God's place!"
123. Max Beckmann, "Adam and Eve, 1917" in C. Schulz-Hoffmann, ed., *Max Beckmann Retrospektive* (Munich, 1984), 201, illustration 16.
124. See the exploration of the Grimms' fairy tale "The Child of Mary" in E. Drewermann, *Marienkind* (Freiburg, 1984), 29–38.
125. On the image of the Egyptian bark of the sun, see N. Jenkins, *Das Schiff in der Wüste*, trans. V. Bradke (Frankfurt, 1980), 139–56.
126. See A Gardiner, *Egyptian Grammar* (Oxford, 1956), 568.
127. See A. Erman, *Die Religion der Ägypter*, 52.
128. I. E. S. Edwards, *Tutanchamun: Das Grab und seine Schätze*, trans. J. Rehork (Bergisch-Gladbach, 1978), 70.
129. S. Schott, trans. *Altägyptische Liebeslieder* (Zurich, 1950), 102–3.
130. On the primeval, partly shamanistic motif of the journey of the soul in folk tales, see E. Drewermann, *Die Kristalkugel* (Freiburg, 1985), 20–34.
131. J. von Beckerath, *Handbuch der ägyptischen Mythologie*, 86, 230.
132. See the illustration in J. Settgast, ed., *Nofretete-Echnaton* catalogue (Berlin, 1976), picture 47.
133. C. Barocas, *Theben: Das Heiligtum Amuns*, trans. C. Callori-Gehlsen (Freiburg, 1983), 48.
134. S. Schott, *Altägyptische Liebeslieder*, 117, n. 58.
135. See E. Eggebrecht, "Die Geschichte des Pharaonenreiches" in A. Eggebrecht, *Das alte Ägypten*, 41–116, 94–100.
136. On the concepts of "eternity" see J. Assmann, *Zeit und Ewigkeit im Alten Ägypten*, 61–69.
137. See E. Hornung, *Tal der Könige* (Zurich-Munich, 1982), 180.

138. See E. Drewermann, *Tiefenpsychologie und Exegese*, 2:105-14.
139. G. W. F. Hegel, *Philosophie der Geschichte* (Stuttgart, 1961), 177-78.
140. S. Morenz, *Gott und Mensch im alten Ägypten* (Zurich-Munich-Leipzig, 1984), 93.
141. Ibid., 76.
142. Ibid., 98-99.
143. On the conceptual and psychological meaning of the "corporative person" see E. Drewermann, *Tiefenpsychologie und Exegese*, 1:271-98.
144. See A. Erman and H. Ranke, *Ägypten und ägyptisches Leben im Altertum* (Hildesheim, 1981), 620-26.
145. See W. Orthmann, *Der Alte Orient*, illustrations 210-16, pp. 317-18; illus. 228-33, pp. 321-22; illus. 236-44, pp. 324-25.
146. See R. Frye, *Persien bis zum Einbruch des Islams*, trans. P. Baudisch (Essen, 1975), 202ff., 217-25.
147. On the veneration of Alexander as the embodiment of Amun-Ra see G. Gottschalk, *Die gross en Pharaonen* (Bern-Munich, 1979), 238-39.
148. Suetonius, *The Twelve Caesars*, "Augustus," 52, p. 80, mentions that Augustus himself forbade anyone to venerate him in the temples and tolerated it in the provinces only when the name of the goddess Roma was added to his. Domitian (81-96) was the first living emperor to lay claim to the title *dominus* and *deus*. Beginning with Aurelian (270-75) this became customary.
149. F. Werfel, *Das lyrische Werk* (Frankfurt, 1967), 276.
150. See E. Dondelinger, *Der Jenseitsweg der Nofretari*, 45.
151. G. W. F. Hegel, *Der Geist des Christentums und sein Schicksal* (Gütersloh, 1970), 86-87.

2. Mary and Elizabeth,
or the Meeting of Two Worlds (Lk. 1:39-45, 56)

1. I. B. Singer, *Shosha*, trans. Joseph Singer (New York: Farrar, Straus and Giroux, 1978), 272.
2. H. Schürmann takes a totally positivistic stance in *Das Lukasevangelium* (Freiburg-Basel-Vienna, 1984), 1:67, where he says: "John belongs to the story of Jesus' birth because God had placed him right at the 'beginning.'" But why did God "place him right at the 'beginning'"? That's the real question.
3. The meaning of the Jesus tradition consists of, among other things, outdoing the John tradition. This can be see from the structural principle of parallel intensification:

Lk. 1:5-25: the annunciation of the birth of John	1:26-56: the annunciation of the birth of Jesus
Lk. 1:57-80: the birth of John	2:1-40: the birth of Jesus

Both of the John-narratives, each of which is divided into two parts (1:5-23, 24-25, and 1:57-66, 67-80), are matched by the two double narratives of the birth of Jesus (1:26-38, 39-56, and 2:1-21, 22-40). In other words, the John-tradition more probably derives from Jewish Christian circles than from the group of John's disciples, and it is passed on only to enhance the figure of Jesus. John and Jesus are coordinated to one another as prophetic promise (Old Testament) and eschatological fulfillment (New Testament).

4. On the figure of the Baptist in connection with the Baptist movement see E. Stauffer, *Jerusalem und Rom im Zeitalter Jesu Christi* (Bern: Dalp, 1957), 80–102.

5. In interpreting mythical or legendary stories of childhood the rule is always that the "beginnings" describe the *essence* of the hero in question. See E. Drewermann, *Tiefenpsychologie und Exegese* (Olten, 1984), 1:350–74.

6. See E. Stauffer, *Jerusalem und Rom*, 49–61; E. Stauffer, *Die Botschaft Jesu damals und heute* (Bern-Munich, 1959), 13–16.

7. It seems that in this passage we find some crucial common ground between the Essenes and the early Church. Both groups rejected the cultic worship in the Temple of Jerusalem and replaced the Temple with the community. Both were thus preparing a form of life that after the destruction of Jerusalem in 70 C.E. would be unavoidable for all Jews: living without the Temple.

8. See E. Stauffer, *Jerusalem und Rom*, 88–102.

9. On the interpretation of the Flood in Genesis, see E. Drewermann, *Strukturen des Bösen* (Paderborn, 1981), 1:191–229; 2:359–430.

10. John was evidently a Nazarene of the deepest dye. See E. Stauffer, *Jerusalem und Rom*, 89–90.

11. See, for example, Tertullian, "On Baptism," 8.

12. See A. Dupont-Sommer, *The Essene Writings from Qumran*, trans. Geza Vermes (Oxford: Basil Blackwood, 1961), "The Scroll of the War Rule," I, 13, p. 171, where the sons of light head into battle with "the army of Belial."

13. See E. Drewermann, *Der Krieg und das Christentum* (Regensburg, 1982), 108–35.

14. Ibid., 65–74.

15. See Karl Marx, *Das Kapital* ([East] Berlin: Institut für Marxismus und Leninismus, 1965), 1:793: "He [E. G. Wakefield] discovered that capital is not a thing, but a social relationship between persons mediated through things [i.e., between the owner of the means of production and the wage-earner].

16. G. Grosz, "Sonnenfinsternis" (1926), Heckscher Museum, New York. "Stützen der Gesellschaft" (1926), Nationalgalerie, Berlin. Reproductions of both in C. M. Joachimides, *Deutsche Kunst im 20. Jahrhundert* (Munich, 1986), illustrations 128–29.

17. See the interpretation of the Exodus in E. Drewermann, *Tiefenpsychologie und Exegese*, 1:485–502.

18. H.-A. Frye, "Die übrigen Erd – und Baumhörnchen," in B. Grzimek, *Enzyklopädie des Tierreichs in 13 Bänden*, 11:234–69.

19. On the parable of the lost sheep see J. Jeremias, *Die Gleichnisse Jesu* (Göttingen, 1962), 132–35.

20. I. B. Singer, *Shosha*, 183.

21. In interpreting the figure of Salome see E. Drewermann, *Tiefenpsychologie und Exegese*, 2:645–48.

22. See J. Jeremias, *Die Gleichnisse Jesu*, 207–11.

23. For arguments against the (mistaken) faith in moral goodness in humans or the moral autonomy of the individual apart from redemption by God, see E. Drewermann, *Strukturen des Bösen*, 3:lxix–lxxxvi.

24. See the excursus, as readable now as ever, "Sünde und Tod, Erbtod und Erbsüde," in O. Kuss, *Der Römerbrief* (Regensburg, 1957), 1:241–75.

25. See E. Drewermann, *Strukturen des Bösen*, 1:179, 210.

26. An essential rule of group dynamics holds that a norm (regardless of whether it is written or unspoken) carries as much weight as the punishment actually meted out for transgressing it. See G. C. Homans, *Theorie der sozialen Gruppe*, trans. R. Grunner (Cologne-Opladen, 1960), 294–97.

27. On the ritualization of oaths in the sense of J.-P. Sartre, as the "brotherhood of terror" within socially internalized compulsion, see E. Drewermann, *Strukturen des Bösen,* 3:243–45, 387–89.

28. Patriarchy appears above all in the Yahwist creation narrative as God's first curse on a human race whose feelings of shame and anxiety make it incapable of love. See E. Drewermann, *Strukturen des Bösen,* 1:90–99, 391–96.

29. See the urgent account in E. Stauffer, *Die Botschaft Jesu damals und heute,* 26–35, where Jesus is treated as the living contradiction to the law, to *every* law.

30. See ibid., 36–39.

31. H. von Kleist, *Prinz Friedrich von Homburg* (1821), in Kleist, *Gesamtausgabe in 7 Bänden,* 3:214–89.

32. On the metaphor of the "lamb," see E. Drewermann, *Tiefenpsychologie und Exegese,* 2:580.

33. On Peter's walking on the Sea of Galilee, see ibid., 2:29–31.

34. See W. Trilling, *Das wahre Israel: Studien zur Theologie des Matthäusevangeliums* (Munich, 1964), 32.

35. On the "maternal" meaning of the Eucharist see E. Drewermann, *Der Krieg und das Christentum,* 309–10.

36. Without this trust, which is an anthropological given, in the "entelechy" of the human psyche there is no purchase for psychotherapy or religion, and the only available option is the terror of socialization by means of heteronomy and violence.

37. See R. Pesch, *Das Markusevangelium* (Freiburg-Basel-Vienna, 1984), 1:170–76.

3. The God of the Shining Light, or the Scene of the Holy Night (Lk. 2:1–20)

1. H. Schürmann, *Das Lukasevangelium* (Freiburg-Basel-Vienna, 1984), 1:97.

2. Ibid., 98.

3. Ibid., 107

4. Ibid., 103.

5. Ibid., 100.

6. Ibid., 101. On this whole complex of questions see the profound critique of H. Gressmann in *Das Weihnachtsevangelium auf Unsprung und Geschichte untersucht* (Göttingen, 1914), 11–13.

7. See E. Schweizer, *Das Evangelium nach Lukas* (Göttingen, 1982), 31.

8. See Schalom Ben-Chorin, *Mutter Mirjam* (Munich, 1977), 75.

9. H. Schürmann, *Das Lukasevangelium* (Freiburg-Basel-Vienna, 1984), 1:112.

10. Ibid., 112.

11. Ibid., 103, n. 40.

12. Ibid., 105, n. 53.

13. Ibid., 103, n. 40.

14. Ibid., 104, n. 51.

15. Ibid., 103, n. 40.

16. See E. Drewermann, *Tiefenpsychologie und Exegese* (Olten, 1984), 2:773–76.

17. On the birth myth of Osiris, see E. Brunner-Traut, *Altägyptische Märchen* (Düsseldorf-Cologne, 1963), 88.

18. On the figure of Mithra see J. de Manasce, "Die Mythologie der Perser," in P. Grimal, ed., *Mythen der Völker,* trans. L. Voelker (Frankfurt: Fischer, 1967), 2:9–49.

19. C. Kerényi, *Asclepios: Archetypal Image of the Physician's Existence,* trans. Ralph Manheim (New York: Pantheon, 1959), 27–28.

20. See O. Rank, *Der Mythus vom Geburt des Helden* (Leipzig-Vienna, 1922), 79–80.

21. Ibid.

22. On the depth-psychological interpretation of the infancy narrative according to Matthew, see E. Drewermann, *Tiefenpsychologie und Exegese,* 1:502–29.

23. Ibid., 1:178–200.

24. See P. Kroh, *Lexikon der antiken Autoren* (Stuttgart: Kröner, 1972), 323.

25. K. Kerényi, *Asclepios,* 28.

26. Ibid.

27. Ibid., 28–29.

28. Ibid.

29. On the symbol of the snakes (as the dogs of the moon) see E. Drewermann, *Strukturen des Bösen* (Paderborn, 1981), 1:38.

30. K. Kerényi, *Asclepios,* 30, 32.

31. See Ovid, *Metamorphoses,* III, 594.

32. See Virgil, *Aeneid,* VIII, 354.

33. K. Kerényi, *Asclepios,* 28–29.

34. Ibid.

35. Ibid., 87.

36. On the symbol of the rooster there is no better commentary than the remark of the dying Socrates to his disciple, "O Criton, we ought to offer a cock to Asclepius. See to it, and don't forget" (Plato, *The Last Days of Socrates,* trans. Hugh Tredennick [Harmondsworth: Penguin, 1969], 183). K. Kerényi, *Asclepios,* 59, observes: "Today we know what he meant. He might just as well have said: 'The sun is rising, the light is coming, let us give thanks.' "

37. Ibid., 88.

38. Hesiod, *Theogony,* 404ff.

39. K. Kerényi, *Asclepios,* 91.

40. Ibid., 91–93.

41. Ibid., 95.

42. H. Schürmann, *Das Lukasevangelium,* 1:99.

43. See E. Drewermann, *Tiefenpsychologie und Exegese,* 1:519–22.

44. On the representation of Asclepius see ibid., 2:174–88.

45. D. Wildung, *Imhotep and Amenhotep: Gottwerdung in alten Ägypten* (Munich-Berlin, 1977), 76–78.

46. On freedom from sickness and death in "Paradise" see E. Drewermann, *Strukturen des Bösen,* 3rd expanded edition, 1:378–89.

47. See R. H. Fuller, *Die Wunder Jesu in Exegese und Verkündigung,* trans. F. J. Schierse (Düsseldorf, 1967), 91–97.

48. The tension of all miracle stories consists, in keeping with their experiential origin, of an opposition between fear and trust. See E. Drewermann, *Tiefenpsychologie und Exegese,* 2:129–41.

49. The star witness for this opinion is J. Jeremias, *Jerusalem zur Zeit Jesu* (Göttingen, 1962), 338.

50. H. Schürmann makes this point quite rightly in *Das Lukasevangelium,* 1:108-9.

51. Accordingly the type of the "shepherd" is to be read, in structuralist terms, as a symbol that mediates between logical (and psychological) opposites.

52. See E. Drewermann, *Tiefenpsychologie und Exegese,* 1:230-50.

53. The first mention of the ox and donkey at the manger is found in the infancy Gospel of Pseudo-Matthew, *The Other Bible,* ed. Willis Barnstone (New York: Harper & Row, 1964), 395.

54. Virgil, Eclogue IV, 20ff. writes: "The goats, unshepherded, will make for home with udders full of milk, and the ox will not be frightened of the lion, for all his might. Your [the Savior's] very cradle will adorn itself with blossoms to caress you. The snake will come to grief, and poison lurk no more in the weed. Perfumes from Assyria will breathe from every hedge" (Michael Grant, ed., *Latin Literature: An Anthology,* trans. E. V. Rieu [Harmondsworth: Penguin, 1986], 134).

55. See E. Drewermann, *Tiefenpsychologie und Exegese,* 2:152-55.

56. See B. Rensch, "Haustierenentstehung," in *Biologie* (Frankfurt: Fischer, 1963), 2:164-67.

57. E. Zimen, "Wildwege" (South German Radio), five-part television series, part 5: "Der Hund" (1), June 21, 1986 (Working Pool of the Broadcasting Corporations of the Federal Republic of Germany).

58. *Apollodorus,* trans. J. G. Frazier, Loeb Classical Library (Cambridge: Harvard University Press, 1989), 2:17.

59. On the depth-psychological meaning of left and right, see E. Drewermann, *Tiefenpsychologie und Exegese,* 2:406, n. 24; 407, n. 25, 27; 558, n. 58.

60. On the image of the Gorgo as a symbol of the fear of castration, see S. Freud, "Das Medusenhaupt, in *Gesammelte Werke* (London, 1948), 24:201-4.

61. On the hermeneutical principle of the inner harmony of all partial elements of a narrative see E. Drewermann, *Tiefenpsychologie und Exegese,* 1:201-4.

62. On the provisional nature of life, in the face of death, see M. Heidegger, *Sein und Zeit* (Tübingen, 1963), 249-67. But see also the critique of J.-P. Sartre, as reported by E. Drewermann in *Struktures des Bösen,* 3:216-18, 246-47.

63. See Kerényi, *Asclepios,* 40-41: "The rites of Eleusis lead us to still greater depths than those of Epidauros. The way was the same, but the sick man who found health at Epidauros turned back sooner than the Eleusinian initiate who made his way to the Queen of the Underworld."

64. T. Mann, *Joseph und seine Brüder* (Frankfurt: Fischer, 1971), 1:141-42.

65. See E. Dondelinger, *Der Jenseitsweg der Nofretari,* table 29, p. 102.

66. Ibid.

67. K. Kerényi, *Die Mythologie der Griechen* (Munich, 1966), 2:185; Ovid, *Metamorphoses,* VIII, 183-235.

68. See A. Erman and H. Grapow, *Ägyptisches Handwörterbuch* (Darmstadt, 1981), 193.

69. See E. Hornung, trans., *Das Totenbuch der Ägypter,* saying 76, p. 156.

70. M. Arnold, *Edvard Munch mit Selbstzeugnissen und Bilddokumenten* (Hamburg: Rowohlt, 1986), 7.

71. On the theme of "night" there is hardly a more urgent commentary than the picture of the same name by M. Beckmann, from 1919, in C. Schulz-Hoffmann and J. C. Weiss, eds., *Max Beckmann: Retrospektive* (Munich, 1984), illustration 19, pp. 204-5.

72. On the living consciousness of banishment in the Yahwist primal history see E. Drewermann, *Strukturen des Bösen*, 1:97-106; 2:232-35.

73. See R. Pesch, *Das Markusevangelium* (Freiburg-Basel-Vienna, 1984), 2:2, 220.

74. On the theme of torture, see the drawings of Karl Schweisg from the "Schlegelkeller" (thrashing cellar) from 1937, in U. Krempel, ed., *Am Anfang: Das junge Rheinland* (Düsseldorf, 1985), 302-3.

75. A reverse Paradise myth of the Aztecs tells how Quetzalcoatl, the mythical ruler of the Toltec land of Tollan, falls into sin because of the seductions of his antagonist, the god Tetcatlipoca. He has to go forth from the Paradise of his peaceable kingdom and all along the way to Tlapallan he leaves petrified footprints. He turns the beautiful and nourishing cocoa trees into thorn acacias; and the corn now tastes so bitter that the Toltecs can no longer eat it.

76. See C. Westermann, *Abriss der Bibelkunde* (Frankfurt: Fischer, 1968), 82; H. W. Hertzberg, *Die Samuelbücher* (Göttingen, 1960), 107ff.

77. On the archetypal opposition between priest and prophet, see E. Drewermann, *Tiefenpsychologie und Exegese*, 2:368-71.

78. See S. Ben-Chorin, *Mutter Mirjam*, 75.

79. See S. Ben-Chorin, *Brüder Jesus* (Munich: dtv, 1977), 28-29, on the Talmudic tradition of Mary's relations with the Roman officer Pandera.

80. Legends about the Christ child in Egypt can be found in the infancy Gospel of the Pseudo-Matthew, *The Other Bible*, 396-97.

81. G. Büchner, "Der hessische Landbote," in *Gesammelte Werke* (Munich: Goldmann, n.d.), 179.

82. Quoted from E. Stauffer, *Jerusalem und Rom im Zeitalter Jesu Christi* (Bern: Dalp, 1957), 20-39, p. 28.

83. Virgil, *Aeneid*, VI, 791.

84. Quoted from E. Stauffer, *Jerusalem und Rom*, 39.

85. G. Wehr, *Thomas Münzer* (Hamburg, 1972), 74.

86. E. Stauffer, *Jerusalem und Rom*, 35.

87. Fyodor Dostoyevsky, *The Idiot*, trans. David Magarshack (Harmondsworth: Penguin, 1962), 385.

88. E. Waldschmidt, *Die Legende vom Leben des Buddha* (Graz, 1982), 48-53 (the prophecy of the seer Asita).

89. *Pindar*, Pythian Odes, VIII, 5, 95, p. 269.

4. "Lord, Now Thou Lettest Thy Servant Depart in Peace, According to Thy Word" (Lk. 2:21-40)

1. E. Brunner-Traut, *Altägyptische Märchen* (Düsseldorf-Cologne, 1963), 192ff.

2. Ibid., 301; J. von Beckerath, *Handbuch der ägyptischen Mythologie*, 30, 84, 226.

3. On the motif of oral conception see E. Drewermann, *Strukturen des Bösen* (Paderborn, 1981), 2:108-15.

4. H. Gressmann, "Vom reichen Mann und armen Lazarus," in *Abhandlungen der preuss ischen Akademie der Wissenschaften* (1918), Philosophisch-Historische Klasse, n. 7.

5. E. Brunner-Traut, *Altägyptische Märchen*, 197.

6. J. Roth, *Die Flucht ohne Ende*, 127-28.

7. On the giving of names in Paradise, see E. Drewermann, *Strukturen des Bösen*, 3rd expanded edition, 1:399–400.

8. Freud himself, in "Bemerkungen über die Übertragungsliebe," X, 317, could observe, "that even the other kind of being in love [i.e., the sort not based on transference], outside of analytical treatment, is more reminiscent of abnormal than of normal psychic phenomena."

9. Thus Nena O'Neill and George O'Neill in *Open Marriage* (New York: Evans, 1972), 242–43.

10. I. B. Singer, *The Reaches of Heaven*. German trans., *Die Gefilde des Himmels: Eine Geschichte vom Baalschen Tow*, trans. H. Neves (Munich: dtv, 1984), 59.

11. H. Hesse, *Stufen* (Frankfurt: Suhrkamp, 1970), 186.

12. Thus H. Schürmann, *Das Lukasevangelium* (Freiburg-Basel-Vienna, 1984), 1:122–23.

13. Plutarch, "Isis and Osiris," in *Plutarch's Moralia*, vol. 5, trans. Frank Cole Babbitt, Loeb Classical Library (Cambridge: Harvard University Press, 1984), chaps. 12–20, 33.

14. Mahapadana-Suttanta (The Great Teaching on Legends), Digha-Nikaya 14, in P. Dahlke, trans., *Buddha: Die Lehre des Erhabenen* (Munich: Goldmann, 1960), 61–86.

15. See L. Frobenius, *Das Zeitalter des Sonnengottes* (Berlin, 1904), 234, 237.

16. H. Schürmann, *Das Lukasevangelium*, 1:122.

17. Marcus Aurelius, *The Communings with Himself*, trans. C. R. Haines, Loeb Classical Library (Cambridge: Harvard University Press, 1979), XII, 32, 26, pp. 341, 343.

18. Thus the famous scene in Fyodor Dostoyevsky, *Crime and Punishment*, in which Rodion Raskolnikov and Sonya Marmeladov, the murderer and the whore, read together the story of the raising of Lazarus (*Crime and Punishment*, trans. David McDuff [New York: Viking, 1991], part 4, chap. 4, 373–91).

19. Thus J. Klepper, *Unter dem Schatten deiner Flügel* (Stuttgart, 1972), 88, says: "If God did not exist, I could look upon nothing in life as more rewarding than to live in this error, that he does. This error would be greater than all truths and realities. All sufferings that result from it make no difference."

5. The Twelve-Year-Old Jesus in the Temple, or Growing Up Means Standing before God (Lk. 2:41–52)

1. E. Brunner-Traut, *Altägyptische Märchen* (Düsseldorf-Cologne, 1963), 193.

2. Ibid., 198.

3. On the rapid growth of the sun, see L. Frobenius, *Das Zeitalter des Sonnengottes* (Berlin, 1904), 234.

4. On the general relationship of the moon to the phenomena of growth and propagation, see E. Siecke, *Die Liebesgeschichte des Himmels* (Strassburg, 1892), 107.

5. To that extent, as C. G. Jung rightly argued, mythology is to be read as projected psychology. See E. Drewermann, *Strukturen des Bösen*, 3rd expanded

edition), 1:xxxi–xlv; E. Drewermann, *Tiefenpsychologie und Exegese* (Olten, 1984), 1:169–72.

6. On the painting of the circle gathered around F. Overbeck and others, see G. Tolzien, "Nazarener," in *Kindlers Malerei Lexikon* (Munich, 1985), 24:179–80.

7. S. Ben-Chorin, *Mutter Mirjam* (Munich, 1977), 89–91.

8. See A. Forge, "Die Baelam: Neuguinea," in E. Evans-Pritchard, ed., *Bild der Völker* (Wiesbaden, 1974), vol. 1, part 1, 74–77.

9. On the dual union between mother and child in the first months of the child's life, see R. A. Spitz, *Vom Säugling zum Kleinkind*, trans. G. Theusner-Stampa (Stuttgart, 1967), 140–47.

10. See E. Drewermann, "Gen. 22:1–9: Abrahams Opfer – in tiefenpsychologischer Sicht," in *Bibel und Kirche* 41 (March 1986): 113–24.

11. S. Freud, "Einige psychische Folgen des anatomischen Geschlechtsunterschieds," 15:17–30.

12. On the story of Rapunzel, see E. Drewermann, *Die kluge Else: Rapunzel* (Olten, 1986), 65–73.

13. On the teaching of the double movement of faith, see S. Kierkegaard, *Fear and Trembling*, with *Repetition*, trans. Alistair Hannay (Princeton: Princeton University Press, 1987), 23–49; E. Drewermann, *Strukturen des Bösen*, 3:497–504.

14. The Gospel of Luke is central, from Luke 9:51 on, as it provides an itinerary of the painful path to Jerusalem, while according to Jesus' twofold prediction of his sufferings in 9:21–22 and 9:44–45, his whole (life-) path is "aimed" at Jerusalem, the city of his death and the city that fulfilled all the Old Testament promises.

15. Kierkegaard also treated this problem masterfully in *Fear and Trembling*, 62–75.

16. Nietzsche, *Human, All-Too-Human*, trans. Helen Zimmern (New York: Russell & Russell, 1964), 3, pp. 4–6.

17. Graham Greene, *The Comedians* (London: The Bodley Head and William Heinemann, 1976), 69.

18. J. E. Rohde, *Naturwunder Küste* (Zurich-Munich, 1979), 74; N. N. Kartaschew, "Alkenvögel," in *Grzimeks Tierleben*, vol. 8, *Vögel*, 2:231–32.

19. Basically the psychic development from child to adult consists in setting free the archetype of the father (or the mother) from the individual parent figures of one's personal biography and anchoring them in the absolute. Becoming a child in the presence of God is the condition of becoming a grown-up in the presence of other humans.

Coda

1. "J. Tauler," in J. Seyppel, *Texte deutscher Mystiker des 16. Jahrhunderts*, 15–16, quoted in G. Wehr, *Thomas Münzer* (Hamburg, 1972), 117.

2. See E. Drewermann, "Aus Schuld geschieden – verdammt zum Unglück," in *Psychoanalyse und Moraltheologie*, vol. 2, *Wege und Umwege der Liebe* (Mainz, 1983), 112–17, 133–35.

3. Ibid., 125, n. 12.

4. John G. Neihardt, *Black Elk Speaks* (New York: Pocket Books, 1972), 17–39.

5. L. Tolstoy, "What Men Live By," *The Portable Tolstoy,* ed. John Bayley (New York: Penguin, 1978), 484–505.